ISRAEL
AT A CROSSROADS

ISRAEL
AT A CROSSROADS

Aba Gefen

gefen גפן
publishing house בית הוצאה לאור
JERUSALEM ♦ NEW YORK

Published in Hebrew under the title:
"Cheshbon Nefesh: Baderech Limdina Palestinait"
by Tcherikover, Tel-Aviv 1999

Typesetting: Marzel A.S. – Jerusalem
Editors: Esther Herskovics and Emma Corney
Cover Design: Studio Paz, Jerusalem

1 3 5 7 9 8 6 4 2

Gefen Publishing House
POB 36004, Jerusalem 91360, Israel
972-2-538-0247 • orders@gefenpublishing.com

Gefen Books
12 New Street Hewlett, NY 11557, USA
516-295-2805 • gefenbooks@compuserve.com

www.israelbooks.com

Printed in Israel

Send for our free catalogue

ISBN 965 229 259 1

Library of Congress Cataloging-in-Publication Data

Israel at a Crossroads / Aba Gefen
Rev. and updated ed. of Heshbon nefesh: ba-derech li-medina Palestina'it

1. Gefen, Aba. 2. Diplomats—Israel—Biography. 3.Israel—Politics and government. 4. Arab-Israeli conflict. 5. Arab-Israeli conflict—1993—Peace. 6. Holocaust, Jewish (1939-1945)—Lithuania—Personal narrative. 7. Holocaust survivors—Israel—Biography. I. Gefen, Aba. Heshbon nefesh. II. Title.

DS126.6.G44 A3 2001 • 956.94—dc21 • CIP Number: 2001023016

IN MEMORIAM

MY PARENTS RUHAMA AND MEIR WEINSTEIN

MY BROTHERS BENJAMIN, JOSEPH AND YEHUDA

MAY THEY REST IN PEACE

CONTENTS

PART FOUR **CAMP DAVID**

PART FIVE **INTIFADA**

PART SIX **MUTUAL RECOGNITION**

PART SEVEN **SOUL-SEARCHING**

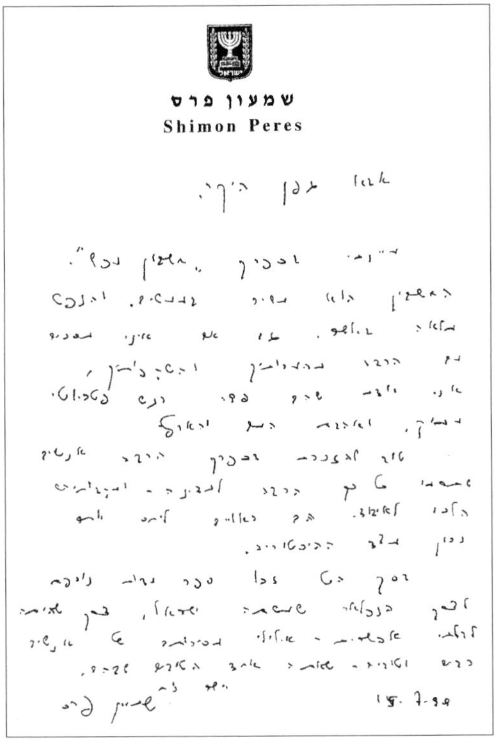
שמעון פרס
Shimon Peres

15.7.99

Shimon Peres
Former Prime Minister of Israel
and Peace Nobel Prize Laureate

Dear Aba Gefen,

I read your book entitled "Soul-Searching."* The search is rich in deeds and the soul is filled with honesty. Even if I do not agree with many of your comments and views, I know that they are the fruits of a deep patriotic sentiment and love for the people and the country.

It is good that in your book you mentioned many persons who contributed so much to the State and whose traces have been lost. They deserve a more proper place in history.

In sum, this is yet another book of testimony on the marvelous path Israel has taken, a path which would have been impossible but for the devotion of many good people — you being one of the best among them.

Congratulations!

Shimon Peres

15.7.99

* Title of the Hebrew edition

List of photos

Sources of the photos: Personal archive of the author; publications of the "Brichah" organization and of the Ministry of Foreign Affairs; and courtesy of Mr. Leon Kahn (Kaganowicz), Anti-Defamation League, the Navy's Museum in Haifa, Government Press Office and the Public Committee for the Liberation of Navigator Ron Arad.

FOREWORD

This book is a revised and updated edition, in English, of the original in Hebrew, *SOUL-SEARCHING — Towards a Palestinian State*.

I describe my life in Israel since 1948, my work at the "*Mossad*" (Israel's Intelligence Service) and my diplomatic service in Israel and abroad. I review the main developments in Israel since its establishment: wars, victories, tremendous achievements in all fields of life, and disturbing phenomena.

I relate in my book the development of the Israeli military conception — from exaggerated self-confidence all the way to a realistic evaluation of the possibilities to provide answers to actual strategic problems. I also tell of the Israeli governments' vicissitudes, from left and right, in their attitude towards the Palestinians — from total disregard to full recognition of their legitimate rights.

I examine the fatal decisions facing Israel at a crossroads of its negotiations with the Palestinians, Syrians and Lebanese, in order to obtain what the people of Israel has been yearning for since its establishment — peace with security.

This book also reflects the principal events in the history of the Jewish people in the twentieth century.

From my earliest days, I lived through the tragedies of our generation and I describe the three years (1941-1944) of my being in hiding under the Nazi occupation in Lithuania; my personal involvement during one year (1944-1945) in the punishment of Lithuanian Nazi collaborators; the ordeal of 250,000 Jewish Holocaust survivors, smuggled across the frontiers of Europe from the countries where their families were annihilated; their life during the years 1945-1948 in refugee camps in Germany and Austria awaiting an uncertain future;

and the stratagems used by the organization *"Brichah"* (Hebrew for flight), which organized their wandering, in order to bring them to Eretz Israel, the Land of Israel.

My book then is the story of one man, and of a nation and a state. It shows that a human being can bear his tribulations, survive, and while grieving the loss of parents, brothers and fellow Jews, witness the renewal of a people and the rebirth of a state after the abyss of the unspeakable Holocaust. The existence of the State of Israel illustrates how different the lot of the six million Jews, assassinated during the Second World War, would have been had the Jewish State already been in existence then. Today, Israel is the main guarantee that Auschwitz, Treblinka and Majdanek will remain only terrible memories of the past, never to happen again.

I wish to express my deep gratitude to my wife Frida, without whose encouragement, patience and advice this book would not have been written.

Special words of thanks are due to my editors Esther Herskovics and Emma Corney and to Gefen Publishing House.

Aba Gefen

Jerusalem, February 2001

PART ONE

DESTRUCTION

WITHIN TERRIFYING EARSHOT OF BRUTAL MURDER

World War II broke out on September 1, 1939, with Hitler's attack on Poland. German forces converged on Warsaw from all sides, crushing the Polish air force within 48 hours and vanquishing the Polish army in one week. Poland was the main biological basis of the Jewish people — more than three million Jews — and was considered the reservoir of Jewish national creative forces.

On January 30, 1939, Hitler "prophesied" that a new world war would lead to the extermination of the Jewish race in Europe, and, with the outbreak of hostilities, the persecution of the Jews sprang into full gear. The frightening predictions of Zeev Jabotinsky, the Zionist Revisionist leader, became reality. Jabotinsky demanded the Jews of Europe leave their continent where — as he put it — there was no future or purpose for them since the earth under their feet was burning. He predicted that "if the Jews will not liquidate the *Golah* (Diaspora), the *Golah* will liquidate them."

Within a year, the Jews of Poland under Nazi occupation were subjected to a series of debilitating decrees and assaults. Jews were prohibited from earning a living, were beaten and robbed, and forced into labor camps and ghettoes. In Warsaw, half a million Jews were crowded into the largest of the ghettoes. Thousands of Jewish refugees from Poland arrived in Lithuania, the country of my birth, but very soon Lithuania also lost her independence — the Soviets occupied it.

I was born in the town of Simnas, in the district of Alitus, the oldest of four sons. My name, Aba-Leib, was given to me in memory of my grandfather Aba-Leib Weinstein, may he rest in peace, who had been ordained as a Rabbi. As was usual in religious circles, my grandfather had many children: seven boys and three girls. My father, Meir, was the youngest. During World War I, my grandfather was killed in one of the pogroms by the Cossacks, who caused the destruction of hundreds of Jewish communities. My father was then 18 years old. Three years later, in Kovno, Lithuania's capital, he met my mother Ruhama Rubinstein, who was on a visit to the big city. It was love at first sight. They got married and settled in Simnas, where my mother's father, Joseph Rubinstein, a well-to-do corn merchant, helped the newlyweds to open a textile store.

After completing the *Heder* (common name for the old-fashioned elementary school for teaching of Judaism), and the elementary Hebrew school in our town, I was sent to Mariampol to study at the Hebrew gymnasium, the first Hebrew high school in Lithuania, where I joined "Beitar" — Zeev

The Weinstein family before the Holocaust
Seated: the parents, Meir and Ruhama
Standing: extreme left — son Benjamin, extreme right — son Joseph, between the parents — son Yehuda, and behind him — son Aba (Gefen)

Jabotinsky's Zionist Revisionist Youth Movement. The situation of independent Lithuania's quarter of a million Jews was good, and they even called it "Little America." Hence very few of the Lithuanian Jews believed Jabotinsky's terrible warning. They continued to live their tranquil lives, blinding themselves with wishful thinking that to them it won't happen, until eventually they themselves experienced the atrocities.

When the Soviets occupied Lithuania, I was studying at the University of Kovno, in the Faculty of Engineering. Together with many other students, I became involved in assisting the Polish Jewish refugees, many of whom tried to find ways to leave Lithuania. On June 14, 1940, the Soviet deportations to Siberia began and among those deported were Jewish refugees, who had not managed to escape. I went to the railway-station, to say goodbye to some of the people being deported, and I heard a man standing behind me, casually say: "God alone knows whether luck is in store for those who stay behind, or for those who are being exiled to Siberia." A week later, this was no longer rhetorical. On June 22, 1941, Germany invaded the Soviet Union. The German air attack on Kovno began at dawn.

Taken by surprise, the Soviet Command abandoned Kovno. The badly prepared and poorly led Soviet forces retreated rather than risk entrapment on Lithuanian territory, whereupon the nationalist Lithuanian guerrillas — known as the Lithuanian Activist Front — established their headquarters in the city and prepared to give the invading Germans a joyous welcome.

Since Lithuania was on the border with Germany, its Jews were the first victims. Even before the Germans entered, the Lithuanian pro-Nazis carried out a pogrom in the Jewish Orthodox suburb of Viliampol, which the Jews called Slobodka and where the famous leading European Yeshivah was located. In addition, the Lithuanian pro-Nazi nationalists conducted mass arrests of Jews and assembled them at various places. On June 24, the day the Germans entered Kovno, I was rounded up along with 20 other Jews and brought to the city square.

Standing in the square with thousands of Jews that had gathered from all parts of Kovno, I watched an approaching group and noticed it was headed by Adolf Blumental, the man from whom my younger brother Benjamin, who was attending the city's technical school, and I had rented a room for the 1940-41 school year. Adolf Blumental had been chief engineer in the Lithuanian air force, with the honorary rank of colonel. When Blumental was arrested along with his wife Zina, a well-known photographer, and son Kolia, he wore on his breast the insignia of the decorations conferred upon him by the government of Lithuania. On Blumental's arrival at the square with the group of Jews, the guerrilla commander — a former air force officer who had served under Adolf and knew him well — separated the Blumental family from the rest. A discussion ensued among the nationalists as to what was to be done with this heavily decorated colonel of the free Lithuanian army. In the end he was told that he and his family could return to their home.

Zina Blumental had noticed me standing there and begged the commander to allow me to join them, saying I lived with them and belonged to the family. The commander consented and I was thus one of the fortunate few saved from the accursed fortress of Kovno, a chain of fortifications surrounding the city. When the Germans entered Lithuania, they started the systematic liquidation of the Jews, and they chose Forts IV, VII and IX of the fortress as spots for the assassination of the Jews.

On Fort VII, from June 25 to July 7, 80-100 Jews were slaughtered each day. On the eve of July 8, 5,000 Jews were executed. The killings were temporarily interrupted the next day when a decree was issued ordering all the Jews of Kovno to be moved into a ghetto, in Slobodka, and every Jew in Lithuania to wear a yellow badge with the Star of David.

The decree also stated that those with permanent residence outside of Kovno could obtain permits to return to their homes. I received such a permit. The Blumentals were confined to the ghetto where their son Kolia was murdered. Zina and her husband, Adolf, were taken off to a concentration camp and he died in Dachau. She survived.

I left Kovno on July 14, 1941, for a three-day hike to my home town of Simnas, 130 kilometers from Kovno, to join my parents and brothers and to share their lot. The Germans had entered Simnas on June 23. In stark contrast to the horrors in Kovno, where the pro-German activists instantly seized and murdered Jews, my brethren in Simnas still dwelt in comparative peace.

They were left in their homes and the men were sent to all sorts of work for the Germans. Everything had been planned so as not to arouse fears and induce the Jews to flee. On August 22, 1941, the German authorities ordered all Jewish males to assemble near the town hall. All obeyed the summons. One hundred were selected and placed in three trucks that left for the town of Alitus. The hundred chosen were all young, healthy and strong men. Among them were my father, Meir, 41 years old, and my brother, Benjamin, aged 17 and an excellent sportsman.

My father, heroically yet with calm logic, saved me from that transport. When we were being lined up for selection, he turned to me and said: "Get out of here and go back home. You've only recently come from Kovno and were not in town when the Germans took a census of the Jewish population of Simnas. Since you're not listed among the Jews here, they are not likely to search for you. Hide at home, son, until the danger is over." I did as he instructed. A few hours later I saw the trucks pass by our home. My father and brother were in the first truck.

On September 1, 1941, we again were told to assemble in front of the town hall. 60 young men and women were selected. This time I was saved by my mother's courage. When the assembly order was announced, she forbade me to go and tucked me into bed, as if I were ill. Within an hour, the activists went from house to house to fetch the absentees. The activist who came to our home turned out to be a long-time employee in the flour-mill of my mother's family. Swayed by her entreaty, supplemented by cash and clothes, he left without me, satisfied with his booty.

On September 10, over 400 Jews — women, children, sick and old people, with only seven young men — were told to assemble by three o'clock in the barracks beyond the town limits. Some thought the intention was to confine us to a barracks-ghetto, others believed that we would be taken to some other city and used there for all kinds of hard labor. The pessimists insisted that the intention was to kill us. My mother did not believe this. She thought, however, that my brother Joseph and I, who were young and strong, might be assigned to harder work. Considering that our youngest brother, Yehuda'le, was only a child, she thought that they might even respect her more for his sake. Turning to me, she said: "I suggest that you, Aba, hide with Joseph in the home of our good friend, the peasant Slavitsky. In a day or two, when you see what develops, you can decide whether to join the others in the barracks or remain in hiding."

Grief-stricken, we took our mother's advice, said goodbye to her and to Yehuda'le, and went to Slavitsky's farm within Simnas. Slavitsky welcomed us very kindly, telling us to hide under the hay in his barn. Hardly an hour had passed when Yehuda'le came running from the barracks to inform us that our friends had already arrived there and had sent him to tell us that we should join them; otherwise it was likely the authorities would discover our hiding place and would kill us on the spot. We tried to persuade our little brother to remain with us, but he stubbornly refused saying: "It will be better for mother if I stay with her."

Slavitsky then entered the barn and told us to leave. He explained that the Jews who knew we were hiding in his barn would not be able to withstand the interrogation about our hiding place, and would thus endanger his life. I implored him to allow us to stay until the evening: as soon as darkness fell, we would go and search for another place. He consented. As we prepared to leave the barn, I made up my mind to keep a diary in which I would record in Hebrew everything that happened to us from that day on. In the evening, we made our way through the fields to the house of the farmer Bogdanovitch who also lived within the town. Bogdanovitch gave us permission to hide in his barn.

On the afternoon of Friday, September 12, Bogdanovitch came to the barn to tell us that the Jews had been moved out of the barracks and led into the woods nearby. The men had their hands tied behind their backs; the women walked arm in arm, as did the children. As we were talking, we heard the sound of intermittent gunfire coming from the woods; it went on for over an hour. We were within terrifying earshot of the brutal murder of the innocent Jews of Simnas, slaughtered only because they were Jews, and among them, our mother and little brother Yehuda'le.

In the evening, Bogdanovitch came again, and his answers to my questions related, in all their horror, to the last moments of the lives of the Simnas Jews. In Simnas there was no need for modern scientific means to liquidate the Jews. The Lithuanians tortured them with simple peasant savagery, until their senses and their human image were obliterated. With no strength to resist any longer, even spiritually, under a hail of blows, from whips and gunstocks, stripped almost to the skin, they were driven to the woods. Still alive, they were forced into a long, deep pit diabolically prepared in advance, and then, in icy cold blood, the Lithuanian activists and German soldiers shot them down. After the slaughter the murderers came out of the woods singing at the top of their lungs.

We were smothered in gloom. Our mood was terrible. We thought we were going mad. I cursed myself for living, yet I didn't want to die, and we had to concentrate on how to save ourselves.

Bogdanovitch suggested that we go to the farmer Smidzun in the village of Glosnik. I reminded Bogdanovitch of his promise to try to get for me the album of pictures I had left in the attic of our house. After two days he brought me my mother's handkerchief containing the album with family photos, as well as my matriculation and student certificates. Looking at the photographs was very depressing. We just couldn't bear the thought that our parents, brothers and other relatives were no more.

Our dear beloved mother used to say that her most fervent prayer was to see me standing under the wedding canopy. But there is the saying, "Man proposes and God disposes." God did not want to fulfill her wish. My wish, too, will never come true — someday to make her proud of me. People were saying that she was crazy about her children. She knew I loved her more than anything. Such a mother is impossible to forget. I swear that she will for ever live in my heart.

And here is the photograph of our dearest Papa. When the Germans entered Lithuania, he repeatedly said that he was praying to be the only victim and that no harm should befall the rest of us. I cannot convey how deeply I loved him.

The author's parents Ruhama and Meir Weinstein

And our brother Benjamin. Sometimes we used to quarrel and even fight, but we were so devoted to each other. If either of us got sick, the other would be distraught with worry. And little beloved Yehuda'le. I looked at his picture and I imagined him alive. I talked to him: I can't believe that God took you, you, who are so much younger than I. The tears in my eyes you don't see are all for you. They bear witness that I will never forget you. I love you so much, my little dear brother.

The author's brother Yehuda'le

The author's brother Benjamin

HOLOCAUST DIARY

On October 10, in the evening, we left the barn. After walking a while we came to a village we thought was Glosnik and began looking for the farmer Smidzun's place, where Joseph had once been. We tried one place and then another, when we suddenly heard footsteps and saw a woman coming toward us who began to shout in Lithuanian: "Yushkovsky, thieves are coming! Thieves!" When we started to run, she shouted even louder. I turned toward her and began pleading with her not to shout: "We are not thieves, but Jews from Simnas, the sons of Weinstein, the shopkeeper." Providentially, she believed me and calmed down. She knew my father. There was not a single peasant in the Simnas area who did not know him, had not bought from him, did not owe him money.

The woman, whose surname was Matulevitch, expressed sympathy for us and invited us to her home to rest a while. She gave us bread and milk and told us of her poverty and about her children: three sons — Sebiastas, Yozas and Vladas — and a daughter, Stase. The boys came to see us. They were young men, strong and frightening, for they might have been pro-Nazi activists, who would seize and turn us over to the police. But no! Upon parting she gave us her blessing: "God be with you, and watch over you."

Once again we got lost. We wandered around until six o'clock in the morning, still unable to find Smidzun's place. Panic overtook us. We must decide quickly. What could we do? We trusted the woman Matulevitch but dreaded her sons. But what option did we have? We had to take the risk. Her parting benediction still rang in my ears. Was it wishful thinking to believe that a Christian woman who invoked God's name, who gave you His blessing, must be a good person who would not betray you to murderers?

We returned to the hamlet of Saulinai, where the woman lived, and came to her house. She and her three sons welcomed us very warmly. I told them I would reward them generously, if we could stay a little longer with them. They agreed and, what had at first seemed like a misfortune — encountering this peasant woman — was becoming a blessing.

During the day, we stayed in our hiding place in the barn and in the evening the woman invited us into her house for supper. After the meal we undressed and she scrubbed both of us from head to toe. It was just marvelous! Who even dreamed of such a reception? We came in wearing dirty, vermin-infested clothing, and the sons gave us their underwear and shirts to change into while the woman washed our dirty clothes.

The next day, she again invited us into her house for supper. After the meal we talked for a while and the woman gave us heart-breaking details of the shooting of the Simnas Jews. She told us that 413 Jews had been killed in Simnas. She said that the Jewish women, wearing only their night-shirts and walking barefoot, kept stumbling and falling, and the barbarians accompanying them would whip them. She said that, when the victims were ordered to jump into the pit, the men did it immediately, while the women tarried, for they held children in their arms, in a last embrace.

The adults understood what it was all about. They knew they were being killed because they were Jews, but the poor little children, who walked wailing and sobbing all the way, what did they know? What could they understand? All they knew was to cry out “Mama, Papa” and cling to them in fear. My little brother Yehuda’le, too, entered the pit tightly holding my mother’s hand. It was their fate that in death as in life they would not be parted, and thus, together, they gave back their lives to the Creator.

One day, the son Yozas came in completely drunk, followed by his staggering brother Sebiastas. I always worried when they were drunk: in their cups — which was often — they would fight with knives. Once they made a hole in my coat, another time Yozas brandished a deadly knife at my throat. If they got tipsy with frightening regularity, it was because the family earned its living by distilling and selling samagon, the home-made vodka.

One day, Yozas told me that the police were coming to search every house for samagon, and, not unreasonably, he told us to quit their place instantly. But where could we head for in broad daylight? After months of having been cooped up in the barn and in the house, we were clothed in rags, and our faces were unshaved and pale as chalk. Any passer-by would know we were fugitives. The longer we lingered in doubt and distress, the more infuriated and nervous the sons became, but the good woman's heart melted in compassion and she decided to hide us in the pigsty. The sons completely lost their temper and the three of them, together with the little girl, left their home.

Weeping bitterly and lamenting our fate, Mrs. Matulevitch dug a pit in the pigsty, pushed us down into it, and covered us with manure. Again we were saved — the police passed by, the sons returned to their mother and we returned to the attic.

The next day, the Matulevitches found out that the police had caught a Simnas Jew, Shimon Cohen, the barber. When the Germans began to remove the Jews from Simnas, Marta, a Lithuanian woman — who was deeply attached to Shimon — suggested that he hide with her family in the country. He agreed and lived with her at her brother's house. But his sweetheart's sister-in-law also became enamored of him. The women detested each other and were sick with jealousy and hatred. Shimon did not realize his danger, imagining he would save himself by proving his devotion to both. But Marta was furious and informed on Shimon to the hamlet's mayor, who told the police. Shimon and the farmer were arrested. A Lithuanian activist named Piletsky shot him and was rewarded with 15 German marks.

Yozas asked me what would happen if we were caught. Would we turn them in? I promised that I wouldn't inform on them. "We shall be shot anyway," I said, "so why should we turn in the people who tried to save us?"

When, years later, the State of Israel was established, Gentiles who saved Jews during the Nazi oppression at the risk of their own lives were recognized as Righteous and awarded a medallion which, in artistry and symbolism, portrays the Talmudic saying: "He who saves a single being saves a whole world." The Righteous stand out as a beacon of light in the blackness of Hitler's occupation of Europe. They represent a slender bridge of indestructible humanity spanning the abyss of Man's malevolence. The Righteous man, as is said in the Book of Proverbs, is an everlasting foundation. The good Lithuanian woman, Ona Matulevitch, who helped my brother and myself save our lives, at the risk of her own, was recognized as a Righteous Gentile. The most famous Righteous are the German Oscar Schindler and the Swede Raoul Wallenberg. While Schindler survived, Wallenberg disappeared.

One day, Mrs. Matulevitch told us that the Russians had surrounded seven German divisions, and people began talking about the Germans retreating. We were told that the Soviets and the British had signed an agreement to open a second front and had already bombed Lithuania and had scattered leaflets advising the population to flee from the big cities. Paratroopers landed near Simnas. Two were caught and four escaped. In Kovno, railroads were bombed and there were 36 casualties, including eight Germans.

On the other hand, rumors were going around that Hitler and the Duce had turned to the Pope, asking him to promote peace between them and the Western Allies and that the Allies might be ready to do it. That burned me up. After all the acts of deceit the Germans had committed, would the Allies extend a hand to them? Even if it meant I could walk out as a free man, I didn't want it. Even if I risked arrest and death, I preferred to continue in hiding if it meant that Hitler's deeds were not passed over in silence.

When the stalks were high, we hid in the wheat fields. I had gathered enough information about the peasants of the area, and knew more or less which of them were enemies of the Jews and would betray us, and which we might trust. So we decided to hide in the fields by day, and go by night to the peasant homes, tap on the window, explain who we were and ask for a glass of milk and some bread.

At the end of July, when the wheat was starting to bend a little, we knew we wouldn't be able to stay in the fields much longer.

When we finally had to leave the fields, I left Joseph in our hiding place in the potato field and went to Stephan Pavlovsky, who lived alone in the countryside, in a four square meter hut. I woke him up and asked him to let us build a hide-out in his barn, with an entrance beneath the wall and, if possible, a direct exit, so that he would not have to bother about our food. He had hardly any food for himself.

He consented and showed me how to fix up a nice nest where no-one could find us. The spot seemed perfect. While we were talking, the subject of arms came up. He brought out a gun, an eight-chamber Montechrist.

He gave me the gun with seven bullets, and I was very happy that I would not need to surrender to the German soldiers or the Lithuanian police should I encounter them. After a few days, we entered the barn.

With winter approaching, I went to visit the Matulevitches to find out whether we could come back to them. They told me that they had already prepared the oven for us, so we returned to their place.

One day, Mrs. Matulevitch visited a neighbor, who told her of rumors that the Maxuks were around (the peasants used to call my father Max, and Maxuk was a nickname for Max's son) and were staying with the Matulevitches.

We therefore had to leave the Matulevitches and went to the Yuchnelevitches. They agreed to keep Joseph for two weeks, so I left him there and went alone to see Pranas Shupienis in Tcherniukishok. He agreed to take Joseph in for a week.

When we started our new phase of hiding — leaving Joseph somewhere for some time, and myself wandering daily from one place to another — I was very worried. But very soon I found out that the same peasants who at first trembled at the very thought of helping Jews had become used to the idea. Once they had provided me with some food, they no longer found it so perilous, and let me sleep overnight indoors or in their barns, and, as time went by, were willing to shelter me for one or two days, and Joseph for longer. I found quite a number of farmers ready to give Joseph shelter for a week or two, either by hiding him in the attic or by keeping him openly.

While I was at Antanas Shupienis, Pranas' brother, a neighbor, Mrs. Apolsky arrived. She told me that two Jews from Simnas, Gamsky and Bialostotsky, had escaped the shooting and had been with them for two weeks. When it became known that the police were on to them, the Apolskys took them to relatives, the Bainorovitch family — a woman with four daughters and a son — in the village of Laukintchai, near the town of Sirey.

I brought Joseph to the Berziunases in Otesnik — they were close friends of my father's and in time were recognized as Righteous — and I went to visit Gamsky and Bialostotsky. I learned that Bialostotsky had died on October 15, 1942.

From the Bainorovitches I went to the painter Zigmunt Emart in Simnas. He gave me a leaflet the Russians were distributing to the German population about what happened at Stalingrad. It was written in German and said that the Red Army decimated the German troops camped outside Stalingrad since November 23, 1942. On February 2, 1943, the Red Army pushed them back. There were 333,000 German soldiers there; 240,000 of them were killed.

On April 20, was our Passover, and I went to visit Gamsky again.

There were Lithuanians who saved Jews for reward; romance, too, was not absent as a factor in the saving of Jews; the Bainorovitches — Gamsky thought — did so simply out of a solicitude to save a fellow-creature from death. As time passed, Gamsky realized that those good people — who were recognized later as Righteous — also had evangelic motives. They did everything they could for him, but — being a very religious Christian family — they also tried to convert him. He had been saved physically, they would say, so the time had come to save his soul.

Each one of the four Bainorovitch daughters was ready to become his wife if he changed his faith, and I am not at all sure that he would not have succumbed if I had not been in the area. I believe that my frequent visits to him and my encouraging him to resist the temptation, gave him strength and kept him from taking a step that he would have regretted afterwards.

I was less successful in the case of two Jewish girls I met while wandering around. One was living with a farmer almost openly as a weaver and the other stayed with a priest completely free. Both sisters converted, and that was very painful for me. I tried very hard to explain to them why they must not adopt the religion of those who slaughtered their parents and entire family. But I did not succeed in changing their minds. However, after the war, they both returned to Judaism. Not all did. In the war, some Jews lost their lives or families, others limbs of their bodies, and there were those who lost their souls.

At the farmer Shupienis' house I found old Mrs. Zimmerman, who did fortune-telling by means of cards. She told my fortune, too. In two days something unpleasant would happen to me and for the next ten days I would be very worried. I shall soon meet two other Jews, a man and a woman. I will aid them, but they will be caught. In four months I'll receive good news. In a year or thirteen months I'll travel to the west, across the sea, and I shall marry a dark woman, who was waiting for me eagerly. I will live 87 years and I will have a two-storey brick house.

Even though I did not believe in cards, I was still frightened by what she told me, and I considered perhaps not helping other Jews because they might be doomed because of me. If two Jews, a man and a woman, were caught because of me, I would shoot myself — I noted in my diary.

Every day, in the morning, I entered in my diary a plus-sign (+) to indicate that we had survived one more day.

While leafing through the diary, I thought to myself: if I survive, these notes will stand as a reminder of our times, a testament to what we have endured.

"The Eternal One shall not fail Israel," I noted in my diary, and added: "Only now am I proud to be a Jew! But only my little notebook and I know it. The war will end and the day will come when I will be able to tell it to them, too — to those who humiliate us today."

There was, however, no sign that the war was ending and we started making plans to escape from Lithuania. We thought about stealing across the border into Romania, which would require traversing Poland; or getting into Russia by way of the battle front, or entering Switzerland by way of Germany. Perhaps to go to Iran and then to Palestine. We were, of course, aware of the fact that those might only remain plans.

When I came to the farmer Yuchnelevitch, he told me that people were saying there won't be any Jews left, so it was pointless to protect me.

One day, I walked by way of the swamps and was soaked up to my knees, when two people passed me. One of them greeted me. I stopped, and when I got a little closer, I recognized him: Pranas Dainovsky. He was a shoemaker in Simnas and a member of the clandestine Lithuanian Communist Party. He was arrested when the Germans entered our town, and released after a short time. A year later, he was arrested again. When we met, he was on leave, for a few days, from the prison. He told me that he had decided not to go back to prison but to join the anti-German partisans in the forest.

When I parted from him, I came to Yermelevitch's in Kalesnik where I heard two encouraging broadcasts — one from the BBC in London, in Polish, and the other from Moscow, in German. Italy had already surrendered, the Italians and the Germans were fighting there in the streets. There were uprisings in Yugoslavia, France, Greece and Albania, and demonstrations in Bulgaria. The

Russians were advancing, and Germany had been given an ultimatum to evacuate all the territories she had conquered.

On November 7, 1943, at night, I heard a radio broadcast from Moscow. It was a very important one. Stalin himself announced that on that day the Russians had liberated the city of Pastov and were also going to liberate the city of Kiev. The population celebrated and sang the praises of the Red Army. Many of the Nazi collaborators were shot. I also learned from the newscast that a meeting had been held in Moscow in which the Foreign Ministers of the Soviet Union, the United States and Great Britain — Vyacheslav Molotov, Cordell Hull and Anthony Eden — had discussed how to proceed with the war.

On December 23, 1943, Pranas Shupienis informed me that there were three Jews staying with Smadziun in the village of Kavaltchuk. I immediately went there and found Zvi (Hershel) Levit and his wife Miriam, as well as Gita Zeliviansky. The three of them came to the outskirts of Simnas on foot, following the road at night, hiding in the woods by day.

They were born in Simnas and from there had moved to Kovno. They told me that the situation in the ghetto of Kovno was becoming increasingly difficult, and rumors were circulating that the ghetto was to be demolished. So they decided to escape to their home-town in the hope of finding friendly peasants willing to help them and give them cover until the storm passed. The three of them knew Smadziun well and went to his place. Smadziun let Levit's wife stay with him, and I took the other two with me.

We left at night, and the three of us stayed one day with Pranas Shupienis, who agreed to give Gita shelter for a month. The next day, Zvi and I went to see the farmer Burbon and I left Zvi there for a few days. On January 10, 1944, Joseph and I went to Strolis in Otesnik, and there we heard about Gita Zeliviansky's tragedy.

Pranas Shupienis, with whom she was staying, was making samagon, like all the farmers did, and one day the police arrived at his place to search for it. When Gita saw the police coming, she thought they were searching for her, and she fearlessly jumped from the window and ran.

A policeman ran after her and caught her. When it became clear who she was, both she and Shupienis were arrested. Gita was taken off to Alitus, where she was shot dead. Poor Gita! It caused me great anguish that one of old lady

Zimmerman's prophecies had come true. She said that two Jews, a man and a woman, might be doomed after meeting me. I had thought that if such a thing happened, I would kill myself. Now I didn't know what to do. What if they caught another one of the Jews I had met? Joseph tried to calm me by saying that it was just fate.

Pranas Shupienis remained in jail for a month. Through the mediation of influential friends he was set free. Much worse was the fate of another friend who had helped us enormously — Stephan Pavlovsky.

Three days after Gita was caught, Joseph and I were at Berziunas' and there we were told that the evening before, eight policemen had come to Stephan Pavlovsky's place. He opened the door for them and they yelled "Hands up!" Pavlovsky was a brave man, and he made up his mind not to surrender. He took out his gun and shot two of them. One died on the spot and the second was going fast. Then Pavlovsky went down to the cellar below his granary. Germans came and set fire to the building, and Stephan was burned alive. Poor Stephan, who helped so many others, was burned alive in the hiding place he had prepared and was so proud of.

A week earlier Joseph and I had passed Pavlovsky's. Two days later we were there again. We sat with him for a long time, until midnight. On the Wednesday of the tragedy, I was at his place toward evening. I wanted to stay with him for a while, but he advised me not to because he was expecting a search. And soon after I left, the police came and it happened.

I left Joseph at Berziunas' and went to the village of Kavaltchuk. While walking, I met a man on a wagon who began talking to me. He offered to give me a ride on his wagon. I introduced myself and asked him who he was. He said he was Gradetzky from Kavaltchuk and invited me to his home. I accepted.

There, he told me that two Jews were staying with Ivanovsky in the village of Skovagol. Gradetzky took me to Ivanovsky, where I met two Jews who had come from Kovno: Leah Port and Samuel Ingel. I stayed over to sleep with them at Ivanovsky's.

Leah and Samuel had escaped from Kovno ghetto and were moving to the woods to join the anti-German partisan groups. Halting near our town, they found shelter for a few days at the farm of the woman Ivanovsky, who was a deaf-mute.

After I spent the night with them and promised to try and find them hiding places, they decided not to continue to the woods, but stay with me. I left them at Ivanovsky's and continued my daily trips in search of new hide-outs.

I went to see Mrs. Zubrowa, the owner of a farm in Metel. She was a very good friend of my father's and let me stay at her farm for a couple of days. She told me to be very careful. "The police have really decided to get you, they are afraid of your diary," she said.

When the barber Shimon Cohen was caught, Yozas Matulevitch told me they wouldn't have killed Shimon if they hadn't found his diary — a thick notebook — in which he made notes about taking revenge. When the Jews were being shot, Shimon was sitting in a tree, and, tied down to the branch by his belt, he recorded in the diary everything he saw, describing in detail how the barbarians tortured children. Yozas made it clear to me that he and Sebiastas were not happy about my keeping a diary and said that they had decided to take my diary from me before we left their place. If we survived, they would return it to me and in the meantime, they would hide it. I told him I would never give him the diary.

Now, the Berziunases were telling me that some of the farmers were saying that because the Russians were drawing near, if I remained alive they would be the first ones to be killed. They claimed that I was very dangerous and must, therefore, be turned over to the police. They said that no good would come of me because I was keeping a diary and writing down everything, and when the time came, I would publish my diary and get my revenge. More than 30 years were to pass before I published my diary.

In 1977, my diary appeared in print as a book, in its original Hebrew. It was then also translated and published in English, French, Spanish, Portuguese and German. Because of its historic value as an authentic, one-of-a-kind document, Yad Vashem (Israel's Martyrs' and Heroes' Remembrance Authority) decided to restore it. Thus, a bundle of papers, notes, pads and copybooks, which were kept in a handkerchief, have become 25 volumes of a book, each piece of paper restored.

When the Jewish American writer Herman Wouk visited our home in Jerusalem, he was very impressed by my Holocaust diary and effusive in his praise of it. I then quoted to him what Menachem Begin had to say about it ("that it was important for the young generation to read it") and told him that

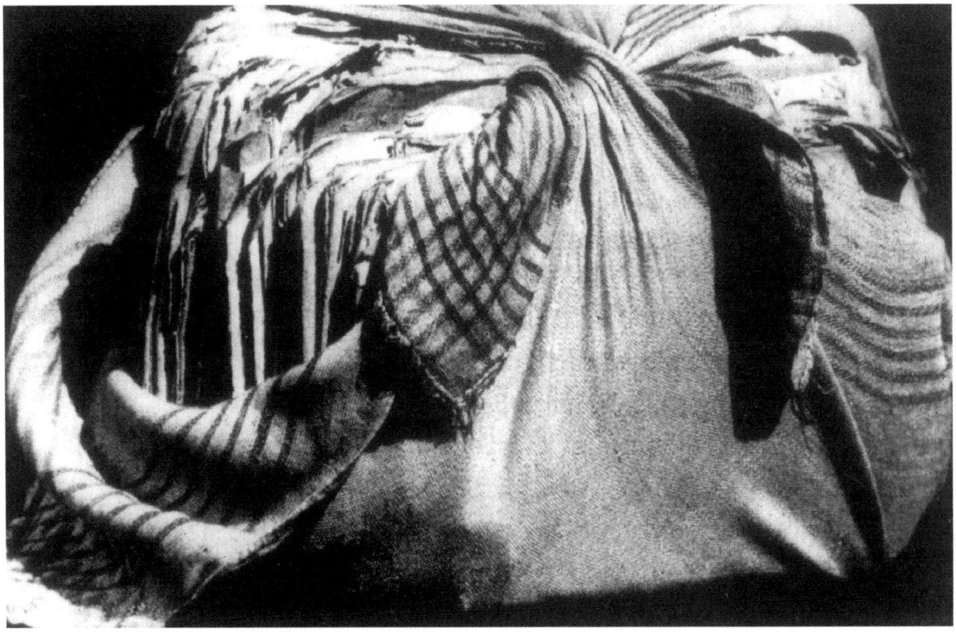

The original Holocaust diary in a handkerchief

The diary restored by Yad Vashem in 25 volumes

Elie Wiesel had written to me "that my diary should be translated into all languages." I added: "Nevertheless, my diary was not a success." "Sorry, you survived" — retorted Wouk — "had you not survived, your diary would have been a world best-seller!"

ON THE COMMON GRAVE

On April 8, 1944, I went to Simnas to see Stase Kazlovsky, who from time to time visited the ghetto of Kovno. She told me she had seen Leib Frank there, a Jew from Simnas. He told her he was planning to escape from the ghetto and make his way to Simnas.

After my visit with Stase, I went to the farmer Yanushon where I found Olga Levin who had escaped from the Kovno ghetto with her son, Abrasha. I also found a Jewish child from Kovno there, who had been sent by a certain Margolis. The Yanushons agreed to keep the child, and for Olga and her son I found a place with Adela Baravik. Olga Levin's husband, Moshe Levin, was the chief of the Jewish police in the Kovno ghetto and was murdered by the Germans.

At Smadziun's in Kavaltchuk, I found Leib Frank and his wife, Rachel. They had arrived from Kovno by car. Rachel was going to stay for some time with Smadziun, and I took Leib to the Berziunases. The Levits were to stay with the Krashnitzkys in Skovagol.

I decided that the time had come for my people to join the partisan movement and play their modest part in combatting the Nazis. It wasn't any more the poorly organized Lithuanian partisan movement, with low morale and negligible exploits, largely ignored by the Germans because of its lack of aggressiveness. The movement had come under close Moscow direction, and had become part of the general Soviet partisan movement which was, no doubt, the largest and certainly the most elaborately organized guerrilla movement in the history of warfare. At its peak, it must have included over 150,000 members — men and women — and it combined all classic features of such movements of the past with modern weapons, means and methods of communication and transport.

Trained commanders were sent to the woods in Lithuania, arms and equipment were supplied in abundance, and a system of controls had been set up to coordinate its operations with the tactics of the Soviet army. On May 31, 1944, I went to see Alphonse Rushkovsky, one of the leaders of the anti-German partisans, and informed him of my decision. He said that he was pleased but they would only accept the young and armed into the movement — no old people and no women in my group. "Let them stay here and look out for themselves!" — he said.

Only Samuel and I carried arms. Joseph and Abrasha would, of course, also be accepted. But all the others who made up my group were for them just "extra mouths" — unwanted competitors in the procurement of provisions from the peasantry. I had also heard that the partisan leadership was disturbingly over-politicized and that it had clashes with the Jewish partisans who tried to assert their Jewish identity in the movement. The Soviets were against the existence of nationally-oriented Jewish combatant units, and among the Gentile anti-Nazi partisans there were Jew-haters and many a Jew died at their hands.

While I was important for them as a partisan, I saw things in a different way. Every Jew was important to me, and I told Rushkovsky that I would join up with the partisans only when I was no longer needed by the Jews, i.e. when the Levits, Franks, Levins, Gamsky, Leah and the two children would be taken in and cared for. He said it was impossible. So I decided not to join them but to carry on as an independent group. I noted in my diary: "As long as I am needed to help even one Jew, I'll stay here. They are willing to fight side by side with us but not assume responsibility for us."

The first week of July planes were flying over and there was a lot of bombing. People were saying that the Germans were in retreat and that the Red Army had already reached Vilno. I went to Amshey's in Verniger to visit Joseph and to start preparing for the return of the Red Army. Joseph was feeling fine and the Amsheys told me not to worry about him. They even agreed to my bringing five or six Jews to their barn. They promised to prepare a proper hiding place. Amshey told me that there was a great uproar in Simnas. The cooperative had been robbed and all kinds of documents destroyed. The Germans had disarmed the Lithuanian police. Everyone was running from Simnas, even the police. Everything pointed to the likelihood that the Soviet army was going to come soon. It was like the beginning of the end.

The Russians were advancing and the front was approaching. On July 20, I slept with Joseph at Amshey's. That place was near the front. I remained with Joseph for a couple of days, planning to go closer and closer to the front, to welcome the Red Army. But first I arranged for everyone in my group a place to stay and wait for the decisive battle between the Russians and the Germans that would break the front in that area.

Zvi Levit and his wife were staying at the Krashnitzkys. They agreed to keep the Levits until the war was over. Leib Frank and his wife were staying at the Berziunases, and Gamsky at the Bainorovitches; Olga Levin, her son, Margolis' daughter and the other girl at Adela Baravik's.

Samuel and Leah asked to join Joseph and myself on our way to the front. We met in the village of Kumatch, where the four of us decided to remain, hiding in a bunker. There was a lot of shooting and for two days the bombs were raining down over our hidden heads. We were almost in the midst of the fire. The moment that we had dreamt of so long, the end of the Nazi presence, was at hand.

After all the suffering and horror that we had endured over the last three years under the Nazi heel, we had no wish to die, at that eleventh hour. In all the years of hiding, flight and constant peril, when I knew that the police was hunting for me, and that a price had been set on my head, I had never feared death so much as in those moments, when I was trapped in a bloody battlefield.

The faith, the trust, the confidence in God, were as a sun lighting up my life throughout the war, and under the rain of shells we prayed silently and hoped God would save us. One must hope, I said to myself: the man who has no hope in his heart is doomed — so long as a man is alive he can hope. And God was with us — something millions of our people could not say.

On July 29, in the afternoon, the shelling stopped, the battle was over, the Germans retreated, and the Russians entered the village of Kumatch.

We came out of our hideout, which was near the woods, and the first thing we saw was Russian soldiers, marching out of the forest, in small groups, each group in single file and all the groups in line abreast, each about a hundred meters from the next. We stood still, waiting for the first group to reach us.

It consisted of 10 men, and lo and behold: the captain in charge was a Jew. His name was Polak. One can imagine his excitement to find himself liberating four Jewish survivors of the Nazi oppression. Our joy was no less: our liberator, the man whom we embraced and kissed, was a brother Jew. Captain Polak asked us for our guns, because if Russian soldiers found us armed, they might take us for anti-Russian partisans. We gave him the guns and we left him as free men starting a new life. It seemed like a dream. In the morning everything around us was in flames, but we came through it untouched.

Lithuania was liberated from Nazi occupation, but the war continued in Europe as well as in Asia. On May 9, 1945, the war ended in Europe with the unconditional surrender of Germany.

Following this surrender, an American-British-Soviet Summit Conference took place at Potsdam, in the outskirts of Berlin, between July 17 and August 2, to discuss future peace arrangements. Since President Roosevelt had passed away in April, the new American president, Harry Truman, participated. In England, Winston Churchill lost the elections, but he attended the opening session of the Conference. Then he was replaced by his successor Clement Attlee. During the Summit, on July 27, an ultimatum to surrender was issued to Japan. It refused and the Allied Forces decided on a nuclear attack, dropping an atom bomb on Hiroshima on August 6. There was a lot of damage and — according to publications in the news media — 71,000 people were killed.

On August 9, the Soviet Union declared war on Japan and the next day a nuclear bomb was dropped on Nagasaki. Japan immediately surrendered. The ceremony of this surrender was held on September 2, 1945, by General Douglas MacArthur, on the deck of the warship "Missouri." World War II was over.

Before World War II broke out, 250,000 Jews were living in Lithuania (including Vilno, called "Jerusalem of Lithuania"), in 240 communities. When the Soviets occupied Lithuania, in 1941, more than 7,000 Jews were deported to Siberia, some for being Zionists, others for being rich people.

During the Nazi rule, 94% of the Jews of Lithuania were murdered. The day of our liberation was, therefore, not a happy one: exactly at the moment the world was to come out from darkness to a new dawn, at a time the Jews condemned to die in concentration camps were being liberated, my brother and I found ourselves in the face of a reality of destruction and suffering. The Jewish people was to be among the victors, but not among the celebrants.

Free of the murderous Nazi menace, my brother Joseph and I first of all went to the Kalesnik woods and flung ourselves on the common grave of our brother Jews of Simnas, where our beloved mother and little brother Yehuda'le were buried.

It was summer, the sun was blazing, but we were shivering all over, weeping, numbly reciting the Kaddish (the prayer for the dead). Was it real or only a dreadful nightmare? The martyrs cried out from the ground to the Lord God, to whom vengeance belongeth, to avenge their innocent spilt blood. To our minds came all our vows, made during the three years of hiding, to wreak vengeance on the murderers of our parents, brothers and other innocent Jews, to exercise retaliation on the twentieth century cannibals for their unspeakable crimes.

A few days after the murder of the Jews of Simnas, while we were hiding in the barn of Bogdanovitch, we heard laborers speaking about the killing of the Jews. One laborer said that one of the victims had been hit by ten bullets, and dozens of people were buried alive, and Mikulsky the woodcutter shouted at him: "Why should you pity the Jews?" I trembled listening to Mikulsky and noted in my diary: "If I survive, that man is dead! I must remain alive to avenge the death of my little brother Yehuda'le."

While I thought of revenge for the blood of the little children who were thrown alive into their common grave in the forest, I felt a murderous rage rising within me and I imagined what I would do if faced with one of the killers. I felt like a beast sure of its prey and remembered the words of the Jewish poet Haim Nahman Bialik in one of his poems: "Vengeance for the blood of a child, the devil has not yet created."

I quoted in my diary Hitler's declaration, "Not one Jew will remain wherever a German soldier has set foot," and I noted: "Some Jews will remain, here and there, and will reveal to the world what has been done to us, and, if they only have the chance, will surely avenge our people." When revealing to the world the crimes that took place, one must, of course, recognize that there were Christians who didn't raise their hands against Jews. But many others who committed sadistic murder on a Friday, were absolved in the confessional on Sunday, and resumed the slaughter on Monday.

While we were hiding at the Matulevitches, we were told that one of their neighbors, a peasant from their own hamlet of Saulinai, a certain Gumovsky, had taken part in the killing of the Simnas Jews. Gumovsky was overjoyed he had hit the Jew Berkson — and those two had been good friends — and shouted: "I hit him in the forehead, damn him, and then I took off part of his nose!"

I noted in my diary: "The blood of the slaughtered must be avenged; God will avenge the blood of His people!"

While I was only dreaming of revenge, the Jewish partisans in the forests actually put it into effect.

The Jewish commanders in the partisan battalions led their men to battle not only with the general military slogans. The order "forward," which was given in the Yiddish language, was accompanied by the call: "For our fathers and mothers, for our children, brothers and sisters, for our people — revenge!"

The aspiration to wreak vengeance on the murderers of the Jews, brought my brother and myself to a meeting with an officer of the Russian counter-espionage, involved in the search after war criminals, to discuss how to proceed. He advised Joseph to join his unit as an interpreter and suggested that I join the local militia, which was the name of the police under the Soviet regime, and help track down the Nazi collaborators.

To begin our searches, I had a list of roughly a hundred Lithuanians from the Simnas neighborhood, who were Nazi collaborators. I gathered all the necessary information about those people at the time, and the first day of my joining the militia, the Russians — using the addresses I had supplied and myself accompanying them — rounded up 40 men, who were taken to Alitus jail. In time, with the aid of myself and other Jewish survivors, the Russians apprehended many of the Lithuanian collaborators, interrogated them and brought them to justice. Hundreds of them were either sent to prison for many years or forced to face a firing squad.

I did not intend, of course, to confine myself to punishment activities, and I did everything in my power to reward the peasants who had helped us in the dark days. Some of the Lithuanians who had helped me survive were nationalists, or men of affluence, not favored by the Soviet regime, and I had to make enormous efforts to have the Soviet authorities modify somewhat their inimical attitude towards them.

From Simnas, I left for the district capital of Alitus and was admitted there to the N.K.V.D. (security service) in the capacity of a district interrogator of the Nazi collaborators. It meant interrogating personally those who were brought to the Alitus prison, as well as to visit the towns belonging to that district and supervise the interrogations there.

When I visited the town of Varena, I found a group of Jewish Holocaust

Aba Gefen and his brother Joseph after their liberation

survivors, who had fought in the partisan movement, and were now roaming the nearby villages and hamlets to revenge on the Nazi sympathizers responsible for the murder of Jews, on farmers who had betrayed Jews to the Nazis, and on civil officials who had collaborated with the Germans.

The group dealt with prisoners who had been proven guilty and sent those in whose cases there was no hard evidence of their participation in the murder of Jews to Alitus. They told me that in many cases they had enough evidence for a conviction, but lacked the ability to compile it in Russian, as required by the

Holocaust survivors' revenge group.
Standing left to right: Pietka Berkowicz, Benjamin Rogowski, Leon Kahn (Kaganowicz). Seated: Yitzhak Sonenzon

Russians, and criminals whom they had spent weeks tracking were set free once they got to Alitus, for lack of proper documentation. We agreed that in the future they would send the prisoners to Alitus, to me personally, and I would interrogate them and document the cases before processing them.

Those were the days of partial retribution, when not only Jewish survivors were anxious to track down the Nazi collaborators, but also Soviet officers were ready to carry out even irregular, and very forceful activities to punish at least some of those who had lent full support to the Germans. Among the Russians involved in tracking down the Nazi beasts and their collaborators, were Russian officers who had liberated the extermination camps of Treblinka and Majdanek. There, Jewish prisoners would immolate themselves on the electrified wire fences — it was better to die that way than in the gas-chambers. The dead were deemed luckier than the doomed living.

In those days, the Soviets were very willing to exact revenge on the Lithuanians, whose thirst for Jewish blood knew no bounds and who eagerly volunteered to finish off the Jews of Latvia and other areas under Nazi occupation. The intellectuals of Lithuania, in this grim ambition, were no better than the masses, often worse. The Lithuanians were among the most vicious collaborators of the Nazis. Wherever they found themselves, they repeated the most abhorrent cruelties such as they had already committed in Lithuania.

CRIMINAL INDIFFERENCE

Lithuanian Jews, who had fled, or been deported to Russia and managed to survive the Nazi horrors, began to return to Lithuania, where they found the country soaked with the blood of their families and friends. When the repatriates heard of the savagery beyond human imagination, many of them refused to believe.

The general public was inclined to doubt the atrocities because of their very enormity and hence, the non credibility of what took place. What happened under the Nazis were things of "another time," of "another planet."

There also were those who ignored the Talmudic saying, "Judge not thy neighbor until thou art come into his place," and could not resist asking: "Why did the Jews not rebel?" They were ready to judge without asking themselves in absolute honesty whether in a similar situation they might not have reacted in the same way. Years later, I even heard people suggest — from the comfort of their peaceful surroundings — to have ready-made prescriptions for what the Jews ought to have done in the countries occupied by the Nazis.

I could not have rebelled when I was arrested unarmed in Kovno and taken with 20 other Jews to the city square.

And my brethren from Simnas, the old and the ailing, the women and children, who — after being confined in the barracks, starved, and tortured — were finally marched barefoot and half-naked, lashed and clubbed, for three endless kilometers, to the Kalesnik woods and the waiting weapons of destruction in the bestial hands of Nazi and Lithuanian murderers — could they have rebelled? Or the thousands who were lined up facing the open pits and shot down by bursts of machine-gun fire! Could they rebel?

When the Germans began to deport the Jews from the ghettoes to the death camps, they told them they were being sent to work camps where they would enjoy better food and accomodations. Postcards arrived in the ghettoes from those camps in which the inmates had been forced to write to their friends: "We are well here. We have work and the behavior towards us is nice. We are waiting for you!" Many went, therefore, to the camps voluntarily, expecting better conditions, and, on arrival, they found a lovely spot: orchestra playing at the entrance, flowers blooming, as though in a rest-camp for German soldiers, and on the camp's gate was proclaimed: "Work makes free."

Once past the portals, they realized the awful truth. Bolts and bars behind an electrified fence and a perimeter of armed guards, kicks and punches right away, often in the face, and an orgy of orders screamed in rage. Complete nakedness after being stripped, the shaving off of all one's hair, and rags for clothes. Then, a march to a barrack, and again selection — to the right and to the left, to hard labor for as long as they could stand it, or to the crematorium; who shall live and who shall die, in the fatal words of a penitent prayer of the New Year and the Day of Atonement. Could they rebel?

Or could Adolf Blumental who saved me from the accursed Fort VII in Kovno, and was himself deported to the extermination camp in Dachau, where he died after having become a "Muselmann" have rebelled? The term "Muselmann" — German for "Moslem" — was coined in the death-camp in Auschwitz, and it referred to a person irreversibly exhausted, worn out, close to death. Blumental was seen walking slowly and hesitantly in the camp, searching in the dung for bones to eat. Could a "Muselmann" rebel?

However, those who thought they could rebel, resist or flee, did try it, even if only to die with honor. Altke Bialotzky, a woman from our town of Simnas, when taken to the pit in the woods, passionately struck a young Lithuanian, Vite Yatkovsky, who had been brought up in her home but now pointed his murderous rifle at her breast. She cried out: "You too, Vite?" That was real heroism!

When the mass graves of the assassinated Jews at Fort IX in Kovno were full to the brim, the Nazi authorities decided to cremate the corpses in order to eliminate the traces of their crimes. A special group of Jews from the Kovno ghetto was set up to carry out the horrendous act of pulling the corpses out of the mass graves and burning them. The group was kept at the Fort under a very heavy guard. They knew that the Nazis would take the greatest care to ensure that no witnesses survived, and they realized that, as bearers of the secret, they must be disposed of and would be shot and burned the moment their task was concluded. So 64 tried to escape. 39 were caught and shot. 25 reached the gates of the ghetto, six of whom were arrested by the ghetto guards. Only 19 succeeded in joining the underground that existed in the ghetto, whose main activity was to send young boys and girls to the forests. All these 19 escapees reached the partisans.

Even in the most terrible of extermination camps, in Auschwitz, there was — in spite of the hopelessness of the situation — an attempt at rebellion by the Jewish "Special Squad." "Special Squads" (Sonderkommandos) were auxiliaries forced to assist in the exterminations. It was their task to maintain order among the new arrivals who were to be sent to the gas chambers, to extract the corpses from the chambers, to pull gold teeth from jaws, to cut women's hair, to sort and classify clothes, shoes, and the contents of the luggage, to transport the bodies to the crematoria and oversee the operation of the ovens, to extract and eliminate the ashes.

Conceiving and organizing these squads was one of the Nazis' most demonic crimes. Their institution represented an attempt to shift onto others — specifically, the victims — the burden of guilt, so that they were deprived of even the solace of innocence. The idea of the Nazis was thus: if they wish so, they can destroy not only the bodies but also the souls.

A group of 400 Jews from Corfu, who in July 1944 had been included in the "Special Squads," refused, without exception, to do the work, and were immediately gassed to death. There were cases of suicide at the moment of recruitment or immediately after.

The "Special Squads," bearers of a horrendous secret, were kept rigorously apart from the other prisoners and the outside world, and were not to escape the others' fate. They knew the Germans would prevent any man who had been part of their group from surviving and telling the gruesome truth. The squads succeeded one another, each remaining operational for a few months. On October 7, 1944, a squad rebelled: it set fire to a crematorium, killed several SS men, cut the barbed wire and escaped; few of them survived.

The finest expression of Jewish defiance against the Nazis was the Warsaw ghetto uprising, a heroic hopeless rebellion, when there was no possibility of getting any assistance from the outside. The fighters of the Warsaw ghetto were few in number, but they made history, redeeming the honor of their people. Mordechai Anielewitcz, commander of that uprising, wrote in his last letter from the ghetto, on April 23, 1943: "The last aspiration of my life has been fulfilled. Jewish self-defense has become a fact."

Not less heroic was the spiritual resistance. Jews — in the ghettoes and extermination camps — clandestinely celebrated the Sabbath, lit candles on *Hanukkah,* gathered for prayers on holidays, and organized schools. Risking their lives, many smuggled into the camps their prayer-shawls and phylacteries, hid them in their barracks under the rafters of the ceiling, and every morning heroically put them on very briefly, saying only *Shmah Israel* ("Hear, O Israel, the Lord our God, the Lord is One!"). Jews marched to the mass graves in prayer-shawls, chanting psalms, while others proudly sang the "*Hatikvah*" (Hope), the Jewish national anthem.

A specific form of Jewish civil resistance was the resolve to bequeath the testimony of all that transpired in the Jewish communities under the Nazis and this became an expression of the people's will. Young and old recorded events — intellectuals accustomed to writing and simple folk who penned painfully. The most famous case of a written testimony from the Holocaust period is the diary composed by Anne Frank while hiding from the Nazis in Amsterdam.

What some transcribed, others photographed. In the ghetto of Lodz, one day a whole family was seen dragging a cart full of dung through the street — father and mother in front pulling, son and daughter pushing from behind. Towards them came the ghetto photographer. He stopped but did not take out his camera, unwilling to film such degradation. But the father bade him proceed: "Let the snapshot be preserved, let others that come after us know how downtrodden we were!" The photographer hesitated no longer.

All that was to be a link between the generation fated to die and the generation to arise after the Holocaust. It bespoke that consciousness of history which Jewry developed when its very existence was at stake: the compulsion to record each daily torment, to maintain a secret archive, to scratch a name on the wall of a prison cell, and next to it add the word "Vengeance!"

A situation in which a hostage is being held by a terrorist or a crazy man is not uncommon in our days. Each time the entire world is surprised anew how mighty governments find themselves helpless when hostages are held by their captors. Now imagine the situation of the Jews when they were hostages in the hands of devouring beasts, who, a long time before the final liquidation, did everything to weaken them physically, to destroy their will, to take away from them their human dignity and to cut them off from the outside world. Systematic starvation, diseases and death made impossible the resistance of the masses who focused only on immediate survival: to get a piece of bread and to maintain the body yearning for warmth and food.

The daily killing, burning and gassing of thousands of Jews, until one-third of the Jewish people was exterminated, was no secret. Tens of thousands of Germans witnessed or heard of the fate of the Jews. The annihilation of Jewry was known to every German military unit, to all its officers and soldiers. The executioners themselves numbered in the thousands. They all spoke freely about this to friends and relatives; many of them related the extermination of men, women and children with the icy coldness of a businessman discussing his balance sheet.

If not for Hitler, there would not have been a Holocaust causing the annihilation of six million Jews, and many research works have been published on Hitler's reasons for hating the Jews so much that no means were disqualified in his eyes to achieve their extermination. There are those who try to discern the source of his wickedness towards the Jews in the Jewish blood which may have flowed in his veins, and there are those who attribute it to the syphilis with which he was infected by a Jewish whore in Vienna. Others add to the personal dimension historical processes, economic factors and cultural and political crises. One thing is clear: without the support of the entire German people, Hitler would not have succeeded in carrying out the murder of the Jews.

Millions of Germans helped to forge, sustain and promote Hitler's power which they knew was being used to kill millions of defenseless men, women and children. They supported an unparalleled villainy of conquest, subjugation, enslavement and murder, and averted their eyes from the trains that carried the Jews to their doom; but all knew of their ultimate fate. They turned their backs so as not to see and not to feel touched by what was happening, deluding themselves that not seeing was a way of not knowing, and that not knowing relieved them of their share of complicity in the evil deeds.

But Nazi Germany is not alone responsible. The guilt must be shared by all who looked on indifferently, when they could have saved so many of those Jews. The free and civilized world abandoned the millions of Jewish victims and made their extermination possible. The origin of the criminal indifference of the world to the annihilation of the Jews by Hitler was the traditional anti-Semitism that had its basis in the lamentable concepts of the Christian Church.

All through the centuries, the Church — in the name of God — vilified, harassed, hounded, tortured and killed the Jews. It ravaged them during the Crusades and the Inquisition. It forbade them to own land or to belong to trade guilds. It drove them to usury and into ghettoes, and then repelled them for their survival and success in spite of all.

The Crusades made the Middle Ages one long martyrdom for the Jews. To bolster racial and religious bigotry, the preposterous ritual blood libel and the monstrous charge of Jewish poisoning of wells were widespread, and the wild charge of Jewish desecration of the Host was propagated. The end-product of this malignancy was the expulsion of the Jews from one country after another. The Spanish Jews were given the choice of exile or baptism. Many of them left, but the Marranos went on living their clandestine lives in Spain, heroically handing on their Jewish tradition in secret from generation to generation, whatever the personal hazard.

The Catholic Church, alarmed by the Reformation, and finding the familiar scapegoat at hand, sought to ascribe that phenomenon, in part at least, to Jewish machinations. The Protestant Reformation, for its part, was at first highly critical of the Roman Catholic Church's policy towards the Jews. It was Luther's hope that his criticism would encourage a wave of Jewish converts out of thankfulness for his professed charity.

When this did not happen, he very soon attacked the Jews in the most vicious denunciations: "What then shall we Christians do with this damned rejected race of Jews?...Their synagogues should be set on fire...Their homes should likewise be broken down and destroyed...All their cash and valuables of silver and gold ought to be taken from them..."

Was not this the kind of ideology that the Nazis put into practice centuries later in dealing with the Jews? "The murder of six million Jews by the Germans" — says Howard Fast in his book *'The Jews'* — "was the final, hideous outcome of a Christian ideology that spent two thousand years teaching mankind to hate the Jews."

The ambition of the medieval Church, it was said, was not to burn but to convert the Jews; modern anti-Semitism was dedicated to the destruction of the Jews. But it was the Church's universal apathy and indifference to modern anti-Semitism that made Auschwitz and Treblinka possible. Had the Vatican done all that was in its power and prestige, things might have been very different.

Pope Pius XII and his assistants knew details of the extermination of the Jews. The Polish ambassador, accredited to the Vatican, came from time to time to report to the Pope about the killings. The Pope resented being bothered by the ambassador, and he is quoted as having said: "I have already heard his complaints a hundred times. Do I have to hear them again?"

Had the Church taken a vigorous stand against the murder of Jews, had the Pope raised his voice, Catholics in Germany, Poland, France and other occupied countries of Europe would have considered it their duty to help save Jews, or at least to refrain from collaboration with the Nazis in their atrocities.

The fate of the European Jews was decided at the Wannsee Conference in Berlin on January 20, 1942, where the heads of the Nazi regime adopted the plan to exterminate eleven million Jews.

In 1944, when the Jews were being exterminated en masse in crematoria and gas-chambers, a young Polish Jew, Samuel Zigelbaum, met in London with an American Jewish officer, Arthur Goldberg, who years later became a justice of the United States Supreme Court, and afterwards the U.S. ambassador to the United Nations. Zigelbaum begged Goldberg to transmit to the leaders of the Allies — American president Franklin Delano Roosevelt and British prime minister Winston Churchill — the supplication of the Jews: "Stop the killing by bombing the extermination sites in Auschwitz and the railroads leading to them."

Arthur Goldberg transmitted the request immediately. The reply was that the Allied forces were busy with their war effort activities and were not in a position to bomb Auschwitz. While the synthetic rubber works seven kilometers from the extermination sites were bombed, as well as the SS hospital some 15 meters away, no action was ever undertaken against the unguarded camp installations easily recognizable by the smoking fires of the crematoria. Samuel Zigelbaum committed suicide in front of the British Parliament in protest against the apathy and criminal indifference of the free and civilized world to the mass spilling of Jewish blood.

The British published in 1939 their "White Paper" barring the gates of Palestine at the very moment when the Holocaust was engulfing European Jewry.

When the Nazis were conquering country after country, heartbreaking tragedy befell the SS "Struma," a converted yacht of about 200 tons burthen. Into it, somehow, were crowded 769 Jews, many young boys and girls among them. It reached Istanbul at the end of 1941. The Turks would not permit the immigrants to stay in Turkey, the British would not permit them to enter Eretz Israel. The ship, perforce, put out to sea, and, at the end of February 1942, it was sunk.

Unfortunately, the Jews of the free world, too, have not reacted to the mass murder of their brethren in Europe as they should have done, and there is also criticism in regard to the behavior by the leadership of the "*Yishuv*" — the Jewish community in Palestine. As a result of their absolute concentration on advancing the idea of the establishment of a Jewish state, they did not do all they could.

PART TWO

HOPE

LONGING FOR REVENGE

In my struggle against the Lithuanian murderers of the Jews, I engaged in two activities: I interrogated those who were brought to the Alitus prison and I searched through the towns of the district. When an interrogation ended, the prisoner was escorted to his cell by a Russian soldier or a Lithuanian militia man. There were cases where one undergoing interrogation tried to escape. He was shot on the spot, the escort filed a formal report about the case, and the interrogator added his signature.

One day, in the town of Yeznas, a gendarme burst in to announce that the picture of Joseph Stalin, the omnipotent Soviet ruler, had been thrown into an outdoor toilet at the local public school. In those days, there could be no bigger crime. I left for the school, accompanied by two Lithuanian gendarmes and a Russian soldier. I asked to see the principal, and couldn't believe my eyes: in front of me was sitting Gedraitis, who had been a teacher in my own town of Simnas. As soon as the Nazis came, Gedraitis was appointed prosecutor-general, and at his command, Jews were murdered in the first days of the Nazi occupation. When the Red Army arrived, he fled to Yeznas and became a school principal.

I was no longer interested in Stalin's picture lying in the outhouse and left the Russian soldier deal with it. I placed Gedraitis under immediate arrest and took him to the militia station. We interrogated him throughout the night, and he recounted everything. He omitted nothing. When he was taken to his cell, he tried to escape to the nearby woods. But a gendarme's bullet brought him down, and I signed a formal report.

It was July 1945, the war had ended, and political factors began to play a determining role in regard to the Nazi collaborators. The Russians started to set many assassins of Jews free, on the pretext of "lack of sufficient evidence." Because of the Gedraitis case, they started an investigation and discovered I had signed a number of reports on escape attempts. They decided to arrest me. A Jewish doctor, employed at the N.K.V.D. headquarters, heard somebody say that a militia major was going to Yeznas to arrest a Jewish interrogator for "complicity in illegal acts of revenge against Lithuanians." The doctor forwarded the information to a friend. Within 24 hours, my brother — who had in the meantime been discharged from the Red Army — came to Yeznas to inform me.

Knowing the Soviet methods of interrogation, it was clear to me that, if I were to be arrested for the Gedraitis case, I might also be forced to tell them what I did in the town of Butrimonis for the Zubrow brothers and be faced with the threat of execution.

While in Butrimonis, I was one day invited for supper by the local Lithuanian pharmacist. I was very surprised because, according to the information we had about him at the militia, the man was an anti-Soviet nationalist whose activities we were following closely. On my arrival at his home, it didn't take me long to realize the reason for that unexpected invitation. A side-door opened, and in front of me was standig Feliks, one of the sons of Mrs. Zubrowa, the Polish mistress of the farm in Metel.

Without wasting time, Feliks explained the purpose of that meeting. He reminded me that in June 1940, the Russians were going to deport their family, for being wealthy and Polish nationalists, to Siberia. It was thanks to the German attack on the Soviet Union that they had not been deported. However, in spite of that, they condemned the persecution of the Jews by the Germans and helped me when I came to them. Now, they needed my help.

He related to me that when times changed and the Russians returned to Simnas, he and his brother, Vacius went into the woods and joined the anti-Soviet guerrillas. He said he knew I wasn't a Communist: I was only pursuing those Nazi collaborators who had participated in the killing of the Jews. He therefore hoped I would be ready to disregard their being Polish nationalists and help him and his brother at a very critical hour in their lives.

He told me that there was going to be a repatriation of Poles from Lithuania to Poland. The head of the Polish Repatriation Commission in Vilno was a relative of theirs, who had offered the two brothers jobs there. But in order to go to Vilno and accept the jobs, they needed certificates attesting that they were respectable Lithuanian citizens. They could not get such certificates in Simnas, so they decided to come to me and beg for my help: they needed official documents, with the seal of the local militia, that before departing for Vilno they were dwelling as peaceful citizens in Butrimonis.

It wasn't easy for me to grant them the required help. It meant risking my own life. I knew the Soviet Criminal Code: if I were caught, they would accuse me of treason for helping persons considered to be "enemies of the people," and I would be punished by imprisonment for up to a life-term and deported to Siberia, or by the death penalty. On the other hand, how could I refuse to recompense somebody who had helped me in my time of need? I finally issued them the necessary certificates, and prayed to God that the N.K.V.D. would not find out about it. Now, I had to flee from Lithuania.

My brother and I arrived at the Polish Repatriation Commission in Vilno, and Feliks provided us with forged papers certifying that we had been born in Poland. On August 25, 1945, we were put on the 46th Polish repatriation transport and succeeded in crossing the border without difficulties.

We arrived in Lodz, where we were told that a clandestine Jewish-Zionist organization called *Brichah* was smuggling Jewish survivors across the frontiers of European states on their way to the Land of Israel. We went to the *Brichah* and after a few days were sent to Cracow.

After two weeks in Cracow, the headquarters of the *Brichah* decided to send off several groups in an attempt to make the border crossing. Instructions were that only "adequate" people could join these groups, in other words, only those devoid of even the most essential personal belongings; otherwise they could not plausibly pass as recently freed inmates of concentration camps with no more than the shirts on their backs.

As my brother and I fulfilled the condition, we were included in the party of adventure. I was put in charge of a group of 20 people and we set forth for Katowice. There we were provided with International Red Cross documentation and a permit for me and my group to cross the Polish-Czech border in transit for Greece, "our mother country": it certified that we were Greek Jews whom the

German invader had transported to concentration camps in Poland, and, now that the war was over, we were returning to our homeland. My brother and I were given the names Joseph Bohiah and Aba Bohiah and were bidden to speak Hebrew throughout the journey and over and over again to proclaim: "*Ani ivri greco*," a strange polyglot rendering of "I am a Greek Hebrew."

In those days, unsettled and nomadic refugees were traipsing across Europe from country to country. The wholesale disorganization and lack of proper frontier controls, made it easy to cross borders with the weirdest of documents. Best of all were Greek papers, apparently approved of by the Soviet commander of the city, because very few in Central Europe knew Greek. Our groups could either pretend not to speak the local language and give no reply, or answer in Hebrew, which passed off as Greek.

On the train, we met several other groups of "Greeks" but avoided all contact with them. Five such groups arrived at the station of Dzerzice, where we stopped for two hours. The Gentiles simply stared at us, and, while some really believed that we were genuine Greeks, others undoubtedly knew the truth and thought: "What does it matter to us if the Jews leave Poland?"

We arrived at Zebzidovice, a frontier stop on the Polish side. Neither the Poles nor the Czechs controlled it strictly, and we entered Bohumin, first border town of Czechoslovakia, without any harassment. We decided to board the first train out. It was bound for Prague, and on the way we changed to one going to Bratislava.

In its 25 rooms, the Yelen Hotel camp in Bratislava could house two hundred refugees under relatively human conditions; the *Brichah* had no choice but to squeeze in up to a thousand people. Consequently, the situation was wretched, the filth and slovenliness were indescribable. Not surprisingly, we could not snatch a moment's sleep that night. Within two days, my brother and I left with a group of 80 "Greeks" for Vienna.

We left in a passenger train, and then traveled in a goods train which crossed the Czech-Austrian border at a point where there were no frontier guards. From the railway station we came to the refugee camp at the Rothschild Hospital.

After the war, Austria — the country of birth of Adolf Hitler — had been, like Germany, divided into four occupation zones: Russian, American, British and French. Vienna lay in the Russian zone, but was in turn subdivided into four sections: the Rothschild Hospital was in the American section. The moment we arrived there, we ceased to be "Greeks" and became Jewish refugees from Poland, protected by the International Committee for the Assistance of the Displaced Jews from Poland, which looked after the affairs of the *Brichah* in Vienna.

In Vienna we were told about the forthcoming trials against the Nazi leaders. The four principal prosecutors of the four main occupation powers had lodged in Berlin an indictment against 24 of the former heads of the Nazi regime (political, military, and economic leaders) captured by the Allies, charging them with numerous crimes against peace, conventional war crimes, crimes against humanity, and conspiracy. The proceedings of the inter-Allied Tribunal at Nuremberg that began on November 20, 1945, were conducted in four languages (English, French, Russian and German), and endured for over 10 months. During the course of the trials one of the indicted Nazis committed suicide, and the tribunal decided that another of them could not then be tried because of his physical and mental condition.

The Nuremberg Trials concluded on October 1, 1946, with a judgment in which 12 of those war criminals were sentenced to death, three to life imprisonment, four to various prison terms, and three acquitted. The death sentences were carried out by hanging on October 16-17, 1946, except for Herman Goering, who took poison and killed himself before he could be executed, and Martin Borman, who had been tried in absentia. Adolf Hitler had committed suicide on April 30, 1945, a week before Germany was forced to surrender.

When the Americans recovered Hitler's political testament, they defined it as "Hitler's final anti-Semitic tirade."

It illustrated vividly Hitler's recognition that he had lost his war against the Jews. He had fought for the "final solution" of the Jewish problem, that not a single Jew be left alive. Having lost this war, he feared to face trial and be confronted with six million would-be accusers. In the last moments of his life, Hitler felt symbolically defeated because he had not succeeded in his vendetta, and the Jewish people continued to live.

Only 24 Nazi leaders were brought to trial in Nuremberg. Many others escaped judgment and were living in prisoner-of-war camps, in relative comfort.

Others were at liberty, watching with hidden disdain the Allies' slow-motioned dilatory judicial organization. They all hoped to escape punishment for their horrible crimes.

Spontaneous acts of vengeance were carried out without authorization, by some soldiers in the Jewish Brigade from Palestine, against German prisoners-of-war who had fallen into their hands during the first days of the surrender by the German forces in northern Italy. These Jewish soldiers also tried to locate Nazi criminals who had not been apprehended.

These soldiers wore the uniforms of the British military police and were equipped with appropriate vehicles. They would come in a team of three to a certain address, find the wanted criminal, pull him out of the house, read out the list of his murderous deeds, and inform him of his death sentence. Then they shot him on the spot. In some cases, they discovered Nazi criminals hiding among the Jewish refugees, after stripping off their clothes and finding they had not been circumcised.

In the hearts of the Jewish survivors, who left behind countries which had become the graveyards of thousands of their brethren, there burned like fire the longing for revenge, and some of them organized the "*Nekamah*" (revenge) group. They were mostly young people who had belonged to the partisan movement during the war. The organization was headed by Aba Kovner, a partisan from Vilno.

The members of the *Nekamah* group did not wish to leave the European continent, soaked with the blood of thousands of their relatives and friends, before dealing a deadly blow to the Nazi criminals. They planted their members inside the camps of the Nazi criminals, and executed some of the assassins. They decided to carry out a massive liquidation and, since they had agreed to accept the discipline of the emissaries of the "*Haganah*" (the Jewish underground self-defense organization in Palestine) they presented the liquidation plan to the latter for approval. The *Haganah*, as an organization, refused to give its approval. So they planned to kill six million Germans, by putting poison in the bread of the prisoners, in revenge for the six million murdered Jews. They succeeded in carrying out a number of liquidations but fell far short of realizing their dreams.

One of the *Haganah* emmisaries attempting to apprehend Nazis still at large,

Asher Ben-Nathan, Commander of the Brichah *in Austria*

was Asher Ben-Nathan ("Arthur"), who had arrived in Vienna to direct the activities of the *Brichah* in Austria. In 1944, Arthur had been on the staff of the Investigation Division of the Political Department of the Jewish Agency in Haifa, collecting intelligence, especially for Jewish volunteers from Eretz Israel who parachuted behind the enemy lines. In that capacity, he and his colleagues assembled vast amount of oral evidence from survivors of the Holocaust, who had made their way to safety, concerning what had happened in the concentration camps and about Nazis known to have been involved in plans to wipe out Jewish populations.

The material was carefully compiled and checked, and on the strength of it, a list was made of the principal planners and executants of the massacre. The list was delivered by the Jewish Agency to the Allies, and was part of the evidence at the Nuremberg Trials.

In the list of the vilest murderers appeared the name of Adolf Eichmann, the fanatical executor of the plan for the "final solution of the Jewish problem," the Devil who undertook to accomplish the largest and bloodiest crime in history, who had said that he would "gratefully go to the tomb with the death of five million Jews on his conscience, for that would be a source of special pleasure." It was Eichmann who prepared and organized the January 20, 1942 Conference at Wannsee.

After the Conference, Eichmann was given extensive powers to direct the deportations of European Jews to the death camps. He determined the pace and the timing of the deportations, and was responsible not only for ensuring the extermination of the Jews, but also for the confiscation of their property, planning the sterilization of people who were only partly Jewish, and deceiving the outside world and hiding the true facts concerning the mass murders. The relatively less gruesome ghetto at Theresienstadt, in Czechoslovakia, was, among others, used for the deception and was under Eichmann's personal direction.

Arthur imagined his chances of succeeding in the search for Eichmann were good, for everything pointed to his still being alive; he was an Austrian and his family lived in that country. Perseveringly, Arthur set out to hunt him down.

Rumors were rife that Eichmann was hiding in a prisoner-of-war camp in the American zone. Arthur asked the O.S.S. (Office of Strategic Services — the American agency that tracked down fugitive war criminals and handed them over to justice), to check; this was done but nothing emerged. Neither Arthur nor the O.S.S. had a photograph of him; thus they lacked a vital means of identification and detection.

Arthur organized a group of young men to track down any Nazi of Austrian origin who might be connected with Eichmann; the Austrian police provided a list of the Nazis in Austrian jails; Arthur visited each of them in his cell. But it was still all in vain.

Arthur learnt that Dieter Wisliceny, murderer of Slovakian Jewry, was in a Bratislava prison. He reasoned that this would be the man to help him in picking up Eichmann's trail. By devious ways, Arthur got to see Wisliceny, who was sure that Eichmann was alive. Thus informed, Arthur could unearth one of Eichmann's mistresses in Austria. One of his agents won her confidence — with cigarettes, chocolates and cash — and she gave him a photograph of her lover. From then on, there were improved prospects for his capture.

BARRIER BREAKERS

After a week at Rotschild Hospital we were "converted" into Austrian-born Jewish refugees. Each of us was given papers attesting his birth-place in a town or village in the American zone of Austria, and that the bearer had been taken to a concentration camp during the war and was now returning home. We arrived in Salzburg in the American zone in the middle of October 1945 and were lodged at the Ridenburg camp. Upon arrival, three possibilities existed for the Jewish wanderer: to settle down in a camp in the American zone of Austria; to go on to Italy, where economic conditions were bad, but with numerous prospects of "*Aliyah Beth*" (clandestine immigration to Eretz Israel), or to go on to Munich, in the American zone of Germany, and settle down in a camp there, with poor chances of getting to Palestine, but with good camp conditions.

In Germany, at the beginning, the American authorities were against separate camps for the Jewish refugees. They had favored the idea of common camps for all refugees, without distinction as to nationality, race or creed: they felt that such divisions meant perpetuating the racist policy of the Nazis. But the refugees demanded that they be left each with his own, and in the end, it was agreed to separate them by nationality and to recognize the Jews as a national group.

General Dwight Eisenhower visited the camps and met David Ben-Gurion, Chairman of the Jewish Agency for Palestine. They reached an agreement that the American zones in Germany and Austria would be used as temporary asylum for the homeless remnants of European Jewry. A delegation of the Jewish Agency, which acted within the UNRRA (United Nations Relief and

Rehabilitation Agency) came to Germany to see that the Ben-Gurion-Eisenhower agreement was faithfully implemented.

Since we had to stay in Salzburg for a while, I offered my services to Pinhas Koppelberg, local leader of the *Brichah,* who was in charge of sending the refugees to Italy. Pinhas was a Holocaust survivor himself and he too, wanted to go to Italy, so was grateful for my offer: he suggested that I stay on a while in Salzburg to replace him. I was attracted by Pinhas' proposal, for I saw that I would derive much satisfaction from the work. But I had little authentic knowledge of the fate of those who did reach Italy. When I remembered everything that these fellow-sufferers had gone through, I was reluctant to be responsible for sending them anywhere, without knowing what exactly was in store for them. I told Pinhas that I would accept his proposal if I were first allowed to go to Italy and find out, on the spot, what had transpired there. He agreed.

Just then, by sheer chance, the president of the Salzburg Jewish Community, Doctor Boris Roisin, asked the *Brichah* for a young man to escort three Jewish girls to Villach, in the British zone of Austria, where a Jewish unit from Palestine was stationed. Roisin busied himself with procuring the necessary papers. I volunteered as an escort, but only on Roisin's promise that he would get me into Italy from Villach. So he gave me two letters: one for Major Sacharov, commander of the unit in Villach, and one for Private Mordechai Surkis, of the Jewish Brigade, in Milan.

In a few days, we were off. We crossed the border without any trouble. At the Villach railway station, we met a soldier in British uniform, wearing a Star of David on his sleeves. He was the first Jewish soldier from Palestine I had ever seen. We explained to him our assignment there and he took us to his camp. Major Sacharov undertook to get me to Milan post-haste.

I left Villach in the guise of a soldier of a Jewish transport unit. Private Alexander, in charge of the transit to Italy, furnished me with a name and army number and familiarized me with such cardinal facts as where I came from, how I had been mobilized and where I had served. That same afternoon I was in Milan, at 5 Via Unione Street, a house that resembled Yelen Hotel in Bratislava in its filth and disorder. The following day I met Surkis, a Pole by birth, who had settled in Palestine in 1933. In 1941, he had enlisted in an artillery unit of the British army, then transferred to the Jewish Brigade.

When Britain declared war on Germany after the Nazi invasion of Poland, the Jewish authorities in Palestine issued a statement supporting the declaration. The war that had been forced upon Great Britain was also the war of the Jews. The *Yishuv* — the Jewish community of Palestine — had a threefold concern in those days: the protection of the Homeland, the welfare of its people, victory for the British Empire. The policy of the *Yishuv*, formulated by David Ben-Gurion, was — to fight the war as if there were no "White Paper" barring Jewish immigration and to fight the "White Paper" as if there were no war.

Thousands of young Jewish men and women were eager to join the British forces. Yet, far from welcoming these Jewish volunteers with open arms to fight in the British ranks, Whitehall put many obstacles in the way. The Mandatory Administration brought to trial Jews who clamored for the privilege of fighting against the Nazis, accusing them of illegal possession of arms. 43 members of the "*Palmach*" — the spearhead of the *Haganah*, the military organization of the *Yishuv* — who belonged to Colonel Orde Wingate's "night squads," and had been trained by the British army for special duties against Arab terrorism, were prosecuted for that "crime"!

But in October 1940, after Italy joined the German axis, the British Government granted the Jewish appeal and approved a limited scheme for the enlistment of Jews in distinct units of the British army. So Jewish contingents, officered by Jews, came into being in Palestine and were soon on active service.

In the end, the advance of Rommel's columns in North Africa, the need for extra manpower, made the recruitment of Palestinian volunteers an urgent necessity for Britain. After lengthy discussions, a Jewish Brigade was formed in September 1944, and the number of Palestinian Jewish soldiers on the Allied side rose to 30,000. They were part of over a million Jews who fought Hitler in the ranks of the Allied armies, among them over half a million in the Red Army, 550,000 in the U.S. armed forces, 200,000 in the Polish army, 65,000 British Jews and additional thousands of Jews from South Africa, Canada and France. The flag and the insignia of the Jewish Brigade featured horizontal blue stripes on a white background, with a blue Star of David in the center. Every Jewish officer and enlisted man in the Brigade was also a member of one of the three Jewish underground groups in Palestine.

Having played their full part in the struggle of the nations championing freedom and peace against the Nazi forces of evil, the officers and men of the Jewish Brigade now devoted themselves to the rescue of their brethren, the survivors of the Holocaust. In their encounter with the displaced Jews, the soldiers from Eretz Israel did a wonderful job of instilling the pioneering spirit of Eretz Israel into the inmates of the DP camps. The Star of David rekindled the wish to live and gave hope for the future. Many Jewish refugees approached the Jewish soldiers and kissed the Star of David on their uniforms. The Star of David, which the refugees wore on their infamous yellow badges, as a symbol of shame, had now become a symbol of honor and pride.

These fighters from Eretz Israel became the soul of the *Brichah,* which, initially, was a spontaneous effort. The flight was disorganized and chaotic at first, lacking explicit direction and clear purpose. It took on form, system and planning when the first fugitives made contact with the soldiers of the Jewish units and the Jewish Brigade. The contacts with the soldiers from Eretz Israel gave the meaningless wandering a specific purpose, a tangible goal, an ultimate direction, in the classic Hebrew term of "*aliyah*" (in English — "ascension" or "going up"), which means the coming of Jews from the Diaspora to live in the Land of Israel. Thus was formed the organized *Brichah,* the biggest illegal emigration movement in our century, whose slogan was: breaking all barriers, ever onwards, to the longed-for shore.

Mordechai Surkis became the first Commander of the organized *Brichah* in Europe, through whose routes passed about 250,000 refugees, 120,000 of them through Salzburg.

Mordechai Surkis, First Commander of the Brichah organization

My conversations with Surkis and with the other *Brichah* people in Milan brought me to the conclusion that I should accept Pinhas' proposal: the chances of getting to Palestine from Italy were good, and that was paramount; any other considerations must take second place. Surkis decided to send to Salzburg — to help us organize the work better — one of the *Brichah* activists, Mula Ben Haim. Mula was a Holocaust survivor and had already organized transports from Romania and Yugoslavia to Greece and Italy.

The main part of the *Brichah* work was the hard and unending labor of the *Brichah'nikim*, the barrier-breakers, who moved the refugees using all possible stratagems: with false papers, along the "black" trails, through forests, over mountains and rivers, through snow and rainstorms, in the shadows of the night.

However, when with the help of our American friends we could make it easier for the refugees, we were happy to do so, and the American officers and men, Jews and non-Jews, did help. They often provided us with transportation for the refugees to cross the borders officially from Salzburg to Munich and from Salzburg to Innsbruck. When the Brenner Pass between Austria and Italy, was practically closed by detachments of French, Italian and British forces, and our transit camp at Innsbruck was flooded with refugees impatiently awaiting entry into Italy, I went to Innsbruck to see what could be done.

I found out that, about 130 kilometers from Innsbruck, the border to Italy could be crossed at the village of Nauders, where there were no British, but only French and Italian guards who had no compunction about admitting any bearer of a paper with a French stamp. Beyond the border there, in Merano, was a convalescent home for tuberculous patients, administered by the American Jewish Joint Distribution Committee ("*Joint*"). I decided to try and transfer refugees to Italy through Nauders on certificates provided by the Americans and stating that the bearers had TB and were going to Merano to convalesce.

Off we went to see an Austrian Jew, Max Feingold, the manager of an automobile company. We told him that we needed a vehicle to drive from Salzburg to Merano. He knew a few things about our business and understood our plans perfectly well. I went to Innsbruck with his truck.

We squeezed 35 people into the truck and set out for Nauders. All that we had was the American certificate.

At the frontier post, the French commanding officer received me most courteously. I explained that I was transporting 35 DPs, all of them Jews who had survived the Nazi concentration camps and been liberated by the American army, to the *Joint*'s convalescent home in Merano. All the expenses were taken care of by the American army, and I hoped that the commanding officer, as a son of magnanimous France, would understand and cooperate. He did — communicating with the gendarmerie in Landeck, explaining the situation and adding that the DPs were escorted by a British and an American soldier.

The gendarmerie allowed our truck to pass. The officer then treated me to a large cup of quality French wine, and I offered him sweets and American tinned fruits. It was all very friendly. The Italian inspection was superficial, limited to noting the number of the vehicle, the drivers' names and my own — in other words, only of the persons who would be driving back.

On the way back, I had a second friendly talk with the French officer and this time tried to be quite frank. He was most perceptive: his people, too, had suffered terribly at Nazi hands, he could understand our feelings, and was ready to help us as necessary. We agreed that I should be back that same night with 45 more people, and I re-appeared at 10 o'clock.

We were determined to use the new route to Italy. But the Americans told us it would be difficult for them to furnish crossing passes to Merano. So we decided to travel on forged ones.

The manifold stratagems that were used by the *Brichah* never constituted an end in themselves, but were an inevitable means; it would have been immoral not to use every possible resort for the achievement of the lofty purpose — to move the survivors of Nazi extermination to their Homeland. The American officers, however, could not, at the outset, comprehend it and were not altogether happy about our infractions, for all our shared interest in getting as many refugees as possible out of their zone. They were very formal at first, probing every issue for its strict legality. But soon they began to judge differently, recognizing that certain things were above the written law, and that not to do all they could to facilitate the Holocaust survivors' return home to Eretz Israel would be a moral wrong.

They evinced humane understanding for our position, and our irregularities were viewed not as an objective but as a recourse, inescapable in the conditions of our lives and work, to what was, by any criterion, a praiseworthy end. As time went on, our American friends helped the *Brichah* to the point of even covering up for its "illegal" actions. When one of them was asked why they were doing it, he replied: "I was with the 42nd Division which liberated the Dachau extermination camp. I was among the first to enter it. I was shocked and I trembled when I saw what had happened there; so I decided to help the survivors of those cruelties in whatever way possible."

To be able to carry out its "illegal" activities, the *Brichah* found a refugee in the DP camp of Bad-Gastein, Eliezer Alpert, who specialized in the manufacture of a variety of rubber stamps. I ordered from Eliezer the Italian, French and American stamps, as well as one of the British liaison officer's in Salzburg. Thus equipped, and after preparing the necessary papers for the passengers, we issued corresponding ones for the vehicles, and got under way to Italy, each refugee carrying an identification card from UNRRA. Our convoy of 45 crossed the frontier smoothly.

At the end of March 1946, I went to Munich to discuss the transport of a thousand pioneers, which was originally to have gone from Germany to Belgium and from there to Palestine. The plan was changed and it was decided to transfer them to Italy, via Nauders. In Munich, I was informed that a transport of 500 children was about to depart for Palestine, on immigration certificates issued by Great Britain. Some children from Salzburg were also to join that group.

The transport had been arranged by "Youth Aliyah," the Jewish Agency's Department for Children and Youth Immigration. It was the first authorized contingent for Palestine, and the Salzburg children — my brother Joseph among them, left for Munich on April 8, 1946. It was a day of jubilation for the *Brichah* in Salzburg.

The next day, Peter Moore and Jimmy Cafin arrived from Milan to Salzburg en route to Poland. They had a letter from the Vatican declaring that the Pontifical Secretary of State supported the rescue of Jewish children, and asking the Polish, Czech and Romanian authorities to advance the humanitarian task as much as possible.

Peter and Jimmy meant to organize the transfer of 3,000 Jewish children to Italy, but the Vatican's letter did not contain a firm commitment on its part to take care of the children on their arrival in Italy. It was our job in Salzburg to "repair" the text of the letter, which we did with the help of Marek, a specialist in manufacturing metal stamps.

One and a half million children were among the six million Jews assassinated by the Nazis. "I did not deem myself justified in exterminating the men," declared Heinrich Himmler, "while allowing their children to grow up to avenge themselves on our sons and grandchildren."

Infants were torn from their mothers' arms and hacked to pieces before the very eyes of their families. Babies were thrown into the air like clay pigeons to see how many bullets would pierce the pitiful target in flight. Children were burnt alive and massacred in ghettoes, asylums, hospitals, prisons and Gestapo torture chambers. They were injected with tuberculosis bacillus and poisoned. Thousands died in the concentration camps, victims of hunger and epidemics.

That any Jewish child at all lived through the terrible massacre of innocent babes was, not infrequently, thanks to adoption by well-meaning Christians. The guns silent at last, some Gentile families were reluctant to give the children back to their folks or to a Jewish institution.

Many stubbornly insisted that they would yield the children to their parents and to no-one else. Some demanded large sums for the succor which they had given, and there was bitter bargaining at times. Others refused to return the children, either because they had come to cherish them and could not bear to let them go, or because they wanted to convert them to Christianity. Often, Herculean efforts had to be made to rescue the orphaned children speedily, lest Christianity take too strong a hold or the anti-Semitism instilled in so many of them become irreversible.

One seven-year-old girl, the sole survivor of her family, had been hidden by Christians who brought her up as a Catholic, and taught to cross herself and curse the Jews. It was not unexpected, then, that when, after much pleading, she was restored to her relatives, the child held back and wept, crying: "I don't want to go with these Jews with the side-locks!"

I myself unearthed a nine-year-old boy during an interrogation of a peasant suspected in having participated in the killing of Jews. He denied it and claimed in his defense, that he had known that a neighbor of his was hiding a Jewish child, but he had not betrayed that child to the Germans. I went to see the peasant and found out that a Jewish child was in effect living with him. It took all my insistence to persuade the man to surrender his foster-son for placement in the Jewish orphanage of Kovno.

Redemption of the children who had survived the Holocaust, and transporting them to the shores of Eretz Israel, was among the paramount missions of the *Brichah*. Most of those children were transported as "illegal entrants." Members of the *Brichah* literally carried them on their backs for kilometer upon kilometer, along lonely tracks, across rivers, over mountains, through forests. The *Brichah* boys were, after all, themselves survivors of extermination. Most of them mourned their own murdered kin, and they felt it their moral duty, their privilege, to save the children with great love and devotion.

BLESSED "JOINT" (AJDC) PARTNERSHIP

In the first week of April I received a very pleasing telephone call from Innsbruck: the *Joint* there had been authorized by the French to send as many people as it wished to Italy over a period of three days. After that, however, the frontier would be hermetically sealed. Would I, therefore, start sending contingents without an instant's delay?

The *Joint*, an American Jewish relief organization, was a blessed partner to *Brichah*'s underground operations. Its representatives in the various countries of Europe did not consider themselves just officials of an overt relief organization whose task it was to feed the European Jews who had survived. They meant to be active partners in a mission to fulfill the longing for safe havens.

Most of the *Joint* representatives were unreservedly sympathetic and helpful to the *Brichah* activities. They not only did everything possible to improve the living conditions of the Jewish displaced persons, by supplying them with food, medicine and clothing, they also helped them cross the European borders, by issuing passes which had been honored by the various frontier guards. The *Joint* representatives were permitted to wear military uniforms with AJDC shoulder patches and to use military vehicles. Those vehicles were often used by the *Brichah* in its illegal immigration schemes.

The *Brichah* operatives also sported military uniforms with *Joint* insignias, which were usually — and most helpfully — mistaken for American Army uniforms by the local police and frontier and customs guards. The moving force behind the *Joint*'s massive support for the *Brichah* was Dr. Joseph Schwartz, the director for the *Joint*'s European Operations.

Dr. Joseph Schwartz

The *Joint* provided the cover for *Brichah* operations throughout Eastern Europe — wherever the *Joint* had reopened its offices. It also paid the *Brichah*'s living and operational expenses (*Brichah* activists received no salaries), and financed large railroad transports of Jewish refugees across Eastern Europe. The *Joint* was totally involved in the activities of the *Mossad* financing the acquisition of ships for the illegal Mediterranean crossings. When I arrived in Salzburg, the head of the *Joint* office there was James Rice. He was later replaced by Leon Fisher.

When we received the call from the *Joint* in Innsbruck, we began to work at a hectic pace, immediately contacting our people in Munich. They, however, informed us that their refugees could not possibly arrive within three days. But transports started coming in from Linz. When the three days of agreement expired, we were asked to stop: in three days we had moved 700 refugees into Italy.

We asked our people in Germany to hold up their transports. Ernst Frank, the head of the *Brichah* there, notified all the exit points forthwith but warned me that a convoy was already on its way, and it was physically impossible to halt it. So nothing could be done and, difficulties or no difficulties, 400 more Jews entered Italy.

A few days later, I was informed that a transport of about 600 refugees was waiting in Landeck railway station on its way to Nauders. It had been sent despite instructions to the contrary. I arrived in Innsbruck in the uniform of a soldier of the Jewish Brigade — Nadaf Ben-Zion, number 32091, where I met with Moshe Vaisand. I set off to the frontier with 370 refugees and we reached the *Joint* convalescent home for tuberculous patients in Merano unscathed. Close behind came Moshe with 220 people.

The congestion in Merano was beyond description: people were literally "housed" on the sidewalks, and a few hundred more were waiting in Innsbruck to cross over.

When I returned to Innsbruck, I learnt that another transport of 300 refugees had come from Lindau to Landeck. We had, therefore, no choice but to try and get them, too, across the frontier. I set out with seven trucks full to overflowing. Thankfully, things went well.

It was a glorious week — 2,000 entrants into Italy. But our rapture was short-lived. Bad news came: the ship "*Fedah*" was at anchor, ready to take 1,200 "*ma'apilim*" (illegal immigrants) to Palestine by *Aliyah Beth*, but they were detained at the port of La Spezia in a convoy of Jewish Brigade lorries. Things became more troublesome, too, on the border between the American and Russian zones of Austria, and on the Austrian-German frontier.

Abruptly, the Czech-Austrian border was closed and refugees were denied entry into Austria. The American army no longer gave us certificates to consign legal transports from Vienna to Linz, and forbade transit from Austria into Germany. We had no choice but to move them on to Germany clandestinely. Yona'le Aizenberg and our other guides were quick to find "black" routes, and along those "illicit channels" we started moving en masse. More than once, in attempts to traverse a forest or ford a rivulet, refugees were caught and sent back to Camp Mulln in Salzburg. But we did not give up. If a group was trapped the first night, it tried again the next, and so on until it finally got across.

One night, a transport of 150 refugees was caught on the border trying to cross it illegally. They couldn't imprison 150 people, so an American sergeant and an Austrian gendarme escorted the group back to Camp Mulln. The American sergeant left and the Austrian gendarme remained to finish up the formalities. I entered into a conversation with the gendarme and convinced him to help the *Brichah*, assuring him that he would not be the loser: he would benefit doubly — as the doer of a good deed and the recipient of a material reward. He was to telephone us where and when he was on frontier duty, so that we could move our transports accordingly, his code name would be "Moishele."

His remuneration was chocolate, American cigarettes and liquor. Moishele helped many refugees cross the frontier safely.

I received a message from the *Brichah* point in Einring, Germany, that the American border police there wanted to know with what papers our transports were crossing the border to Germany. They had gone to the Einring refugee camp and asked to see the documents of arrivals. Our people there, of course, showed them nothing and hurried away to warn me. We knew that showing our legal papers might get our American friends in Salzburg in hot water.

The American army command in Austria was not in the slightest interested in looking after refugees and was only too glad to be rid of them, which is why it helped us to get the largest possible number into Germany. However, its counterpart there hardly welcomed the influx; it was aware of the limitations on Jewish entry and could not fathom why, nevertheless, so many were entering legally; the frontier guards had reported that the refugees had American papers, and the American border police in Germany wanted to see those documents.

On the morning of June 18, Yona'le set out with 130 people and crossed the frontier with no trouble, returning at midday.

An hour later he left again with 106 more. At Freilassing, Yona'le saw that the station was full of American military police. Accurately guessing that they were there to "welcome" him, he ordered his "wards" to get off the train and scatter.

The Americans gave chase, but only caught 18, Yona'le among them, who was charged with illegal crossing. The papers that were taken away from Yona'le were signed by me as civil director of Camp Mulln, and Captain Nowinski, head of the U.S. Army's DP Section, agreed that I should go to Germany to liberate Yona'le.

I came to the military command in Bad-Reichenhall and asked Lieutenant Evans to release Wilhelm Rechnitz. On this occasion, Yona'le carried the papers of an Austrian citizen.

After telephoning his superior, Colonel Kent, Lieutenant Evans ordered me into the corridor in the custody of an armed soldier. I was under arrest.

After more than three hours in the corridor, I was taken to the headquarters of the Border Police, thoroughly cross-examined about Camp Mulln, the papers and our links with the American army; and what were the names of the officers who stamped our papers with the 42nd Division seal? My answers did not satisfy them and I was, therefore, sent to a German jail. There I met Yona'le. I was hungry and asked for food; a jailer brought me a crust of bread, Yona'le got nothing. The warden showed me a written order from the American officer to the effect that Wilhelm Rechnitz was to be given food only once a day.

Next morning, a parcel of food arrived from Salzburg, with a message that Captain Nowinski was intervening vigorously — the American commanding general in Salzburg, even the Supreme Command in Vienna, had been apprised.

Within a few minutes, we had a most welcome visitor, Leon Fisher, director of the *Joint* in Salzburg. He telephoned Lieutenant Evans and asked why I had been arrested, but all that Evans could say was that it was on orders from Colonel Kent. Fisher instantly called Kent, identified himself and explained that he had come on behalf of General Collins, Commander of the 42nd Division, to find out why Aba Weinstein and Wilhelm Rechnitz were in custody. Kent answered that Rechnitz had attempted to get Jews across the border with false papers and Weinstein had interceded for him.

Captain Stanley M. Nowinski, head of the U.S. Army's DP Section

"If that is so," said Fisher, "I have come to intercede for Weinstein now; will you arrest me also?"

Colonel Kent, of course, disclaimed any such intention.

Fisher went on: "In the name of the commander of the 42nd Division, I demand that you set both men free here and now; they crossed the frontier legally in broad daylight, under orders from the American army in Austria. If you want them for questioning, they will come whenever you say. You can always find Aba Weinstein through Captain Nowinski of the DP Bureau of the 42nd

Division; he is civilian director of the Camp Mulln and you may contact him directly by phone 1478."

Kent, vastly impressed, ordered our instant release. The German jailers were amazed. As the warden turned around, I took away from his desk the order putting Yona'le on "short commons" as a souvenir.

When we later had problems with the Americans in face of the "hunger escape" from Romania and the army did not supply food rations for the thousands of Jewish refugees arriving in Austria, the *Joint* filled the gap and enabled us to carry out our work.

After 31 years, on arrival in Bucharest as Israel's ambassador, I renewed my contacts with the *Joint*. I found there the *Joint* acting within the Jewish community. Thanks to the *Joint*, there were "kosher" restaurants in 15 towns, including Bucharest, and there was no hungry Jew in Communist Romania. Families of sick people and invalids received hot meals at their homes. Thanks to the *Joint*, Romanian Jews had "Matzot" for Passover, and in 1979 I attended the inauguration of a new Jewish old-age home in Bucharest, built by the *Joint* at the cost of a million dollars.

This was a very fine modern building which was, in fact, a hospital for elderly people. It had laboratories with advanced equipment and institutes for physiotherapy. This home was intended for the hospitalization of people with heart and kidney diseases as well as for some mentally ill patients. The emphasis there was on occupational therapy and the atmosphere was one of creative activity. I felt really good to see the *Joint* continue its blessed activities.

AMERICAN MAGNANIMITY AND HELP

On July 4, 1946, in broad daylight, a nine-year-old boy, the son of a shoemaker, appeared at the militia station of Kielce, in Poland, and said that he had been held captive by Jews for two days, that he could identify the place of his detention (the Jewish Committee's house), that he had been there in a cellar and that he had seen other Christian children murdered there by the Jews, presumably for ritual purposes. The story was hair-raising, but the commander of the militia accepted the testimony of the boy without any doubt and ordered his militiamen to go to the Committee's house and surround it from all sides. The boy, of course, went along, too.

As a crowd began to assemble, the boy repeated his story, with no sign of disapproval by the militia, to an incensed audience. The crowd became a mob, a priest appeared on the scene and did nothing to calm the audience, and soon the attitude of the mob toward the occupants of the house became threatening. At about 11.15 a.m. the crowd, including the militiamen, attacked the building. Defenseless youngsters were dragged outside and a number of them were brutally murdered. The mob then pillaged the house, and finding very little of any value there, turned to the office where the Committee staff were assembled. The mob dragged them out, and outside, in the courtyard, the Jews were put to death with bricks, knives and sticks.

In the meantime, workers from factories came and joined the crowd, while other Jews were attacked and killed in other parts of the town. When evening came and relative calm was restored, 41 Jews were dead, and many dozens injured. The murder of 41 Jews in the pogrom created an acute feeling of vulnerability. The reaction of Polish Jewry, which now included tens of thousands of repatriates from the Soviet Union, was an immediate and overwhelming desire to leave Poland as quickly as possible. Thousands — abandoning all property, including personal belongings — fled by a number of perilous routes into Czechoslovakia, and on to Austria.

With the aid of Rabbi Philip Bernstein — the American Supreme Commanders' special adviser on matters affecting Jewish refugees — approval was granted for the entry of a hundred thousand Jewish refugees into the American zones of Germany and Austria. Captain Nowinski informed me that the *Brichah* would be assigned seven additional transit camps. Captain Nowinski's never-ending willingness to assist greatly eased the work of the *Brichah* in Salzburg.

On August 17, 1946, I went with Nowinski to see Colonel Linden, who was acting, in General Collins' absence, as Supreme Commander in the American zone. He thanked me for our cooperation in the army's work with Jewish refugees; without our help, he confessed, he would have had a great deal of trouble.

That day, two *Brichah* members were married at Camp Mulln. Two special guests were present: Captain Nowinski and Rabbi Eliezer Silver, President of the Union of Orthodox Rabbis and of the 'Agudath Israel' (Israel Association) movement of the United States. On his return to the United States, he wrote the following in the New York Yiddish newspaper, "The Day":

> ...One day, L., a pleasant Jewish captain, came along and told me that Aba, the *Brichah* commander, would be coming to one of the camps and wished to have an interview with me. Among the refugees, Aba is a sort of Ataman, a king of the indigent, the 'boss' of the disorganized Polish *Brichah*. Aba is a legendary figure, something like a Jewish Robin Hood. He wields more authority than the leader of an established army...After talking for several hours with the leader of the largest Jewish exodus, of which the least said the better, I gave a speech."

I smiled at his hyperboles: "Ataman," "Robin Hood," "legendary figure." But I could understand. He was not referring to me in person, his words were the perfect definition of how the refugees regarded the *Brichah* and its members, whom they considered as their angels. What could be more natural than that its men be highly respected, almost worshipped, by the refugees, as the heroes of many a wonderful and thrilling tale?

A few days after the wedding, I came to Captain Nowinski and proposed a representative body for the *Brichah* transit camps, asking for the army to provide a headquarters from which we could supervise them.

On August 27, thanks to Nowinski, the "Committee for Assistance to Jewish Refugees" (CAJR) was born, and a bright new era began.

Nowinski equipped me with a document, as Chairman of the CAJR, with my photo on it showing me in military uniform, tantamount to an authorization to wear a uniform. Nowinski also installed an army telephone in the private room I kept, enabling us to get into direct touch with any American garrison anywhere in Germany or other parts of Europe; this was an incalculable boon. When I went to see Nowinski, for the first time in my uniform, he did not conceal his friendly amusement at my military style. You might say that the *Brichah* was by now a sort of illegal organization with official status, to such a degree that, more than once, the Americans sought our aid to get certain people, in whom they were interested, across the frontier.

For instance, one day, I was invited to dine with Major Lifshitz, a good Jew and a patriotic American, who was in charge of the O.S.S. activities in Salzburg. He asked me to move to Germany, over the pathways of the *Brichah*, a person working for him.

At the end of November 1946, we received the visit in Salzburg of Ephraim Dekel. Born in Russia, Ephraim had emigrated to Eretz Israel

Ephraim Dekel, Second Commander of the Brichah organization

HEADQUARTERS
ZONE COMMAND AUSTRIA
DP & PW Section

APO 541, US Army
7 November 1946

This is to certify that Weinstein, Aba, is the chairman of the Committee for Assistance to Jewish Refugees, (C.A.J.R). This committee is engaged in Welfare work with Jewish Refugees in US Zone Austria. Mr. Weinstein, as chairman, is working in coordination with DP Section Zone Command Austria.

Stanley M Nowacki
Capt Inf
Asst DP Officer

The document certifying Aba Gefen as Chairman of the CAJR

in 1921, joining the *Haganah* a year later. After carrying out largescale clandestine operations, he was given command of the European *Brichah*, replacing Surkis who returned to Eretz Israel. From Salzburg, Dekel went to Basle to attend the 22nd Zionist Congress.

On December 9, 1946, in the uniform of a British officer, I, too, left for Switzerland. It was the first Zionist Congress held after the Holocaust, in the very hall where 49 years earlier the founding Congress had been convened by Theodor Herzl.

In Paris, Herzl had been correspondent of the Vienna "Neue Freie Presse" during the 1894 trial of Captain Alfred Dreyfus, an Alsatian Jew in the French army, accused of espionage for Germany. Against all the evidence, Dreyfus was found guilty and his appeal dismissed; clearly he was a victim of that same ideology which was to destroy millions of Jews in the Nazi gas-chambers half a century later.

The trial convinced Herzl that, as long as Jews remained a minority, prisoners of circumstances and policies which they could not control, their constant lot would be discrimination, or worse. For him, then, the solution was the fulfillment of the age-old dream, of the yearning of thousands of years: the Return to Zion. In 1896, he published his book "Der Judenstaat" (The Jewish State), in which he articulated his ideas. These ideas had been inherent in Judaism since God made His Covenant with Abraham. They had been the theme of the first Jews who went into exile — "By the rivers of Babylon we sat and wept when we remembered Zion" — and of Israel's prophets and visionaries throughout the centuries of agonizing Diaspora. The Jewish people remained faithful to the Land of Israel in all the centuries of their dispersion.

In the Diaspora, in prayer, a Jew turned eastward, to Jerusalem, and all the synagogues were so oriented. Morning, afternoon and evening, Jews prayed to return to the Land that God gave to Abraham, Isaac and Jacob.

The Jewish people enjoyed self-rule in Eretz Israel for some two thousand years. With the destruction, in the year 70, of the Second Temple, the Romans interrupted Jewish sovereignty, and from that time until 1948 the country was never independent: it became the province of many empires. The Romans, however, only shattered the Jewish State, they did not destroy the Jewish presence in Eretz Israel. Jews in greater or smaller numbers lived on there, considering themselves always to be the representatives of the whole exiled nation. And unbrokenly, the stream of home-coming Jews from East and West into Eretz Israel kept flowing. But it was Herzl who in 1897 lent priority to the concept of a Jewish National Home. He considered the Jewish State to be a necessity and was confident that the Jews who wanted it, would win their State and be worthy of it.

It was in 1917 that Britain, in the Balfour Declaration, made known its sympathy with the idea of a Jewish National Home. The Balfour Declaration marked a decisive diplomatic victory in the contemporary chronicles of the Jewish people. It was the turning point. It also heralded a British military campaign which, a month later, led to the liberation of Judea from the Turks. On the first day of *Hanukkah,* (the Festival of Lights) — which commemorates the triumph of the Hasmonaeans, the Maccabees, over the Graeco-Syrian king Antiochus IV Epiphanes, who at one time sought to extirpate the Judaic faith — General Allenby entered Jerusalem. Among his troops were three Jewish "Gdudim" (battalions), fighting units of volunteers from England, the United States, Canada and of "sabras," those born in Palestine, led by Zeev Jabotinsky and Joseph Trumpeldor.

Even the Arab leaders welcomed the Balfour Declaration. On March 3, 1919, the day after Dr. Chaim Weizmann had presented the Jewish case to the Paris Peace Conference, Emir Feisal, representing the Arab case, wrote the following to Felix Frankfurter, a prominent American Jewish jurist: "We Arabs, especially the educated among us...wish the Jews a hearty welcome home.... The Jewish movement is nationalist and not imperialist. Our movement is nationalist and not imperialist. And there is room for us both."

In 1920, at the San Remo Conference of the Allies, the Palestine Mandate was finally settled, and Lloyd George, Britain's Prime Minister, parted from Chaim Weizmann, president of the Zionist Organization, with these words: "Now you have your State. It is up to you to win the race."

At the Congress in Basle, in 1946, the nervousness and confusion prevailing in Jewry, in the aftermath of the Holocaust, was tangible. Few of the delegates expected the British to discharge their promises and obligations. A majority trend crystallized that favored activism and the need to fight against the British in Eretz Israel for the independence of the Jewish people in their own Land, for the establishment there of a Jewish State.

Intensification of "*Ha'apalah*" (illegal immigration), by all ways and means, was held to be one of the most important and rewarding methods. The Congress decided that it was essential to get the remnants of European Jewry to the shores of Eretz Israel, above all, its youth, as a fighting force.

A representation of the Holocaust survivors met at the Congress with David Ben-Gurion. They put forward the position that it was forbidden to forget and to forgive, and that the Holocaust might repeat itself. They demanded to increase the struggle for the establishment of the Jewish State which would not only be able to absorb the survivors but also serve as a stronghold for the Jews, to make sure that such a disaster would never recur and Jewish blood would never be shed in vain, and to defend the Jewish people in every corner of the world.

This unequivocal demand by the Holocaust survivors strengthened the activist camp in the Zionist movement headed by Ben-Gurion, and he declared at the Congress: "The last testament of the millions who went to death was: only because we were a people without a homeland and a state did we perish, and victory of freedom and justice will not be established unless the historical distortion is repaired — and the Jewish State will be resurrected."

In Basle, Ben-Gurion spoke of the eventual departure of the British from Palestine and foresaw an invasion by all the Arab states so as to conquer the country and put an end to the Zionist enterprise. Ben-Gurion emphasized that it would be impossible to detain and repel that invasion by means of settlements, illegal immigration and political struggle — only an organized military force could do it. The Congress decided to struggle for the establishment of a Jewish State in Eretz Israel and entrusted Ben-Gurion — in addition to his position as Chairman of the Jewish Agency for Palestine — with the responsibility to prepare the *Haganah* to become the army of the Jewish State when established.

The *Haganah*, rigidly subordinate to the civil authority of the Jewish Agency, was formed in 1920, when the problem of protection of the Jewish community in Palestine became an integral part of its economic, political and cultural development. The *Haganah* grew out of "*Hashomer*" (the Watchman), a small self-defense body stemming from a militia of fighters and farmers, pioneers in

Jewish villages, who stood guard over remote outposts lying isolated amidst hostile Arab populations.

The Arab attack on Tel Hai in 1920, on Jewish Jerusalem in the same year, and the riots in Yafo in 1921, all demonstrated the need to organize Jewish self-defense in a new way; provision had to be made for procurement of arms and the training of young men and women to meet the mounting threat of the now systematic Arab terrorism. It was clear that the British would not be willing to sacrifice their soldiers to save Jewish lives. And it was no longer enough to furnish watchmen for the farm villages. The towns, too, had to be defended. The entire *Yishuv* must look to its security. The handful of vigilantes, who went out at night to guard the crops, would become a central instrument in the shaping of Palestine's political destiny. Without it, settlement, *aliyah* (immigration), and communal defense would have been impossible.

The military strength of the *Yishuv* was mainly marshalled in the *Haganah*. But there were two dissident Jewish underground groups: "*Irgun Zva'i Leumi*" — National Military Organization, and "*Lohamey Herut Israel*" — Fighters for the Freedom of Israel; both were militantly anti-British and responsible for numerous attacks on British targets. These two organizations differed sharply with the *Haganah* as to the best way to thwart British policy.

On my return to Salzburg, our American friends wanted to hear from me about the Congress and about any progress towards solving the problem of the Jewish refugees living in the DP camps. I informed them in detail about the proceedings in Basle and told them, with conviction, that the great day was drawing near, the day on which we would see Eretz Israel as our own. American magnanimity, friendship and help were a source of strength and hopefulness for all of us, engaged in making the *Brichah* play its part in the struggle for the establishment of the Jewish State and have the gates of Eretz Israel thrown open to mass immigration.

"FIFTH POWER"

The American army provided the refugees in the camps food to the value of 1,500 calories per person, and supplied these rations in accordance with the lists of refugees forwarded by the military camp commanders. The camp commanders received those lists from the civil directors of the camps, who had been appointed by the *Brichah*.

Since the 1,500 calories were insufficient, we did not report to the camp commanders the real numbers of refugees we were moving out of the camps, and we thus received more rations, which we called "angels." The army finally discovered the existence of the "angels," and headquarters summoned me and demanded an explanation. I gave the reasons and they accepted them, but asked me to keep the percentage of "angels" in a camp below 25%.

At a meeting with Colonel Hill, the new head of the DP Bureau in the American Zone, he confirmed to me that there was a new policy: the Austrian frontier was sealed, the camps would be under close control, the number of refugees found in each would be taken as its definitive capacity, and there would be no more "angels": not a single additional refugee could enter Austria. I asked smilingly whether departure, too, was banned, and he replied very seriously that it would not be. It was the shortest — and least satisfactory — conversation I had ever had at the DP section.

A short time after this very unpleasant meeting with Colonel Hill, Captain Ross, the Deputy Chief of O.S.S. (Office of Strategic Services) came to see me. The O.S.S. was an American civilian information service, founded in 1943 during the war by the Roosevelt Administration, separate from the military information service. The O.S.S. was established with the purpose of uncovering in the United States Nazi and Fascist espionage nets.

In Europe, in the framework of the American army, it dealt with the tracking down of war criminals and their being put to trial. Many intellectuals were recruited into this service, and the chief of the office in Salzburg was a Jewish professor, Major Lifshitz. Ross was his deputy. With the onset of the Cold War, the order of priorities of this service changed. The hunt after the Nazis was forsaken in favor of the war against communism. The activity of this service was now to discover Communist agents infiltrated among the Jewish refugees coming from the Soviet Union.

The O.S.S. tried to achieve this goal by interrogating the refugees of the *Brichah* transports. In time, the O.S.S. was dismantled and replaced by the C.I.A. (Central Intelligence Agency).

At our meeting, Captain Ross recited a long list of complaints against the *Brichah* as obstructing his work. The *Brichah* people, he said, had lately stopped offering him interpreters, had begun making technical difficulties for him in other ways — not giving him rooms to work in, not providing him with desks — and they were recommending to the refugees not to reply to the interrogators' questions. He said he knew that the *Brichah* had an enormous prestige among the refugees who were calling it the "Fifth (occupying) Power," and if we would not tell the refugees to collaborate with the O.S.S., they would not do so.

I replied that I was not surprised about technical difficulties put in his way, but I said it was not true that the members of the *Brichah* obstructed his work: each refugee determined his own attitude — if he wished, he spoke, if not, he held his tongue. I explained to him that our people were not instructing the refugees to collaborate with his agents, because we were not happy at all with their recruiting ex-Nazis and war criminals for their anti-Communist purposes. We would like to see their Nazi collaborators in jail and brought to trial, but we were not inimical to the American intelligence activity.

It is well known today that, because of the Cold War, many Nazi criminals succeeded in being integrated within the Western Intelligence services in general, and those of the United States in particular, and they exploited for their benefit the rivalry between the Allies and the Soviet Union. In time, it became clear that the Allies' use of those Nazi criminals made it possible for the ideologists among them to create a wide assortment of neo-Fascist organizations throughout the world, as well as an apologetic literature of Nazism and Holocaust denial.

Ross understood our position on the interrogations, but he wondered why I was not surprised about the technical difficulties put in his way. "They do so on my orders," I answered, "and for a very simple reason: relations between the *Brichah* and the army have deteriorated lately. Some officers have been putting pressure on us in a variety of matters. So we try to retort in kind: negative tit for negative tat; and since we see a chance to impede their work, we do so — unhesitatingly." I also asked him why his agents were questioning the refugees about the *Brichah* work, the papers we use, the irregular routes which our transports follow into Germany, and so on. "Why are the Americans harassing us?," I asked.

Grateful for frankness, he promised to stop the interrogations. The Americans, he said, were not making things difficult out of spite; on the contrary, they admired our work. But there was a political angle: the unfriendly British complained about the American army's help to *Brichah*, so the army put on an occasional show of obstruction, intercepting our transports, for example. After each such interference, however, the army would aid us generously by way of indemnity.

Meir Sapir, Third Commander of the Brichah *organization*

As the work of the *Brichah* in Austria intensified, so did the counter-action of the British Intelligence Service. It sent in agents from all corners of the empire, to find out about the sailings of the illegal immigrant boats, in order to stop them and deport the refugees to the camps in Cyprus.

On 9-10 May 1947, the third European *Brichah* convention was held in Fuschel, near Salzburg, with delegates from all centers. Also present were Moshe Sneh — of the Executive Committee of the Zionist Organization, Chaim Pozner — the Jewish Agency's treasurer in Europe; Yehuda Golan — the Jewish Agency's representative in Salzburg; the *Joint* representatives, and Ephraim Dekel — European commander of the *Brichah*. Following the convention, Ephraim was to leave for Eretz Israel and be replaced by Meir Sapir from Kibbutz (collective settlement) Kinneret.

After the convention, a farewell party for Captain Stanley M. Nowinski, who was returning to the U.S., was held in the *Brichah* premises in Salzburg. All American officers who were in close contact with us were present. Arthur, commander of the *Brichah* in Austria, spoke, eulogizing the work undertaken by Nowinski and the invaluable collaboration and help that he had extended to us.

Ephraim Dekel spoke on behalf of the central Jewish institutions in Eretz Israel, and, adding their praises, announced that the *Brichah* had planted 36 trees in Nowinski's name in the forests of "Keren Kayemet Leisrael" (Jewish National Fund), as a token of thankfulness for his unforgettable aid; the numerical value of the Hebrew letters forming the word "Chai," which means alive, is 18, so that we were wishing Nowinski "Long life!" twice over.

I presented Nowinski with a letter of appreciation and gratitude, in the name of the "Committee for Assistance to Jewish Refugees," the body that he had helped to form as cover for the *Brichah* work. I also gave him a photograph on which appear all the *Brichah* activists, with five American officers, *Brichah*'s closest friends — Captain Nowinski, Captain Mikelson, Lieutenant Richard Seibert, Lieutenant Morley and Rabbi Eugene Cohen.

We bade farewell to Nowinski as to a dear friend, a truly righteous person, our unfailing protector in all our troubles and mishaps, who had undergone so much, had risked his career and endured baseless vilification for his humanity. Even after he had been downgraded at General Headquarters and given a less responsible job, because of his intimacy with the *Brichah*, his dedication and friendship did not flag and he continued to stand at our side unhesitatingly.

No words of mine can adequately describe the value and extent of his efforts on our behalf. Whenever we found ourselves in a tight corner, there he would appear like an angel out of the blue and pull us out. I endeavored to resort to him as little as possible, but he was always ready to give us a hand and reduce the

The Brichah *activists in Salzburg*

hardships of the refugees, so as to send them with the least possible delay to where a happier life awaited them, though he was fully aware that these contacts might do him professional harm.

We never publicized Nowinski's intervention, nor did he wish for publicity, which might be imprudent, even harmful. We trusted him implicitly; we only kept from him one secret — though he may well have guessed the truth himself — our use of "home-made" American seals.

Nowinski expected no rewards from us. He considered it his plain and simple duty, as a human being, to do his utmost for the survivors of a people that had lost six million of its sons and daughters during World War II.

We remember Nowinski with overflowing love and grateful affection, and all Americans who will read these words of homage to Nowinski will be proud of him and thank him for rendering a service to the United States. By helping those survivors, Nowinski was contributing to the American people with the merit of his noble attitude and deeds.

After Nowinski's departure, we had difficulties now and then. But generally, Nowinski's seeds bore fruit, and we could always find American officers and men ready to uphold his wonderful tradition.

A short time after Nowinski's departure, a farewell party was held in Vienna for Arthur. The speeches evoked the happy period during which Arthur had headed the *Brichah* and his invaluable contribution to it. Arthur won the trust of everyone with whom he came in touch. His courage and determination could surmount any obstacle, and his companions lauded his persuasiveness, recalling various episodes.

Smuggling the frontier into Italy across the Alps

Moving the refugees through forests and over rivers

After Arthur's departure, I took a week's holiday in Italy, stopping on my way at *Brichah* points in Saalfelden, Innsbruck and Merano. From Saalfelden, the people went to Italy either through Innsbruck or directly across the Alps. Innsbruck was the easier route and we often managed to transport the refugees by train, our people having reached an "agreement" with the train-conductors. This was most useful, especially for the aged, women and children; others went by night, over ploughland and hills.

Direct passage to Italy was much more difficult, indeed out of the question for any but young persons — it meant climbing a steep mountain, along narrow tracks wide enough in some places only for Indian file, and then an eight-kilometer ravine and a second mountain twice as high as the first. It was very rough going, and ropes had to be used to hoist up the climbers from point to point. Only those whom the Lord called a stiff-necked people could make it.

In Innsbruck, I witnessed the nocturnal preparations of a transport to Italy — aged, weak and ailing people, pregnant women, children and babies. A similar group had crossed the frontier the night before, by a new route. The people in that transport were told what to expect, but they were in high spirits all the same.

I crossed the frontier to Italy with the group. I reached Merano and went to see the frontier post for the mountain track from Saalfelden. Undoubtedly, the method of *Brichah* work there was unusual: the job was actually done by the Italians themselves, and thanks to the friendly behavior of the kind Italians, thousands of Jews were able without trouble to enter Italy.

The frontier post was 1,621 meters up in the Alps, and in the hut of the frontier guards lived some of the *Brichah* boys. A hundred meters further on was an Italian dwelling to which the refugees from Austria, detained by the Italian frontier guards, were being taken.

The Italians would notify their superiors that a group of people had been apprehended trying to cross the frontier and lodged in the dwelling. When the order came to return the refugees to Austria, the guard commander would send a token handful back, turning the rest over to the *Brichah* boys, who saw to getting them to Merano. The *Brichah* trucks were parked opposite the hut of the guards. And even the token handful were only taken to nearby woods and there set free. Needless to say, they did not return to Austria, but went back to the dwelling.

In Merano, on July 27, we learned that the 4,500 refugees, who sailed in the subsequently world-famous "Exodus 1947," were being returned to France. 3,500 grown ups, 400 of whom were pregnant women determined to give birth

"Exodus 1947" ship of "illegal" immigrants to Eretz Israel

to their babies in Palestine, and a thousand children were involved. They had been taken in June by the *Brichah* from the refugee camps in Germany to France and handed over to our colleagues of the *Aliyah Beth*.

As the ship drew near the shores of the Promised Land, it was attacked by British warships, cannon fire and gas. Under the smoke screen, destroyers surrounded the ship and boarding parties scrambled over its rails: hundreds of British soldiers in full combat dress, using clubs, pistols and grenades against wretched refugees. There was hand-to-hand fighting between the refugees and the insensitive troops. One crew member and several refugees were killed by British gunfire, many more wounded. After resistance collapsed, the ship was towed to Haifa and the refugees transported by British destroyers back to France.

At Port du Buc, the refugees would not leave the ship; the French were prepared to offer asylum to any refugees who sought it, but emphatically objected to accepting refugees forced to disembark. When the French advised the English that they would not permit forcible disembarkation of refugees on French soil, the British decided to take them to the camps in the British Zone of Germany. Anger and indignation swept the Jewish inmates of the camps in Germany and Austria because of the "Exodus" refugees being shipped back like animals, in their wire cages, to DP camps in the country that symbolized the graveyard of European Jewry.

In the meantime, a tide of refugees left Romania and it was called the "hunger escape." It was a headlong flight precipitated by the insecurity of crossing the Black Sea, by fear lest the Iron Curtain would descend, and by widespread hunger. In Vienna, there were already eleven thousand Romanian refugees, crammed within three camps with a normal capacity of a thousand. Once in Austria, the Romanian refugees began to press us to take them on to Italy: they were over-optimistically convinced that they could then reach Eretz Israel without trouble or delay. We finally started sending groups of them to Innsbruck en route to Italy. But in Innsbruck, too, they had to await their turn, which again created problems, and on September 27, a terrible thing happened there. A hundred armed men, most of them Romanian Jews, entered the premises of the *Brichah*, killing Eitan Avidov, from Eretz Israel, and gravely wounding two other members of the *Brichah*.

It is, of course, conceivable that the crime was not premeditated, and I am sure that its perpetrators regretted it. It was the result of wild and unwarranted agitation by a few hot-heads of the Zionist Revisionist Party who denounced the *Brichah*'s alleged political biases, and accused it of discrimination; the unhappy circumstances of the Romanian refugees created an inflammable situation.

The murder was a grim mirror of the political squabbling in Eretz Israel. The death of Eitan was a direct outcome of the senseless internecine strife developing in Eretz Israel, which gravely endangered the fight for independence. It inflamed the camps in Austria and Germany, and there were many there asking for revenge. But when Eitan's father, Yani Avidov, active himself in *Aliyah Beth*, arrived in Innsbruck to take his son's body back to Eretz Israel for burial in his native village of Nahalal, he appealed, standing by the coffin, for moderation and conciliation, so that the sacred work might go safely on. It was difficult to explain a crime with a background of internal politics to the French and Americans, to whom ideological differences between Jewish organizations were an enigma.

The British exploited the incident, and the danger was so real that a frontier, indispensable for our work, might have had to be closed. It took desperate efforts, and all our contacts in Paris, to persuade the French not to issue orders that would have made *Brichah* activity in Austria much harder.

PART THREE

RESURRECTION

THE HOMELAND' S GATES WIDE OPEN

When Meir Sapir, the third commander of the *Brichah* organization, arrived in Salzburg, I informed him of my plans to get married. I applied to end my work in Salzburg and go to Eretz Israel. He agreed and said I would go, together with my future wife and her mother, by "*Aliyah Daled,*" which meant illegal immigration on false passports. The date of my wedding with Frida Szmulowich was fixed for October 21, 1947. Rabbi Abramowich, an American chaplain, and Rabbi Bohm, a refugee from Hungary, officiated.

The ceremony and wedding-dinner took place at one of the American clubs in Salzburg, "Sternbraeu," which the army placed at our disposal, and the *Brichah* once again used the opportunity to illustrate its friendship with the Americans. Among the guests were all the officers — and there were many of them — who in one way or another were connected with our work.

My wife Frida was born in Lida, near Vilno. Her father, Jacob, had been a respected and well-off businessman; her mother, Liba, was active in many of the charitable organizations. When, following the German invasion of Poland, the country was divided between Germany and Russia, the Russian army entered Lida on September 18.

Large enterprises were confiscated at once, and Frida's father, together with her elder brother, Samuel, fled to a still free Lithuania, making their way safely across the perilous frontier. The mother, and her two other children, Eliezer and Frida, were to follow. In the midst of their frantic preparations for flight, on the fateful day April 13, 1940, they were deported.

Frida Gefen's family.
From left to right: the mother Liba, the brother Samuel, Frida, the brother Eliezer, the father Jacob

When the Szmulowiches arrived at the railway station, they met other families there. Hundreds of Jews and Poles alike were bundled into freight-cars, packed like sardines, to be railed to Siberia in inhuman conditions. In the wagon in which the Szmulowiches traveled, were 52 people. During the trip, the Russian soldiers periodically counted the exiles, according to lists, to make sure nobody escaped. After a few days of traveling, the deportees began complaining about the lack of water and air. After that, they were allowed once a day to get buckets of water and to answer nature's call near the wagon, in the presence of the guards. It was very humiliating.

They traveled 17 days, and on their arrival in Siberia, the whole transport of deportees was brought to a station called Tokushy. The occupants of each train-car were sent to a different "kolchoz," a Russian collective farm. From Tokushy the Szmulowiches later moved to Petropavlovsk. Eliezer was drafted to work in the mines, Frida worked during the day as a clerk, and in the evening she went to school. Mother stayed at home.

The Szmulowiches remained in Siberia until 1946, when, thanks to the Polish-Russian agreement for the repatriation of Polish citizens from Russia, they returned home. There, the Jewish repatriates were welcomed with violence and death threats for those who had survived Hitler. The Szmulowiches could not remain in Poland and joined the stream of refugees making their arduous way to the American Zone of Germany. Thus they arrived at the refugee camp in Bad-Reichenhall, where I met Frida.

From the day I met my mother-in-law, I felt she was an extraordinary person, and as time went on, I heard from various people, who were with her in Siberia, about her goodness, friendliness and hospitality, as well as her bravery under Stalin's tyrannical anti-Jewish regime. In spite of the threats, she organized — in her small one-room apartment in Tokushy — a Friday night and Sabbath "*minyan*" (the requisite number of ten males for congregational worship). When she was arrested, during a year in jail she kept "*kashrut*" (Jewish dietary laws) and lived only on water, bread, onions and garlic. Not a morsel of "unkosher" food was brought into her home during the entire six years of exile.

She opened her home to everyone — whether wanderer, exile or refugee. Any Jew who needed shelter for an hour, a day, or months, found a place at her house. No-one left her place hungry — if nothing else, he received at least a baked potato, a slice of bread with onion or a bowl of soup. It's hard to understand what that meant in those dark and difficult times. She was loved and respected by all the exiles.

While the mother, with her younger son and daughter, languished in Siberia, the father and the older son were wandering in another part of the world. As long as Lithuania was free, they could live there at ease and hoped to be joined by the other members of the family. But when the Russians occupied Lithuania in 1940, it became a deadly risk for them to stay. In Kovno, they learnt of the possibility of getting a Japanese transit visa for Curacao, and they were among the lucky 5,000 Jewish refugees who received visas from the Japanese Consul, Chiune Sugihara, who issued them without authorization from Tokyo. In Japan, they all concentrated in Kobe, and in 1942, after the outbreak of war between Japan and America, they left for Shanghai where they remained until 1947, when a kinsman secured visas to Mexico for them.

Once in Mexico City, they arranged papers for the mother and daughter —

the son Eliezer had married in the meantime and, via Marseilles, had smuggled himself into Eretz Israel. But by the time the Mexican visas came, Frida and I had decided to get married and go to Eretz Israel. Her mother, having shared such difficult years with Frida, was reluctant to be separated from her daughter, and, despite her ardent longing to be reunited with husband and son, made up her mind that the family reunion must take place in Eretz Israel and not Mexico. She would join Frida and me on our "illicit" vessel journey to Eretz Israel rather than go legally and comfortably by plane to Mexico.

My wife and I left Salzburg for Eretz Israel on November 25, 1947. First, we went to the refugee camp in Bad-Reichenhall — where we were joined by my mother-in-law — and then to Munich, whence on November 29 at 5 o'clock in the afternoon, we left for the refugee camp in Bergen-Belsen. Before leaving Munich, we heard the radio news about the debates at the General Assembly of the United Nations regarding the rcommendations of the United Nations Special Committee on Palestine (UNSCOP). It was appointed by the General Assembly of the United Nations at a special meeting convened in May 1947 after Britain had submitted the Palestine problem to the UN. The Committee consisted of 11 members, representing the governments of Australia, Canada, Czechoslovakia, Guatemala, India, Iran, The Netherlands, Peru, Sweden, Uruguay, and Yugoslavia.

The Committee members heard oral testimonies, received written communications from individuals and organizations, and visited Palestine, neighboring countries, and the camps of displaced persons in Germany and Austria. The displaced Jews, who at the beginning had presented a moral and humanitarian problem, had now become a strong political factor. When the UNSCOP members met with them, they heard for themselves the anguish and agony which those refugees had undergone; they saw with their own eyes the suffering of the people, and were moved by their talks with many of them.

Thus the *Brichah* work — the concentration of the quarter of a million Holocaust survivors in the occupation zones of Germany and Austria — directly influenced the Committee in its report, published in August 1947. Andrei Gromyko, the Soviet Foreign Minister — whose speech of support for the partition resolution was a decisive factor in its approval — referred in his address to the hundreds of thousands of Jewish Holocaust survivors and to their

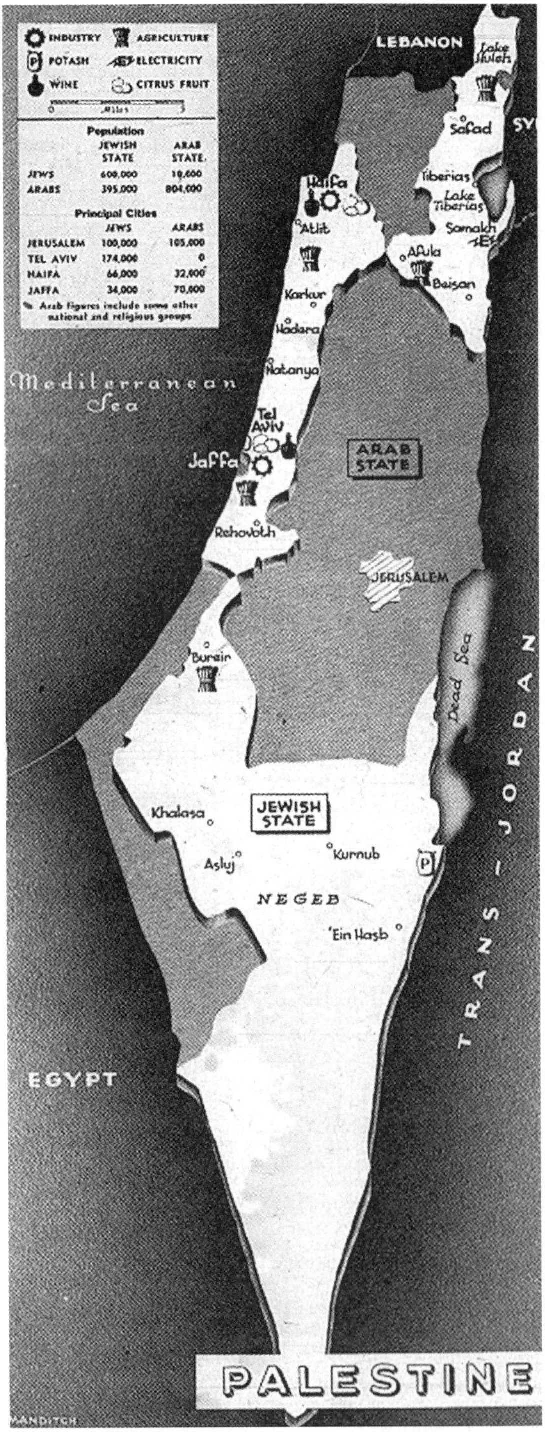

The U.N. Partition Plan dividing Palestine into two states: a Jewish one and an Arab one

yearning to establish their own state. UNSCOP unanimously resolved that the British Mandate be terminated, and while the minority proposed the establishment of a bi-national federal state, the seven-member majority recommended the partition of the country into an independent Jewish state, an independent Arab state, and a "corpus separatum" consisting of Jerusalem and its environs as an international enclave.

All night, in the train from Munich to Bergen-Belsen, we were not very optimistic — the chances were uncertain. We could not close our eyes: there was the fear that, because of one or two votes, the partition proposal might collapse. To our joy, arriving next day at lunchtime, we were welcomed by inscriptions on the walls of Bergen-Belsen: "Long live the Jewish State," "Long live Ben-Gurion!" In the refugee camp of Bergen-Belsen, the people embraced and kissed each other. The General Assembly adopted the UNSCOP report, by a vote of 33 in favor, 13 against, and 10 abstentions. "Historical justice" — Ben-Gurion called the U.N. resolution. The generation which had suffered the most terrible of tragedies, the Holocaust, was now to witness the greatest of salvations, the establishment of the independent Jewish State.

At the conclusion of the First Zionist Congress in Basle, Theodor Herzl noted in his diary on September 3, 1897: "If I wished to sum up the Congress in one sentence — something I would be very careful not to do publicly — I would say: in Basle, I have founded the Jewish State. If I said it today in a loud voice, it would arouse a general laughter. Maybe in five years, for sure in fifty years, all will recognize it." Exactly fifty years after Herzl wrote those words, the U.N. General Assembly adopted, on November 29, 1947, a resolution on the establishment of a Jewish State. Herzl's prediction came true.

After 1,800 years of exile and Diaspora, an independent Jewish State was to be established in Eretz Israel despite the Holocaust which has destroyed the biggest reservoir of Jews, whom the Zionist visionaries had foreseen as the citizens of the state to rise.

Herzl spoke of millions. He said not all Jews would come to the Jewish State, but most of them would. Now that the Jewish State was to emerge from the destruction of our people, caused by the same diabolical ideology which had brought a Jewish officer in the French army, Alfred Dreyfuss, to trial and transformed an assimilated Jewish journalist into the visionary of Jewish national resurrection — there were in Eretz Israel only 650,000 Jews. The joy in the streets of Eretz Israel burst all bounds and crowds went out to dance; they danced the whole night through.

But the joy of liberation was soon tempered when home-going celebrants learnt of the first victims, murdered by Arabs as they traveled in a bus from Netanyah to Jerusalem. Seven Jews were killed in the first few hours in an outbreak of Arab terrorism. Roads were mined, villages isolated, convoys ambushed.

By the end of the first week, 105 Jews had perished. Apartments in Jerusalem were blown up, more than 50 men, women and children were killed. 35 Hebrew University students were massacred on the road near Jerusalem. The Jewish Agency building was bombed, with heavy casualties. A convoy was set afire on the road to Hadassah Hospital on Mount Scopus and in that dastardly outrage 77 Jewish doctors, nurses and scientists met their death. While the Jews accepted the United Nations resolution, the Arabs rejected it and resolved to oppose it by force.

The Jews still did not have free access to Eretz Israel, and my wife, my mother-in-law and I still had to reach the country clandestinely. We landed there on February 24, 1948, each with the passport and name of someone else; only the photographs were ours. My mother-in-law traveled as Bertha Halpert, my wife as Paula Lehrer, and I as Menashe Klein.

The *Brichah* had to continue its work until the proclamation of the Jewish State. Only then did the homeland's gates swing wide open to receive the hundreds of thousands of Holocaust survivors who poured into the country, arriving from the displaced persons camps in Europe and from the British detention camps in Cyprus. The mass immigration of Jews had begun.

WAR OF INDEPENDENCE

Less than two months after our landing in Eretz Israel, the United Nations, confronted with a challenge to its moral authority, convened a second special session of the General Assembly, for April 16, 1948. The decisive factor for the approval of the Partition resolution was that it was supported by both the United States and the Soviet Union. This joint American-Soviet support, which was in those days a very rare occurrence at the U.N., was given for opposite considerations: those were the days of the Cold War.

The strategic aspirations of the West and of the Communist Bloc collided in various parts of the world, especially in the Middle East. From Moscow's point of view, any weakening of the Western presence in any place had to serve the interests of the Soviet Union. It strived, therefore, to shake the British hold on the Middle East. Moscow hoped that political independence in Palestine, be it as a bi-national state or as two separate states, would open the country's gates to Soviet penetration.

The American considerations were humanitarian — the wish to help the suffering Jewish people. But there were also pre-electoral considerations in the United States, as well as political interests to strengthen the position of the West in the region and prevent Soviet penetration. For these reasons, the prime interest of the Americans was to ensure calm in Palestine. Since two peoples competed uncompromisingly in Palestine, simple logic dictated separation between them, partitioning the country in two.

The United States delegation at the U.N. voted in favor of partition in accordance with President Harry Truman's instructions who overruled the position of his State Department. Veteran American diplomats were unreconciled, however, and soon after the partition resolution was adopted, supporters of the Arab cause — missionaries, oil lobbyists, Arabists — organized a powerful committee to demand its repeal.

The U.N. Security Council proved impotent to cope with Arab pressure and belligerence, and the United States put forward a proposal for the establishment of a "temporary" trusteesship for Palestine, which was, in effect, a new version of the Mandate. On an American initiative, the Swedish diplomat, Folke Bernadotte, was appointed U.N. mediator in the Arab-Israel conflict. Bernadotte recommended a new solution to the conflict which included transferring the Negev from Israel to the Arabs, internationalization of Jerusalem, joint Arab-Israeli use of the Haifa port and the Lod airport. If those recommendations had been accepted, the Partition Plan would have been canceled. Bernadotte was killed in Jerusalem by an organization calling itself "the homeland's front."

The attempt to block the establishment of the Jewish State failed. The *Haganah* forces, in combat with Arab armies and irregulars, secured well-organized Jewish political authority over a substantial part of the country, and Ben-Gurion decided to proclaim the Jewish State while many hesitated and considered the act crazy. George Marshall, the American Secretary of State, cautioned not to proclaim the State because it would be attacked by all Arab countries. If this happened, he said, the United States would not supply Israel with any arms for her defense and would declare an embargo on arms shipments to the Middle East. "You will be erased from the face of the earth," Marshall warned. Ben-Gurion did not succumb to fear. He was convinced that the right moment had come and it was necessary to jump into the "cold water." At the meeting of the provisional government of the state-in-formation — six members voted in favor and four against. The decision was taken on the edge of one vote: had there been a stalemate, five against five, the State of Israel would not have been proclaimed.

On May 14, 1948, in the afternoon, my wife and I stood amidst an enormous crowd in front of Government House in Haifa, waiting for the dream of 2,000 years to come true. At that historic moment, on the top of Government House, a banner fluttered, bearing, in giant letters, the words yearned for so long: "The State of Israel is born." It was four o'clock, and simultaneously, in a short

David Ben-Gurion proclaims the establishment of the State of Israel

ceremony at the Museum of Tel-Aviv, 240 men saw a new page written in Jewish history, as David Ben-Gurion read the Proclamation of Independence of the newly-born State.

The governing paragraph in Israel's Proclamation of Independence reads: "Accordingly we, the members of the National Council, representing the Jewish people in the Land of Israel and the Zionist Movement, have assembled on the day of the termination of the British Mandate for Palestine, and, by virtue of our natural and historic right and of the resolution of the General Assembly of the United Nations, do hereby proclaim the establishment of a Jewish State in the Land of Israel, to be known as the State of Israel."

Eleven minutes after that proclamation, President Truman granted de facto recognition by the United States, much to the dismay of the State Department. After two days, the Soviet Union granted de jure recognition.

The "*Vaad Leumi*" (National Council) had established a Central Enlistment Bureau for the army and I was accepted, in March 1948, to work at that bureau's office in Haifa. Five days after the Proclamation of Independence, I was sent to work at the Haifa port, which was considered a vital defense position, and I was mobilized into the paramilitary unit established there.

The infant State of Israel was invaded from all sides by seven Arab States: from the north came the Lebanese army; from the northeast, the Syrians; Jordan's Arab Legion and the Iraqi forces attacked at the center; and from the south, the Egyptian army moved up, supported by bomber planes. Units from Saudi Arabia and Yemen, too, joined the invaders.

The secretary-general of the Arab League, Azzam Pasha, boasted in Cairo: "This will be a war of extermination and momentous massacre which will be spoken of like the Mongolian massacres and the Crusades." As Jewish dead were piling up, it seemed that the miracle of the rebirth of the Jewish State, rising out of the very ruins of our people, would not be realized.

"Independence is never given to a people," said Chaim Weizmann, Israel's

Prof. Chaim Weizmann with the American president, Harry Truman

first President, "it has to be earned, and, once earned, must be defended." Our independence was earned and defended. Self-reliance became the inevitable posture for a people for whom no-one else would risk any blood, even when destruction stared it in the face. There was, however, an exception — the "*Machal*," Jewish volunteers from abroad, mainly from the United States and Canada. They were World War II veterans and they poured in to Israel to fight for its independence. Arms deals with Czechoslovakia brought to Israel about 50,000 rifles, more than 6,000 machine-guns and 75 war planes.

The War of Independence endured for more than 13 months, including 61 days of continuous combat, and was won. It was in the ghettoes, in the forests and in the extermination camps that the spirit of Jewish heroism had been ignited, to reach its greatest incandescence in that war, and in the other wars that Israel had to fight later on. The war ended officially on July 20, 1949, with the signing of the Armistice Agreement with Syria. Similar agreements had been signed before with Egypt, Lebanon and Jordan. Iraq, whose troops were stationed in heavy concentrations on the west bank of the Jordan, refused to sign an international agreement with Israel.

When the fighting ended, Israel's frontiers were not those recommended by the United Nations. Israel's rule extended over the whole of Galilee; the entire coastal strip, except for the Gaza Strip in Egyptian hands; the whole of the Negev; and West Jerusalem, with a sizable corridor to the coast. Its area of effective jurisdiction was over 20,000 square kilometers. Judea, Samaria and East Jerusalem, including the Old City, were under Jordanian control.

The Jewish State was ultimately not established by the U.N. partition resolution, which was only an important link in a chain of events that brought the state into being. Under international law, Israel became an independent state when it proved its viability as a legal unit by meeting the four cumulative conditions — nation, territory, government, independence — which emerged from the throes of its War of Independence.

Once the war ended, my mother-in-law advised her husband in Mexico that she had reached her terminal stop and would no longer wander. Let him join her in Israel. He did. They happily settled in Haifa on Mount Carmel. The son Samuel married in Mexico and remained there.

In the War of Independence, 4,783 soldiers were killed, 900 of whom were

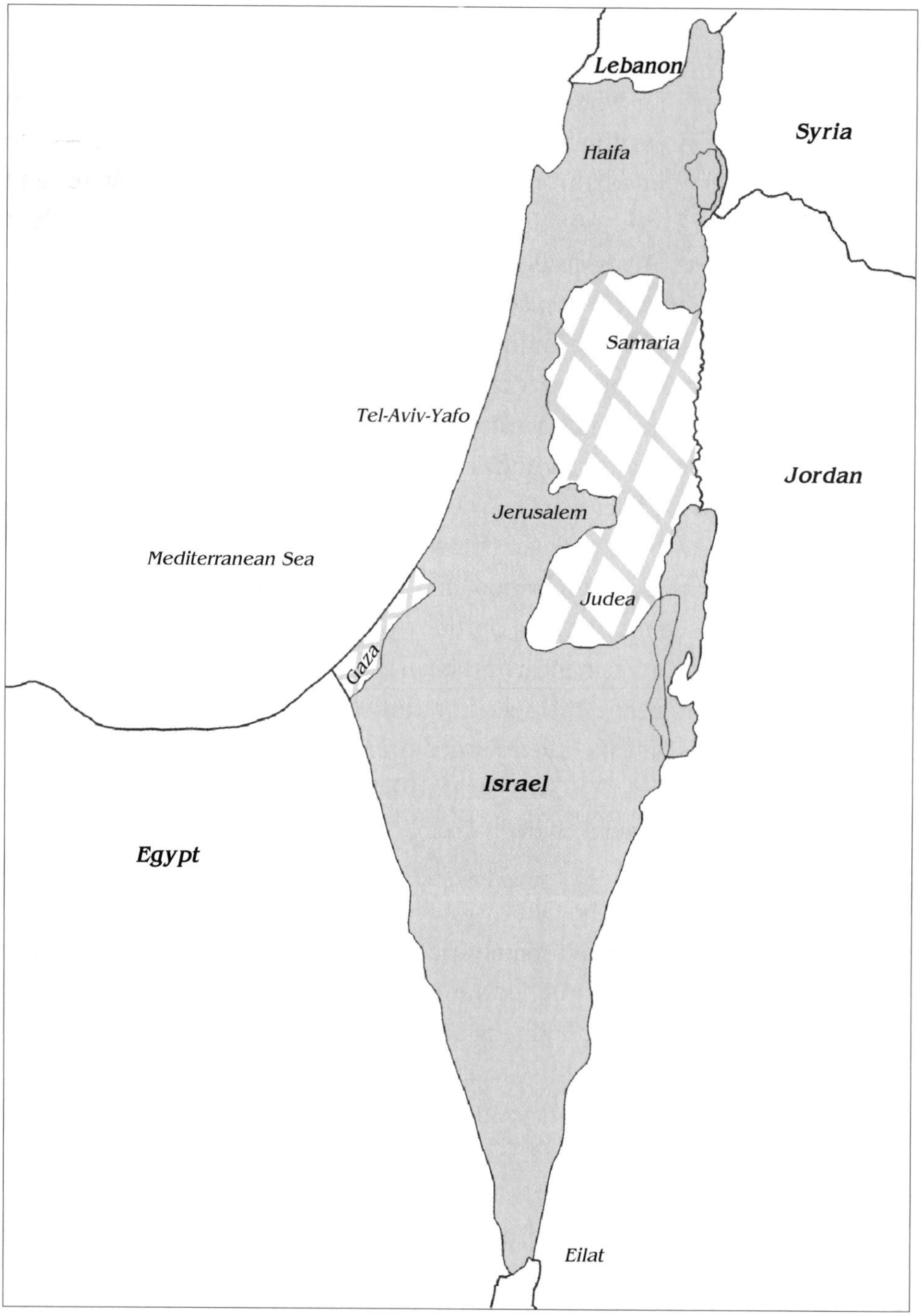

The map of the armistice borders

new immigrants Holocaust survivors who were sent to the fronts upon their arrival in Israel, and 2,000 civilians. One victim per 100 Jews living here. Israel mourned with praise and pride its beloved and faithful sons and daughters, who gave up their brave and glorious lives in the flowering of their youth. They will be forever engraved in the nation's heart.

Hundreds of thousands of new immigrants began pouring into the country. In the first four months of Israel's independence, when the country's fate was still in the balance, some 50,000 immigrants reached her shores. By September 1948 the stream had become a flood. While it had taken 30 years under British mandatory rule for the Jewish population to increase to 650,000, between May 1948 and December 1951, 687,000 newcomers had landed in Israel. Among them were: 50,000 Yemenite Jews, most of them children, who arrived in 380 flights in the "Magic Carpet Operation;" 130,000 Jews from Iraq in the "Ezra and Nehemiah Operation," who were flown to Israel within a few months straight from Baghdad to Lod. Only 6,000 Jews remained in Iraq. Later, the Iranian Jews were brought to Israel, by plane, from Teheran to Lod.

During the year 1949 alone, 250,000 Jews arrived in Israel. They were lodged in military camps and later transferred to civilian transition centers ("Ma'abaroth," in Hebrew), throughout the country, from Kiryat Shmona to Beer Sheva. Those were crowded camps of tents, huts, barracks and shacks. The living conditions were shameful and many families were housed in big barracks, with little privacy, no electricity, heating arrangements or sufficient blankets and warm garments, but with putrid stinking cesspits; in many places, real hunger reigned. Most of the new immigrants in the transition camps were unemployed, although some were engaged in relief work.

Israel found itself under an almost impossible burden of immigration and absorption. An austerity regime was proclaimed: basic food provisions were rationed. Only pregnant women, children and people with ulcers received additional rations. All the rest received food coupons. A "black market" of basic provisions developed; the Government established a headquarters to fight against this "black market," and special courts were established for the speedy judgment of the black-marketeers.

In 1949, the first elections for the founding legislative assembly took place. This became the Knesset, Israel's Parliament, composed of 120 members and elected for four years. A government of 12 Ministers was formed. Professor Chaim Weizmann was elected as the first President of Israel, and on May 11, 1949, Israel was admitted as a full-fledged member-state at the United Nations.

While I was working at Haifa Port, Asher Ben-Nathan ("Arthur"), who had been a *Brichah* commander in Austria, became a senior official at Israel's Foreign Ministry, in charge of the operational activities abroad of the Ministry's political department. (In time he became director-general of the Defense Ministry and ambassador in Paris and Bonn). The main task of the political department was to collect, outside Israel's borders, information in the political and military arenas and to act against Arab arms purchases. Arthur invited me to enter the Foreign Ministry and be sent to Rome, Italy, to work in the political department there. Rome was then one of the major world centers for espionage.

Israel's first Foreign Minister, Moshe Sharett, requested all Israeli diplomats to change their names to Hebrew ones, and so — instead of Weinstein — I became Gefen, the Hebrew word for vine. In May 1950, I left for Rome as attache at Israel's legation there, which in time became an embassy. A month later, my wife joined me, together with our one-and-a-half year old daughter, Ruhama, a name given to her in memory of my mother, may she rest in peace. In Rome, a son was born to us, Meir, a name given to him in memory of my father, may he rest in peace.

During my four years of service in Rome, I studied at the university there and in 1955, returned to present my thesis on the subject "The State of Israel and its Declaration of Independence," for a doctorate in political sciences. To enable me to travel to Rome, I received a special grant from Foreign Minister Sharett, whom I had met in Rome in 1951 when he came there for a visit during which he met with Pope Pius XII.

In Rome, we went to see the Arch of Titus that marks the Roman victory of 2,000 years ago, over the Jews; the conquest of Jerusalem and the razing of the Second Temple. A panel is engraved on the arch showing the carrying of the "*Menorah*" (seven-branched candelabrum) — part of the spoils brought back by the Romans — in the triumphal procession following the subjugation of Judea.

After the United Nations General Assembly had approved the partition of Palestine, thousands of Jews assembled at the arch for a thanksgiving prayer that the Jewish State, destroyed two thousand years ago, had been built anew.

When the State of Israel had to choose an emblem, it decided on a *Menorah* patterned after that on the Arch of Titus.

My official position in Rome was principal assistant to the head of the consular section. In fact, I was assistant to Avraham Kidron, the head of the Foreign Ministry's political department in Italy. Kidron had additional assistants and his team was in charge of recruiting agents and collecting material in all the fields of Israel's interests.

In the autumn of 1951, after the dissolution of the political department of the Foreign Ministry, the Israeli intelligence community was reorganized and the *Mossad* became the main body for the collection of intelligence and for the execution of special activities abroad. Avraham Kidron returned to Israel and I was appointed to replace him in Italy.

TREASON IN *MOSSAD*

In the summer of 1952, we discovered that a member of our personnel in Rome, Ted Cross, had betrayed us. Ted Cross worked for the Israelis and the Italians, at the same time selling information to an Arab country. The news about his betrayal reached the *Mossad* in Israel from an Arab source, and I was asked to despatch Ted as quickly as possible to Israel. Before I spoke to Ted, I flew to Zurich and from there I asked, by telephone, one of our important agents in an Arab country to leave immediately. Ted might have informed his operators about this agent, and luckily, he managed to leave before it was too late.

When I returned from Zurich, I told Ted that he was invited to come to Israel for consultations. He replied that for family reasons it was impossible for him to leave Rome. This was absolutely untrue. It was well known that his marriage was on the rocks and that he was constantly traveling abroad to spend time in the company of his lovers.

So it was decided to bring Ted to Israel by force. I was ordered to rent an appropriate apartment on a quiet street and to prepare there a big box fit for Ted's measurements — almost two meters high — as well as wax and seals of diplomatic mail, which I did. After a few days, a team of five persons headed by Isser Harel, then chief of Israel's Security Service and later head of the *Mossad*, arrived in Rome. Among the five was Harel's deputy in the Security Service, Amos Manor, who later replaced him as chief.

Harel explained to me the procedure of the operation: I would arrange a meeting with Ted in darkness at one of our usual meeting places. Ted would take the right front seat in the car, next to me. In the rear would be hidden one of the members of the team from Israel. The moment Ted took his seat, the man from behind would press on his face a pillow soaked with chloroform and throw him down on his seat. Ted was supposed to fall asleep instantly, and I would take him to the prepared apartment. There, he would be put into the box, the box would be packed as diplomatic mail, sealed with the proper seals, and taken to the airport where an El-Al plane would be waiting to bring it to Israel. This was the first time the *Mossad* tried to abduct somebody to Israel. The next *Mossad* abduction took place eight years later when Adolf Eichmann was brought to Israel.

I didn't like Harel's plan at all and told him that we wouldn't need it. I undertook to make sure that Ted Cross would within a week fly to Israel of his own free will. I was convinced that Ted's refusal to go to Israel was temporary. It was clear to me that Ted could not give up his connection with us. He did not receive money from the Italians, but the very fact that he maintained relations with us and with them made it possible for him to sell information to the Arabs. If we cut off relations with him, the entire basis for his supply of material to the Arabs — among it a lot of false information, the fruit of his wild imagination — would disappear. His main income came from us: his salary, the money he succeeded to exact from us for his inflated ostentatious expenses, and the money for his supposed informers.

I was sure that if I would handle him properly, without raising any suspicion, he would board the plane of his own free will.

Harel rejected my proposal to wait and demanded that I carry out the abduction as it has been decided in Israel. "This is an order," he said angrily, "it is inconceivable that the head of the Security Service and his team waste a week in Rome without doing anything and wait until you succeed in convincing Cross to board the plane for Israel."

I cabled Avraham Kidron at the headquarters of the *Mossad* and told him about my hesitations to execute the original plan; I asked to accede to my request to let me do it my way. Kidron consulted Reuven Shiloach, then head of the *Mossad*, and cabled me that my proposal had been approved, and added: "You surely understand what a responsibility you are taking upon yourself and what will happen if you fail." I did not fail. After five days I accompanied Ted Cross in my car to the airport. Since those were days of economic austerity regime in Israel, I stopped on my way at the market and bought a few kilos of apples, asking Ted to deliver them to Kidron. After a few hours I received a cable from Kidron saying: "The apples arrived. Thank you!"

The five days of my negotiations with Ted on his voyage were nerve-racking days of tension. We met every day, in the afternoon, at my home and spent many hours of repeating the same things again and again ad nauseam. He asked all the time to hear my opinion on whether he should go to Israel or not, and my answer was always the same: "I understand that you have hesitations. Since I don't know what your hesitations are, I cannot, as a friend, tell you to go. If you tell me what your hesitations are, I will be able to advise you. Otherwise, I will never tell you to go."

After three consecutive days, during which I did not try at all to influence him to go, Ted began to explain his hesitations. He related to me about the inflating of his expenses, about the exaggerated false bills he presented, and claimed that he was afraid it had finally been discovered. He then asked me what his punishment might be. I replied: "They won't put you into jail, but you will have to return all the money you received by fraud. I am not advising you to go, because I don't know what they really know in Israel about your deeds. Only you can decide."

At the end of our meeting at my home on the fifth day, following a four-hour conversation, I told him that I had received instructions from Israel to severe relations with him completely and to inform him that, since he refused to come to Israel, his work with us had come to an end. He was very surprised and immediately agreed to go.

The five days of my negotiations with Cross were even more nerve-racking for Isser Harel than for me. He almost "exploded" for having to waste a week in Rome, together with his team, without doing anything. He had to wait for my daily reports to find out what had transpired. Harel was in those days the symbol of conspiracy — in time, no more — and refused to meet with me anywhere in daylight.

On his arrival in Israel, Ted was arrested, tried, found guilty of treason and of sabotaging Israel's intelligence work, and sentenced to 14 years in jail. For good behavior and because of his precarious state of health, he spent only half that time in prison. After his release, he remained in Israel and tried to rehabilitate himself as the owner of a fish restaurant on the Caesarea beach. After a few years he passed away.

In December 1953, I met in Rome the Israeli intelligence officer Major Avraham Zeidenberg, on the eve of his departure for Cairo on a false German passport in the name of "Paul Frank." He was going to Cairo as the representative of a German company manufacturing electronic products. Zeidenberg was to replace Avraham Dar who had set up in Cairo, in 1951, a now dormant espionage net. The assignment of that net was to execute special operations to harm vital strategic military targets before the outbreak of a war.

Despite the Israeli-Egyptian Armistice Agreement, Israel assumed that there existed the danger of an Egyptian attack. Avraham Dar arrived in Cairo on a false British passport in the name of "John Darling," a merchant. Dar contacted a group of Jewish youngsters, members of Zionist youth movements, lacking any experience in the field of activity for which they were chosen. They were, however, indubitable Jewish patriots and expressed their readiness to help Israel. Some of those youngsters went to Israel, via France, and were trained there in the technique of secret writing with invisible ink, in methods of espionage and sabotage. In time, they were given communication instruments and were asked to acquire chemical materials in pharmacies and set up a secret workshop for the preparation of explosives.

On the night of July 22-23, 1952, a group of Egyptian "Free Officers" seized control of Cairo, and soon afterward of the whole country, without bloodshed. King Farouk was forced to abdicate and left the country unharmed. A new government was set up, headed by General Mohammed Naguib, considered a hero of the Palestine war. The real leader of the revolution was Lieutenant Colonel Gamal Abdel Nasser who had also fought in the Palestine war. After a short time, Nasser deposed Naguib and took power into his hands.

In 1953, Nasser began to negotiate with London an agreement on the full withdrawal of the British forces encamped along the Suez Canal. The civilian and military equipment of the British, the installations and the military camps were to be delivered to the Egyptians. The departure of the British army would remove the foreign barrier between Israel and Egypt and thus turn the Canal area into a "take-off plank" of the Egyptian army into the Sinai desert and towards the State of Israel.

This possible development aroused heavy fears in Israel which knew the danger represented by Nasser who had been defeated and taken prisoner by Israel's forces in the Negev. Nasser's aspirations for vengeance were no secret. He did not hide his belligerent intentions from the public in his own country or in the rest of the world.

Israel considered the British presence on the Suez Canal as vital. Israel thought that as long as British forces were in the area of the Canal, they would keep the Egyptians busy. It seemed to Israel that the British presence there might cool off the enthusiasm of the Arab warmongers who were speaking loudly of a "second round" in their war against Israel. It was clear that the British would not stipulate the evacuation of the Suez Canal with an abolition by the Egyptians of their blockade against Israel. The Churchill Government's plan of evacuation encountered sharp resistance in many circles of the governing party, and in certain circles in Israel percolated the idea that there was still hope to dissuade the British from leaving the Canal.

In those Israeli circles the idea was raised to implement in Egypt some unconventional acts that would prevent the evacuation of the Canal or at least cause its postponement. They recommended that the members of the dormant Israeli espionage net in Egypt execute some sabotage acts directed at American and British institutions. Assuming that the Americans and the British would consider those sabotage acts as hostile deeds executed with the inspiration of the Egyptian government or by the "Moslem Brotherhood" organization, it would cause a confusion in Egypt's relations with the United States and Britain and strengthen in Britain the opposition to the evacuation.

When Zeidenberg replaced Dar, I was instructed to be his liaison-man in Italy and during our meeting in Rome I introduced to him my assistant, Benjamin Rotem, who would be his liaison-man after my eventual departure from Italy. I delivered to him the detailed "order of the operation" and gave him $1,000, secret ink and details about two post office boxes put at his disposal for his correspondence from Egypt: one in Germany, the other in Austria. I also improved in his false German passport a correction made in Zurich. There, the word Tel-Aviv was erased from his passport in an unsuccessful manner and I had to amend it to ensure it would not be readable.

Zeidenberg is also known under the code-name of "The Third Man," because he was the third "hero" among the Israeli intelligence officers to testify in the investigation on the subject: "Who gave the order to activate the dormant net in Egypt?"

In time, it became clear that the plan of activating the secret net was naive, lacking any political understanding, irresponsible and very dangerous. The activation of the net was implemented without the knowledge of Moshe Sharett, then Prime Minister.

The "senior officer" who transmitted the order to do it was Benjamin Gibli — he claimed that he received an order about it from the then Defense Minister Pinhas Lavon, but Lavon denied it.

The net was activated by Zeidenberg in July 1954 in a series of sabotage acts of small dimensions and on a very amateurish level: an explosion device, prepared in a primitive way, set on fire a post office box of an American citizen; another "bomb," equally benign, exploded in one of the departments of the United States Information Service in Cairo; and finally, a matchbox, full of explosive material, blew up in the pocket of a Jewish youngster's coat while he was about to enter a cinema to place the "bomb" there.

An Egyptian security man detained the youngster. Following his detention, all the members of the secret espionage net, local Jewish youngsters, were captured, as well as the Israeli Major Meir Binet (Max Bennet), a Jew of German origin.

Bennet was sent to Egypt by the Israeli intelligence as a representative of a German firm. Bennet succeeded in becoming friends with General Naguib himslf. Bennet was supposed to fulfill his mission as an isolated spy, without any relation to the sabotage net. He was caught by the Egyptians through the fault of the net members who did not follow strictly the rules of precaution, separation and conspiracy. The net collapsed like a house of cards, and the entire affair ended with the nickname of "the security mishap." At the beginning of December 1954, the show-trial against the 11 accused of spying for Israel opened in Cairo. On January 27, 1955, the Egyptian military court announced its verdicts: two of the accused, Dr. Moshe Marzuk and Shmuel Azar, were sentenced to death; two others to life imprisonment with hard labor; four to seven years; two released. Meir Binet committed suicide before the verdict was announced — he cut his veins with a rusty nail which he had pulled from the door of his cell.

Avraham Zeidenberg himself was not bothered despite the fact that he was the commander of the net and all the threads led to him. He managed to wind up his affairs, sell his car and leave for Europe. He presented himself to Benjamin Rotem at Israel's embassy in Rome and told him how he had miraculously managed to slip away, at the last moment, from arrest, trial and the death sentence. In time, all his stories were revealed as pure lies and inventions. Zeidenberg had betrayed Israel and handed over to the Egyptians the net which he commanded. His apparent escape was carried out in collaboration with the Egyptian intelligence people who wanted Zeidenberg to appear in the eyes of his Israeli bosses as a wise agent crowned with the aura of a hero.

The Egyptians had an interest in Zeidenberg's continuing to act in the center of Israeli intelligence in Europe as a double agent, and they achieved their goal: Zeidenberg's Israeli commanders trusted his stories and he continued his work in Germany and Austria on the basis of his invented past as a member of the Nazi S.S. At a certain moment, Zeidenberg received an order to cease any contact with the Egyptians.

However, very soon, the Israeli security services realized that Zeidenberg was still meeting with Osman Nuri, the Egyptian military attache in Germany. During Zeidenberg's stay in Cairo, Nuri was the head of the Egyptian counter-intelligence service.

Suspicion arose that Zeidenberg was an Egyptian spy. He was brought to Israel, tried, and sentenced to 12 years' imprisonment.

SINAI CAMPAIGN

In March 1951, while we were in Rome, Israel's Foreign Minister, Moshe Sharett, submitted an official note to the four Allied governments (United States, the Soviet Union, Britain and France) which claimed global recompense to the State of Israel from the German Federal Republic for the properties of the European Jews. In September, 1951, the West German chancellor, Konrad Adenauer, declared its country's readiness to negotiate reparations. At the beginning of 1952, the issue was introduced into the agenda of the Knesset, causing a big uproar among Jewish people and stormy street demonstrations in Israel. Menachem Begin, the leader of "*Herut*" (Freedom Party), led the protest against the reparations.

Prime Minister David Ben-Gurion gave the full weight of his authority to the Reparations Agreement with Germany and introduced the term of "another Germany." This issue created a difficult moral problem. On the one hand, there was no desire to conduct relations with Germany since it was still considered an outcast in the family of nations. The question raised was whether perhaps Germany was eager to pay reparations in order to be forgiven for its crimes. The opponents called it "harlot's pay."

On the other hand, there was the issue of whether it was right that the murderers should also inherit, especially when Israel so desperately needed the money to accept and absorb more than a million immigrants, most of them Holocaust survivors. This mission was impossible with only the contributions of the Jewish people. In addition, Israel needed money for the purchase of arms and of other equipment for the military and for its maintenance.

The Knesset approved the reparations proposal by 61 votes for and 50 against, with nine abstentions. The reparations agreement between Israel and Germany was signed in Luxembourg, in September 1952, by Moshe Sharett and Konrad Adenauer, despite the warning by Menachem Begin, that this would cause a "war of life or death." The agreement was ratified and took effect on March 21, 1953.

In February 1953, after a bomb placed by a fanatic exploded in the courtyard of the Soviet Embassy in Tel-Aviv, the Soviet Union broke off diplomatic relations with Israel. Relations were restored a few months later, but Soviet support for the Arabs at the U.N. encouraged the Arabs to strain every nerve to defeat Israel by political and economic pressure. The Arab States had laid down their arms in exhaustion and defeat, but there was no disarmament of their spirit or emotions. While Israel regarded the Armistice Agreements as the end of the war and as a peace settlement in embryo, the Arab governments saw them as a temporary phase in a continuing war.

The Syrians interfered with Israel's irrigation projects in the northern demilitarized zone, and opened fire to stop Israeli development work. They also attacked Israeli fishing boats and patrol vessels in an attempt to drive them out of the Sea of Galilee. At home, they called for the destruction of the "Jewish cancer." In Lebanon, too, there were calls for the liquidation of Israel.

The Jordanians began harassing Israel's frontier villages. Numerous attacks were carried out by infiltrators and Jordanian troops on Israeli civilians and soldiers. The infiltrators attacked Israeli buses and killed tens of people. Legionaries shot from the Old City wall, killing Jews in Jerusalem.

The Egyptians sent into Israel bands of terrorists, organized among the Palestinian refugees in the Gaza Strip. The infiltrators, known as "*fedayeen*" (suicide fighters), penetrated deep into Israel territory from all sides: from the Gaza Strip, from Jordan, as well as from Syria and Lebanon. In Gaza, a Palestinian army was formed, well trained and equipped, whose purpose was — in the words of Egypt's President Gamal Abdel Nasser — to "liberate Palestine." The Egyptians were trying to make the Negev uninhabitable. Egypt also intensified its blockade on Israel in the Suez Canal and confiscated cargoes destined for Israel. It occupied the uninhabited islands of Tiran and Sanafir in the Red Sea at the entrance to the Gulf of Aqaba, established a garrison at Sharm el-Sheikh, interfered with international shipping to and from Eilat, and banned planes from flying over the Straits to or from Israel.

Israel reacted with heavy reprisals, which increased the disagreements between Prime Minister David Ben-Gurion and Foreign Minister Moshe Sharett. Ben-Gurion was a born national leader and fighter, who believed, to use his own words, that "what the Jew does is much more important than what the Gentile says." Golda Meir wrote in her memoirs that Ben-Gurion thought in terms of sovereignty and security, and believed that, ultimately, history would judge Israel on the record of its deeds, not its statements or its diplomacy.

Sharett, on the other hand, was a born diplomat and negotiator, immensely concerned with the way in which policy-makers elsewhere reacted to Israel and what was likely to make the Jewish State look 'good' in the eyes of other foreign ministers or the U.N. How Israel was judged by her contemporaries, rather than by future historians, was what mattered to him most.

Until the 1950s, Ben-Gurion and Sharett worked together, in spite of being so different in their basic personalities. But the question of Israeli retaliation for terrorist activities became a major area of conflict between them.

Sharett was just as convinced as Ben-Gurion that the incessant incursions across Israel's frontiers by gangs of Arab infiltrators had to end, but they disagreed sharply on the methods to be used. Sharett believed that well-worded protests to the U.N., skillful diplomatic notes and repeated presentation of our case to the world would eventually succeed, whereas armed reprisals could only result in a storm of criticism and make our international position even less comfortable than it was.

But Ben-Gurion still saw his primary responsibility not to the statesmen of the West or to the world tribunal, but to the ordinary citizens who lived in the Israeli settlements that were under constant Arab attack.

In the meantime, a defense treaty between Iraq and Turkey, linked to an earlier one between Turkey and Pakistan, was signed in Baghdad on February 24, 1955. Britain and Iran joined in. The U.S. did not formally participate in the pact, but its spiritual father was John Foster Dulles, the American Secretary of State, and the main support in arms and money came from the United States.

The pact alienated Egypt. Nasser interpreted it as an effort by Washington and London to divide the Arab world into rival blocs corresponding to the East-

Moshe Sharett raises the Israeli flag at the United Nations

West division. His position as the leader of the Arab world was being challenged, and he responded with an arms deal with the Soviet Union via Czechoslovakia. The massive Egyptian-Czech arms transaction was followed by a Syrian-Czech one. Weapons of a destructive capacity hitherto unknown in the region poured into Egypt at a rate beyond all previous experience: large quantities of tanks, artillery, jet planes and submarines were on their way to Egypt.

Israel now saw itself faced with possible dangers far greater even than those involved in the daily border attacks. The border conflicts were threatening Israel's short-term tranquility, while the pursuit of Arab favor by the major powers was undermining its long-term security. The actions of the major powers were all destined to appease the Arabs, by rearming them under defense pacts and arms deals. The Western powers, however, gave no clear reply to Israel's appeals for arms to redress the balance. Israel had neither an assured source of arms nor a guarantee of its security and integrity, and a wave of anxiety swept the country.

On July 26, 1956, Egypt announced that it had nationalized the Suez Canal. Britain and France now found themselves with a growing apprehension over the threat posed by unfettered Egyptian control of the Suez Canal to their communications and interests.

France had long since reached a point of complete exasperation with Egypt. While the U.S. still refused to sell arms to Israel, it consented to France supplying Israel with advanced Mystere aircraft. Now, also large quantities of French heavy armaments were being sent to Israel and unloaded in secret. Once French and Israeli policies vis-à-vis Nasser had converged, Britain, too, joined.

On October 17, 1956, Egypt and Syria signed a military pact. On October 25, Jordan joined the pact. The three armies were put under the command of

David Ben-Gurion and Moshe Sharett at Sde Boker

Prime Minister David Ben-Gurion with American president, Dwight Eisenhower

Nasser. The noose was tightening around Israel's neck. If resistance were not shown now, soon it might be too late. Sharett had to leave. Golda Meir was named Foreign Minister, and on October 27, Ben-Gurion submitted to the cabinet a proposal for a large-scale operation to demolish the bases of the *fedayeen* and the Egyptian army in the Sinai Peninsula and the Gaza Strip, and to occupy the shore of the Gulf of Aqaba in order to safeguard navigation. Israel mobilized its forces and, on October 29, its troops moved into Sinai, capturing vital points in the heart of the peninsula, and threatening the Suez Canal. Israeli fighter planes established air superiority over the combat areas.

On the afternoon of October 30, Britain and France issued an ultimatum calling on both sides to stop fighting and withdraw to 16 kilometers on either side of the Suez Canal. The same day they vetoed a U.S. sponsored resolution in the Security Council calling for immediate withdrawal of Israeli troops. Israel accepted the Anglo-French demand, but since Egypt rejected it, Israel's advance continued. In the course of five days Israel's army captured Gaza, Rafah, Al Arish, as well as thousands of prisoners, and occupied most of the peninsula east of the Suez canal. Israel lost 231 men.

The British and French invaded Egypt after having bombed its airfields. But the invasion proceeded very slowly and did not achieve its goals. Soviet-American pressure forced the British and French to withdraw.

Heavy Soviet-American pressure was put also on Israel to withdraw, and they threatened her with sanctions. The General Assembly of the U.N. called on Israel, on November 2, 1956, to withdraw her forces from Sinai. Ben-Gurion stated that Israel would leave Egyptian territory when arrangements had been made for a United Nations emergency force to enter the area and replace British and French troops, who had seized part of the Suez Canal.

The emergency force of 4,500 men took over its task in December. Israel finally withdrew in March 1957, also from Gaza. Following the Sinai Campaign, the American administration began to pay more heed to Israel's security sensitivity and already at the end of Eisenhower's term, Israel was promised to be given "Hawk" missiles for her defense against the new "Mig" planes Egypt and Syria were receiving from Moscow.

Aba Gefen and his wife at a reception by the Peruvian president, Manuel Prado

Israel's achievements in the Sinai Campaign were: the Egyptian army had been demolished, the *fedayeen* gangs in Gaza destroyed, the maritime blockade broken, the Red Sea opened to navigation, and the threat on Israel's existence removed, though, unfortunately, only temporarily. The U.N. assurances expired after 10 years, but Israel was given 11 years of calm on the border with Egypt and eight years of tranquility on her borders with Jordan and Lebanon.

When the Sinai Campaign began, I was — after two years in the research division of our ministry — preparing to leave for Lima, Peru.

We arrived in Lima in November 1956. We were told that Lima was called the City of the Inquisition. When I accompanied our ambassador to present his credentials to the president of the state, Manuel Prado, we traversed a street along which, some 400 years earlier, Jewish martyrs, the Marranos, nominal converts from Judaism to the Christian faith, had been dragged to the pyre.

SIX-DAY WAR

In 1959, we returned from Lima with our family enlarged. Our son Yehuda was born in the Peruvian capital, and we named him after my youngest brother, may he rest in peace.

We found a different Israel. In the period before the Sinai Campaign, many in the world still doubted Israel's durability. In 1959 nobody questioned it any more, and the people of Israel themselves looked to the future with vitality and optimism. This was in spite of its difficulties in the international arena and internal governmental crises following various affairs, such as the problem of "Who is a Jew?," the sale of arms to West Germany, and the riots following a local affray in a cafe in the neighborhood of Wadi Salib in Haifa.

On the international scene, Israel found itself in many respects entirely alone. France continued to be an ally and a good friend, a few other European countries were sympathetic. Though the Americans became more alert to the danger of neglecting Israel's security risks, our relationship with the United States continued to be strained. With the Soviets it was much worse than strained.

In Asia, our campaign against Egypt had evoked disapproval, though it had also inspired respect. In spite of having established diplomatic missions in some of the Asian countries, we were misunderstood there and not popular; the Asian Moslem states were openly hostile to us. The so-called "Third World" — in which the leader of India, Nehru, and the leader of Yugoslavia, Tito, played a decisive role — looked toward Nasser and the Arabs, and away from us.

Still, the world was not made up exclusively of Europeans and Asians, to use Golda Meir's words; there were also the emerging nations of Africa, then on the

President Yitzhak Ben-Zvi departing on a tour to Africa

verge of achieving their independence. Israel believed that it could contribute a great deal to those black states-in-the-making. In a world neatly divided between the "haves" and the "have-nots," Israel's experience was beginning to look unique because it had been forced to find solutions to the kinds of problems that large, wealthy, powerful states had never encountered.

Israel couldn't offer Africa money or arms but, on the other hand, it was free of the taint of the colonial exploiters, because all that Israel wanted from Africa was friendship. True, it hoped to have their support at the United Nations.

A separate department for relations with Africa was established at the Ministry of Foreign Affairs, and I was attached to it. In addition, a department for international cooperation was formed and between 1959 and 1973, thousands of Israeli experts in agriculture, hydrology, regional planning, public health, engineering, community services, medicine and scores of other fields were sent to Africa; also thousands of Africans in various fields were trained during those years in Israel. In the wake of the Yom Kippur (Day of Atonement) War, in 1973, most of the African states, unfortunately, severed their relations with Israel.

From the African department, I was transferred, at the end of 1959, to head the Foreign Ministry's director-general's bureau. While I was working there, a wave of anti-Semitic events erupted in 28 countries which continued also at the beginning of 1960: from painting Nazi swastikas to attacks on synagogues and the destruction of gravestones in cemeteries.

Every day, telegrams arrived from around the world about such incidents, and it was decided to present official protest notes to the governments in all the countries where those events were taking place. Foreign Minister Golda Meir, together with the director-general Yaacov Tzur, prepared the text of the instruction to our diplomatic representations.

Since such an act was to be a diplomatic precedent, Golda Meir decided that it could not be done without the approval of Prime Minister David Ben-Gurion, and I was asked to obtain his consent.

I contacted Yitzhak Navon, who was Ben-Gurion's secretary, and he arranged a meeting for me with Ben-Gurion. When I brought him the draft of the telegram, he read it attentively and approved it without changing or adding a word.

I sent out the telegram to our representatives in the following countries: Argentina, Austria, Australia, Belgium, Bolivia, Brazil, Canada, Chile, Cuba, Denmark, Ecuador, England, Finland, France, Germany, Greece, Italy, Mexico, The Netherlands, New Zealand, Norway, Panama, Peru, South Africa, Sweden, Turkey, United States and Uruguay.

In all the countries, except one, Israel's protest was received as a natural act and their governments expressed official regrets for the anti-Semitic outbursts. Only in South Africa, in a conversation with its Foreign Minister, did our ambassador feel that the Minister feared lest our protest be interpreted as interference in the internal affairs of his country. After a few months, the anti-Semitic outbursts ceased.

On May 11, 1960, a team from the Israeli *Mossad* abducted Adolf Eichmann in Buenos Aires while he was walking home from a factory in which he worked. At the end of the war, Eichmann had been taken prisoner, but his true identity was not discovered and he succeeded in escaping under a false name, Ricardo Clement, with papers prepared by friends in the Vatican. He was kept in hiding for 11 days and on May 22, he was brought to Israel on an El-Al plane which had brought an Israeli official delegation to Buenos Aires to participate in the celebrations of Argentina's 150th anniversary. The delegation was headed by Minister of Education and Culture, Abba Eban, who knew nothing about the operation. On May 23, Prime Minister David Ben-Gurion informed the Knesset that Eichmann was to be tried in Israel.

Eichmann's trial opened in April 1961. He was brought to justice in Jerusalem, in the sovereign Jewish State. He was indicted for crimes against the Jewish people, crimes against humanity, and crimes of war, under the Nazi and Nazi Collaborators (Punishment) Law of 1950. Day by day, for two years, the mystery of man's infinite degradation was demonstrated in gory detail.

The trial was exemplary in its dignity and judicial precision. The court of three judges heard hundreds of witnesses who unfolded stories so macabre and agonizing that the whole nation was stunned by a new flow of grief. In his memoirs, while in jail, Eichmann wrote that in the autumn of 1941, Hitler personally ordered the extermination of the Jews. Of great significance was the justice meted out to the odious monster, and the effect of the trial on world opinion and on Israel's young generation was electrifying. The raison d'être of Israel's struggle for freedom and security was made crystal clear.

Eichmann was found guilty. Sentence of death was passed and upheld in the Court of Appeal, and he was hanged.

When Eichmann was brought by the *Mossad* to Israel, Argentina asked that the Israeli ambassador be recalled and delivered a complaint to the United Nations Security Council. But the formal irregularity of the capture struck most of the world as subsidiary to the greater drama: here was an arch-criminal, an assassin of Jewish masses, brought to trial in a Jewish homeland.

Israel did everything possible to restore normal relations with Buenos Aires, and, accidents and unpleasantnesses notwithstanding, matters began to improve. In 1963 a new Israeli ambassador, General (Res.) Joseph Avidar, was appointed to Buenos Aires, and I — having served for a short time as our Foreign Ministry's spokesman — was sent to our embassy in Buenos Aires as First Counselor. As time went by, relations with Argentina returned to their traditional cordiality.

While we were in Argentina, important internal political changes took place in Israel as a result of the security "mishap" of 1954 in Egypt and the resignation of Lavon as Defense Minister.

In March 1963, Isser Harel, the head of the *Mossad*, resigned. The reason for it was an instruction from Ben-Gurion to stop the secret activities against the German scientists in Egypt — sending of explosive envelopes, abduction of some scientists and threats on their families. Ben-Gurion feared that the *Mossad's* activities against those scientists might harm the relations being developed between Israel and Germany, following Ben-Gurion's historical meeting, in March 1960, at the Waldorf-Astoria Hotel in New York, with the German chancellor, Konrad Adenauer.

In March 1965, when Ben-Gurion was already in retirement, the Knesset approved the establishment of diplomatic relations with Germany — 66 voted in favor, 29 against, 10 abstained.

Levi Eshkol was elected Prime Minister when Ben-Gurion resigned in June 1963. Eshkol was a man of vision and action. His personal charm conquerred many people. His visit to the United States, in June 1964, was the first visit of an Israeli Prime Minister at an American president's invitation. Following this

David Ben-Gurion with German chancellor, Konrad Adenauer

Prime Minister Levi Eshkol with President Lyndon Johnson

meeting, a close friendship was established between Eshkol and President Lyndon Johnson. When France ceased its arms deliveries to Israel, Eshkol acted to convert the United States into the main supplier of arms to Israel.

The trend of the Eisenhower administration, during its second term, was to improve relations with Israel. This trend continued during the presidency of John Kennedy and it matured with the American decision, in 1962, to sell arms straight to Israel. That decision presented a signal that the United States would not agree to a violation of the arms balance between Israel and the Arabs and served as evidence that it wished to prevent a feeling of isolation in Israel.

During Johnson's presidency, relations with Israel continued to improve and, at the same time, the courting of the "revolutionary" Arab regimes was abandoned. During Eshkol's second visit to the United States, in January 1968, he obtained an increased supply of "Skyhawk" and "Phantom" planes and an American commitment to preserve the arms balance between Israel and the Arabs. From the United States, Eshkol traveled to Toronto for the weekend and he was in an exalted mood. He was received by Ontario's Prime Minister, John Robarts, and met with the Jewish leadership and a group of principal contributors to the United Jewish Appeal. In Toronto, Eshkol addressed a public assembly and an artistic photo of him was taken which later served as the prototype for the Eshkol stamp issued by Israel's postal department.

Eshkol's election to Prime Minister had been well received not only by the government's coalition parties, but also by the opposition. He succeeded in introducing correct personal relations between the two camps and showed significant tolerance towards rivals of the past, by, for example, permitting to bring to Israel the remains of Zeev Jabotinsky for burial in a state funeral on Mount Herzl.

But in the field of foreign affairs, the new government showed hesitancy. This invited criticism from within the Labor Party, at a time when in the Arab world, the previous request for the "return of the Arab refugees to their homes" was replaced by the demand for the "restoration of the legitimate rights of the Arabs in Palestine." Thus they negated absolutely Israel's right of existence and declared that only the Palestinian Arabs possess the right of self-determination

Foreign Minister Golda Meir with President John Kennedy

Aba Gefen with Prime Minister Eshkol in Toronto

and the country belongs to them alone, whereas the Jews have no right whatsoever to sovereignty or political independence there.

In May 1964, less than a year after he had taken over as Prime Minister, Eshkol was faced with the establishment of the so-called "Palestine Liberation Organization" (PLO), headed by Ahmed Shukeiry, and the adoption of the "Palestinian Covenant," the basic document of the PLO and its constituent organizations. Later, Shukeiry was replaced by Yasser Arafat and in 1968, the Covenant was formulated anew by the Palestinian National Council (PNC) at its meeting in Cairo.

The "Palestinian Covenant" was to serve as an ideological basis for the struggle against Israel, and in the name of it, Arab spokesmen swore to eliminate Israel. Eshkol's Government was accused of a lack of resolve on Israel's rights and needs. On the eve of the 1965 parliamentary elections, the Labor Party split: David Ben-Gurion, Moshe Dayan, Shimon Peres and Joseph

Almogi formed a separate list for the Knesset. In addition, there were the *Mossad* setbacks, in 1965, in Egypt and Syria.

In Cairo, Major Zeev Gur-Arye, nicknamed "the spy on the horse," was caught. In Syria, the Israeli spy Eli Cohen, who had succeeded in establishing close ties with the Syrian leadership, was publicly hanged in the Damascus city square. On the other hand, a year later, the *Mossad* had one of its biggest successes. It brought to Israel an Iraqi fighter pilot, Munir Radfa, who landed in Israel with his "Mig 21" plane, considered the best Soviet plane in the service of the Egyptian, Syrian and Iraqi air forces. It was the first plane of the "Mig 21" model to reach the West.

Two Arab Summit Conferences, in 1964 and in 1965, sought to keep the prospects of armed conflict with Israel alive, in policy and rhetoric, and to keep the pot simmering sufficiently to prevent any long-term tranquility. In 1966, Nasser became impatient, and, being convinced that the Arabs could achieve Israel's elimination, a joint Arab command was established under the leadership of Egyptian General Abdul Hakim Amer, to plan an eventual military assault. "*Fatah*" (the military arm of the PLO), developed the ideology of a "people's war" and engaged in a series of terrorist activities inside Israel's territory.

The constantly increasing terrorist incursions, carried out by *Fatah* from Syrian territory, were fully supported by the Syrian *Ba'ath* regime, and created ever-growing tension. The revolutionary *Ba'ath* regime in Syria, established in 1963, sought to appear as the foremost champion of the Palestinian cause and the most extreme in its hatred of Israel. It thus became Moscow's favorite ally.

On November 3, 1966, Egypt and Syria signed a war alliance. The raids into Israel continued, and there was a chain of mutual commitments between Syria, Egypt and the Soviet Union to keep Israel under murderous harassment while protecting Syria from reprisals. After several terrorist raids, the Syrians attacked Israeli farmers in the Sea of Galille area. The exchange of fire escalated from machine-guns to artillery and from artillery to aircraft. In an air encounter on April 7, 1967, six Syrian Mig aircraft were brought down, two of them in the territory of Jordan. The extent of the Syrian defeat was unexpected.

The leaders in the Kremlin were furious: this debacle might completely undermine the Arab States' trust in Soviet protection. The Soviets were afraid to participate directly in the fighting, which might have invited a confrontation with the United States. So they prodded the Egyptians to rescue Syria from its self-inflicted humiliation, and supplied Cairo with false information about Israel concentrating massive armed forces on the Syrian border. It was, of course, a gross lie, and Levi Eshkol invited the Soviet ambassador and his attaches to get into a car, without prior notice, and search for the "massive Israeli concentrations" which they said were lurking in the north. The ambassador replied that his function was to communicate Soviet reports, not to test their veracity. At the same time, however, the secretary-general of the United Nations reported publicly that no exceptional Israeli troop concentrations had been noted at all.

On May 15, 1967, Israel's Independence Day, Nasser began dispatching, with ostentatious publicity, large numbers of Egyptian troops into Sinai, convoys being deliberately routed through Cairo's busiest streets on their way to Ismailia. On the same day Egypt demanded the withdrawal of the U.N. Emergency Force (UNEF) from the Gaza Strip and Sinai borders and Sharm el-Sheikh.

Back in 1957, Israel had agreed to withdraw from the Sinai Peninsula after satisfactory arrangements had been concluded for the deployment of the UNEF on the borders between Israel and Egypt. Israel had been given assurances, by the U.N. as well as by the U.S., that the dangerous situation to its security on its border with Egypt would never recur.

These assurances were null and void ten years later. Because, confronted with Nasser's demand, U Thant, the secretary-general of the U.N., replied that any such request would be regarded as a demand for its complete withdrawal. Nasser then officially requested the evacuation of the force, and on May 19, the UNEF Commander, General Rikhye, told Israel that the force would cease to function the same day.

On May 22, Nasser made his fatal step, imposing the blockade at the Straits of Tiran for Israeli shipping and on ships carrying any cargoes to Israel. Charles de Gaulle, however, warned Israel not to react militarily to Egypt's blocking of the Straits.

Egypt brought up 90,000 troops against Israel's southern region, concentrated 900 tanks with their advanced force within swift striking distance of Israel, and occupied the entrance to the Straits of Tiran. Nasser declared he was now prepared to wage total war on Israel.

Radio Cairo announced: "The existence of Israel has continued too long. The great hour has arrived. The battle has come in which we shall destroy Israel."

In Israel, a troubled sense of renewed vulnerability was developing. In sight again was the spectre of genocide and the destruction of everything that Israel had achieved in the 19 years of its existence as an independent state. Egypt no

David Ben-Gurion with the French president, Charles de Gaulle

longer even pretended that its actions were intended to protect Syria, speaking openly and clearly of its preparations for the destruction of Israel.

In Israel, under the looming shadow of war, the organization and training of the reserve units was accelerated greatly, while older men, women and schoolchildren helped to keep the home front going. Many worked overtime without pay to get in the harvest, maintain supplies, and fill export orders. The Government announced that ample supplies of food were available and kept the warehouses open until late at night for shops to replenish stocks. The country anxiously awaited a government decision to end the uncertainty, and army leaders pressed for action. Widespread demands were made for the establishment of a government of national unity to fortify public confidence and, specifically, for the appointment of General Moshe Dayan, who had been Israel's chief-of-staff in the Sinai Campaign of 1956, as Defense Minister.

On May 30, King Hussein of Jordan arrived in Cairo, signed a military pact with Egypt and placed his forces under Egyptian control. Five days later, Iraq followed Hussein's example and also signed a military pact with Egypt. Egyptian, Saudi Arabian, and Iraqi troops were sent to Jordan, and Iraqi, Algerian, and Kuwaiti forces to Egypt.

On June 1, Dayan was appointed Defense Minister, which enhanced military morale. With the inclusion in the government of Menachem Begin, the opposition leader and previous chief of the *Irgun Zvai Leumi*, as minister without portofolio, the formation of the government of national unity had been completed. On June 3, Radio Cairo quoted an order of the day by General Murtaji, commander of the Egyptian forces in Sinai, hailing "the Holy War to restore the rights of the Arabs stolen in Palestine, and to reconquer the plundered soil of Palestine."

The world's reaction was, unfortunately, the same tragic apathy and deplorable indifference which cost the lives of a third of the Jewish people under Hitler, and the Jews saw the State of Israel, which had become the symbol of Jewish survival, in danger of destruction. The Jewish State, founded after six million Jews had been slaughtered by Nazi Germany and built up in part by the shattered remnants who escaped the gas-chambers and by refugees from Europe and Arab lands, was now being threatened with annihilation.

Surrounded by Arab forces that were likely to attack at any moment, Israel could delay no longer. On the morning of June 5, Israel's air force attacked the airfields of Egypt, and destroyed most of its planes on the ground. In less than three hours, Israel had achieved complete superiority in the air, and conveyed a message to King Hussein of Jordan, expressing the hope that he would stay outside the conflict, promising him that Israel would attack nowhere unless it was in retaliation. Hussein, however, made a fateful mistake: his forces launched an unprovoked destructive assault all along the armistice line, occupied U.N. headquarters in East Jerusalem, and indiscriminately shelled the Jewish areas in the west of the city, killing many and wounding hundreds. Israel repelled the attack, destroyed the Jordanian air force, and inflicted heavy casualties on the Syrian and Iraqi air forces.

By dawn on Friday, June 8, the entire Sinai peninsula was in Israel's hands and its forces were encamped along the Canal and Gulf of Suez; the Gaza Strip had been taken, and Israel's naval forces had captured Sharm el-Sheikh; all of Judea and Samaria were in Israel's hands, including the Old City of Jerusalem, which was taken by a paratrooper unit, under the command of General Motta Gur who liberated the Western (Wailing) Wall and the Temple Mount, proclaiming: "The Temple Mount is in our hands." When Moshe Dayan paid his first visit to the Old City of Jerusalem, on June 7, he said: "We have unified Jerusalem, the divided capital of Israel. We have returned to the holiest of our holy places, never to depart from it again."

With the fighting over in the south and the center, the Israel air force opened fire on the heavily fortified gun positions on the Golan Heights, and in two days Israeli forces reached the town of Kuneitra, on the main road to Damascus. The Security Council of the United Nations called for a cease-fire, and with the acceptance of it by Israel, Egypt, Jordan, Lebanon and Syria, the Six-Day War came to an end.

When the war was over, there was great exhilaration in Israel. In one of her greatest hours, she had gained prestige and was admired by the entire world, loved and revered by the Jewish people. She held 68,572 square kilometers of territory previously in Arab hands: 1,150 sq. km. on the Golan Heights; 5,879 sq. km. in Judea and Samaria; 362 sq. km. in the Gaza Strip; and 61,181 sq. km. in Sinai. All those areas, except for Jerusalem, were to be administered, under

The paratroopers at the Western Wall

the cease-fire agreements, by the Israeli military government. But from this war, too, Israel came out bereaved: she suffered 776 deaths and 2,586 injuries.

Israel's soldiers fought heroically, buoyed up by the knowledge that they were not alone, that they had an uncompromising ally: the Jews all over the world who saw the state, established for all of world Jewry, in mortal danger, and themselves jeopardized with it. The Diaspora Jews were for the people of Israel an inspiring source for their infinite fortitude, partners of merit in a victory that averted a second Holocaust.

We were then still in Buenos Aires, except for our daughter Ruhama, who, at the age of 18, had returned to Israel and enlisted into the army. During the Six-Day War, she served with the navy in Haifa.

Toward the end of the Six-Day War, the song "Jerusalem the Golden" by Naomi Shemer became the hymn of victory. The paratroopers sang it at the

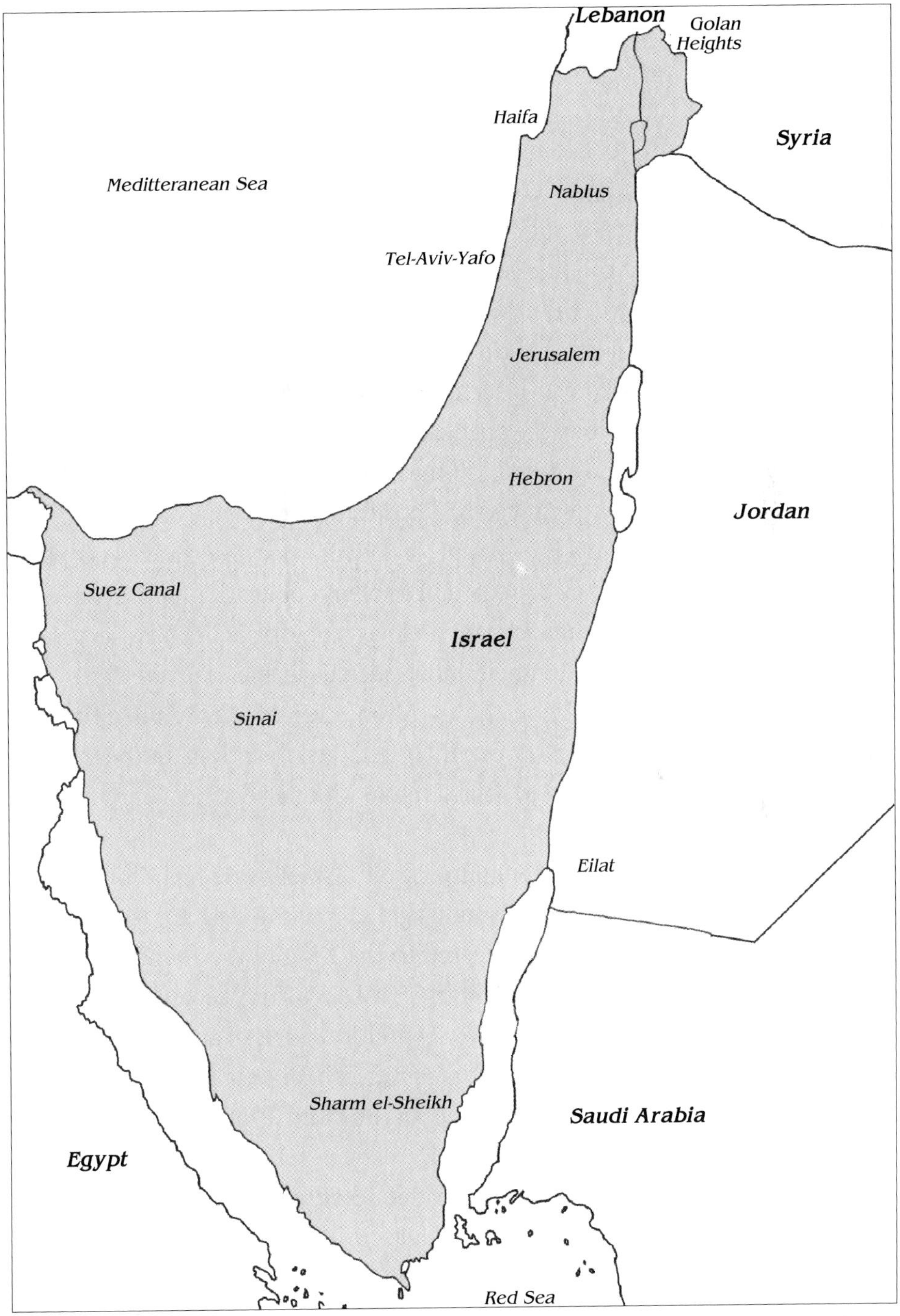

Map of Israel following the Six-Day War

Western Wall, after the take-over of the Old City. Baruch Tenenbaum, the representative of Israel's Ministry of Tourism in Buenos Aires, returned from Israel and brought the song, and the entire Israeli community in Buenos Aires gathered at his home to listen to it. In Jerusalem, the 19-year-old barriers between the eastern and western parts were removed, and the City of God, spiritual shrine and center of all the Jews on earth was again united.

A law was passed by the Knesset, extending the limits of Jerusalem and the jurisdiction of Israeli law to the eastern part of the city, which during the War of Independence had been sundered from us. It was occupied by Jordan and for 19 years Jerusalem the Golden was bisected by barbed wire and concrete barriers.

Arab legionnaires all along the artificial frontier through the heart of the city opened fire at will, wounding and killing Israelis. The Jewish Quarter of the walled city was practically destroyed and scores of synagogues laid waste. The ancient Jewish cemetery on the Mount of Olives was desecrated and partly demolished. In contemptuous disregard of a solemn obligation in the Armistice Agreement signed by Israel and Jordan, no Jews from Israel or elsewhere in the world were allowed access to their most sacred shrine, the Western Wall, steeped in Jewish history, religion and tradition. Even Moslem Arab citizens of Israel were not permitted to carry out their personal devotions in the territory under Jordan's rule. In May 1967, the Temple Mount became a camp for the Jordanian militia.

Jerusalem would not have been united under Israel's rule had King Hussein not ignored Prime Minister Eshkol's message, asking the king not to join in the Six-Day War. This message was delivered to the King in the framework of his secret contacts with Israeli personalities. Hussein's first secret meeting was with Ambassador Yaacov Herzog, Eshkol's political adviser, and it took place in London, in September 1963, a short time after Eshkol became Prime Minister. Hussein held two more secret meetings, in 1964 and 1965, with Ambassador Herzog and Ambassador Ehud Avriel, respectively. At those meetings, understandings on the use of common water resources had been reached, and border security arrangements made, and Hussein asked for Israel's assistance in obtaining American aid.

In September 1965, Eshkol sent Foreign Minister Golda Meir to Paris, to meet the king there, and this was Hussein's first talk with a top Israeli political personality. Golda Meir had met, in 1948, King Hussein's grandfather, King Abdullah, and tried, without success, to dissuade him from joining the war against Israel. Now, in Paris, Golda Meir proposed to Abdullah's grandson, King Hussein, the signing of an Israeli-Jordanian peace treaty within the then existing Israeli borders, each side committing itself to respect the territorial integrity and independence of the other, and with guarantees by the Big Powers. But Hussein committed his biggest mistake: he did not sign peace with Israel. If he had not missed that opportunity, wars would have been prevented, many thousands of lives saved, and developments in the Middle East would have been completely different.

Hussein ignored the fact that Nasser had called him "an imperialistic lackey," "a treacherous dwarf" and "the Hashemite harlot." He also preferred to ignore what was clear and evident to all, that the PLO, though its intention was to fight Israel in the undefined future, actually wished to destroy Hussein in the more immediate present. Hussein rejected Israel's hand extended for peace, its most generous offer to agree to the best imaginable conditions for Jordan.

Three weeks after the end of the Six-Day War, Hussein met again secretly, in London, with Ambassador Herzog. At that meeting, in July 1967, it was Israel's turn to disregard the opportunity of peace. Hussein proposed a peace agreement based on significant border changes; he was willing not to oppose the emigration of the majority of Arab refugees to distant countries, was ready to solve the problem of the Moslem holy places in the framework of a unified Jerusalem, and asked to meet personally with Levi Eshkol or Moshe Dayan.

Dayan strongly believed in the possibility of signing a peace agreement, which Hussein could present as a "reciprocal and honorable arrangement," as he requested. Eshkol, however, refused to meet with Hussein and did not let Dayan do so either. The Government of Israel had not yet decided on a clear policy as to the future of the administered territories, while Menachem Begin's position was not to give up even one inch of land. Eshkol was, therefore, afraid of internal political complications, especially since the general view in those days was that, in the Jordanian arena, time was working in favor of Israel.

In August 1967, an Arab summit conference convened in Khartoum, the capital of Sudan. The conference resolved that there would be no peace with Israel, no negotiations with Israel, no recognition of Israel, and Hussein's readiness for the above mentioned compromises very soon petered out. At the next secret talk with Herzog, in November of the same year, Hussein agreed only to very minor border changes. He would not concede the Mount of Olives or even one Arab village, and announced Jerusalem was not negotiable. When he was later presented with the "Allon Plan," he rejected it as he had done with every other Israeli proposal for a territorial compromise.

In April 1987, King Hussein met in London, at the residence of Lord Victor Mishkin, with Israel's Foreign Minister Shimon Peres and his deputy Yossi Beilin. Jordan's Prime Minister Zaid Rifa'i was also present. The participants reached what was called the "London Agreement." This agreement was similar to the understandings crystallized in Hussein's talks, in July 1967, with Yaacov Herzog. But the "London Agreement" was never activated. Eight months later, the "*intifada*" broke out, and King Hussein decided to renounce his claim on the West Bank.

In 1991, Hussein met with Yitzhak Shamir, then Prime Minister, on the eve

Aba Gefen with Foreign Minister Yitzhak Shamir

of the Madrid Conference on Peace in the Middle East. The idea of meeting Hussein came to Shamir's mind immediately after having been elected Prime Minister following Menachem Begin's resignation in August 1983. Before making any preparations for such a meeting, Shamir wanted to know what had been discussed at the previous meetings with the king. Being an adviser to Shamir, I was given all the relevant secret files of the Prime Minister's and Foreign Minister's bureaus and was asked to sum up all past meetings.

I presented a report with a summary of the 24 meetings with the king that had taken place until then. Shamir met with Hussein when I was already in retirement.

Today it is public knowledge that in the course of many years, beginning long before the Israel-Jordan Peace Treaty was signed in 1994, King Hussein met secretly at least 16 Israeli personalities: Golda Meir, Moshe Dayan, Yigal Allon, Yitzhak Rabin, Yaacov Herzog, Ehud Avriel, Gideon Rafael and Chaim Bar-Lev — may they all rest in peace; as well as Shimon Peres, Abba Eban, Yitzhak Shamir, Ehud Barak, Simha Dinitz, Elyakim Rubinstein, Yossi Ben-Aharon and Ephraim Halevy. The meetings took place in London and Paris, on the Israeli-Jordanian border, on boats in the Aqaba Gulf, in Aqaba and in the desert, in Herzliyah and in Tel-Aviv.

All the discussions were conducted in an atmosphere of friendship and contributed to the easing of tensions, so that the calm on the border continued with practical security arrangements, and altogether, the situation with Jordan was satisfactory. The biggest obstacle preventing the secret talks with the King from bringing about a formal peace treaty with Jordan were the three "no"s of the Khartoum Conference. At the same time, the Soviet Union undertook to rehabilitate the Egyptian and Syrian armies, initiating a vast airlift of planes, tanks, and other equipment to replace their losses, and sending in thousands of Soviet advisers and experts. The Soviets embarked on this dangerous path in contradiction to their own support of the U.N. Security Council's resolution 242, adopted unanimously on November 22, 1967, which emphasized the need to work for a just and lasting peace in which every state in the Middle East can live in security.

At the Suez Canal, which Nasser had blocked immediately after the Six-Day War, in September 1968, Egypt started massive artillery shellings on the Israeli positions. It was the beginning of the War of Attrition, its purpose being to weaken Israel by border infiltrations, shellings, and terror.

Israel paid a high price in the War of Attrition — 721 killed — but it was not weakend. Egypt was. The Israeli reprisals by land, sea, and air caused the destruction of the canal cities, the flight of their inhabitants and many casualties. In August 1970, Egypt accepted a cease-fire.

On September 28, 1970, Nasser died, and Egypt's new president, Anwar Sadat, decided to exploit the cease-fire period for the preparation of a new *"Jihad"* against Israel, and declared: "Egypt is committed to the liberation of the whole of Palestine and the annihilation of the Jewish State — politically, militarily, socially and spiritually." But in February 1971, Egypt announced, unexpectedly, to Ambassador Gunnar Jarring, the U.N. secretary-general's mediator between Israel and Egypt, its desire to sign a peace treaty with Israel if the latter would agree to withdraw to the old international borders.

This announcement was a change in Egyptian policy and showed that the new Egyptian president intended to deviate sharply from the positions of his predecessor.

This unexpected situation required a thorough evaluation by Israel and a special effort to penetrate the obscurity that concealed the real significance of the Egyptian proposal. Israel did not welcome the Egyptian proposal with warmth. Instead, it published a cautious statement in which it defined the Egyptian announcement as positive, while immediately adding that it would not withdraw to the June 1967 borders. The American administration exerted pressure on Israel and warned that it was disregarding a golden opportunity for a peace treaty with Egypt. It was only seven years later, in 1978, that Israel agreed to the conditions she rejected in 1971. It is reasonable to suppose, that had she accepted the 1971 offer, the Yom Kippur war in October 1973, would have been avoided.

PART FOUR

CAMP DAVID

YOM KIPPUR (DAY OF ATONEMENT) WAR

A short time after the Six-Day War, I was appointed Consul General of Israel in Toronto, Canada. I arrived there at the beginning of September 1967, together with my wife and two sons. A year later, having concluded her military service, our daughter Ruhama joined us, and enrolled at the University of Toronto, to study English language and literature. During our four-year stay in Toronto Ruhama married Dr. Sol Goldstein, a Canadian-born Jew, and they named their first-born son Benjamin, after my brother, the fourth member of my immediate family killed by the Nazis, may he rest in peace.

While we were in Toronto, Israel was struggling against a hostile alignment, led by the Soviet Union, which had broken off diplomatic relations with Israel because of the Six-Day War. In Canada, there was a local partner to that alignment — the official organ of the United Church of Canada, the "United Church Observer."

The "Observer" was treading the perilous path of encouraging Arab terrorism: if it did not openly promote it, certainly it did not shrink from condoning the terrorist activities. The "Observer" printed articles calling for unreserved aid to the anti-Israeli terrorists and inviting donations for *Fatah*, which was tantamount to subsidizing the terrorist groups. The editor, Reverend Al Forrest, supported the belligerent and irrational Arab leaders, proclaiming a *Jihad* (a holy war) against Israel. He identified himself closely with those who had admitted to most despicable atrocities and told a reporter: "You can't be long with these [Arab] commandos without sympathizing with their cause."

The Canadian poet Irving Layton, responding to the anti-Israeli campaign of the *Observer*'s editor, wrote: "In the Middle Ages it was the poisoning of wells. In the 1970's it's the whole world that Jews are threatening, according to that fine and upstanding United Churchman.... With a stroke of the pen he promoted them from mere well-poisoners to world destroyers."

During our stay in Toronto, I was often invited by synagogues to address their congregants on political events and these meetings were often reported in the news media, thus serving as a platform for Israel's public relations. In a talk at Beth-Tzedek synagogue, I harshly criticized the United Church for its attitude. The daily newspaper "Globe and Mail" published an editorial attacking me personally for "having insulted a distinguished Canadian population" and called on Canada's Foreign Minister, Mitchel Sharp, to declare me a "persona non grata." When that editorial appeared, Israel's Minister of Education and

Aba Gefen with Minister Yigal Allon in Toronto

Culture, Yigal Allon, was in Ottawa on a mission of the United Jewish Appeal (UJA), from where he came to Toronto. Our ambassdor in Ottawa, Ephraim Evron, showed him the editorial.

When I received Allon at the Toronto airport, he patted me on the shoulder with affection and said: "Gefen, it is sometimes good to tell people what you think about them."

I had known Allon since 1946, when he was the Commander of the *Palmach* and, together with Israel Galili, head of the *Haganah*'s headquarters, visited the Jewish refugee camps in Europe. I took them in my car across the Austrian-German border. I very much appreciated Allon's attitude towards my confrontation with the "Observer" and his remarks encouraged me to continue the struggle against Israel's enemies in Canada.

In February 1970, the United Church of Canada sponsored in Toronto a public meeting on the Middle East crisis, and invited an Arab representative and me to present our positions. The Arab representative was the Director of the Arab Information Center in Canada, Ibrahim Shukrallah, stationed in Ottawa. All the news media were invited, and part of the proceedings were televised; the auditorium was packed. It was the first time, since the establishment of Israel, that Arab and Israeli diplomats had appeared on the same platform.

When question-time came, I found myself facing a hostile axis — Palestinian refugees, Canadian-born Arabs, the editor of the *Observer*, and a Jew from New York who declared himself anti-Zionist. I rejected their hostile arguments and stressed that their whole attitude was pure anti-Semitism, which is evident in either case: when an individual Jew is deprived of his civil rights, or when Jews as a people are deprived of their right to corporate existence.

When the Israeli minister, Joseph Burg, of the National Religious Party, arrived in Toronto on a mission of the UJA, I arranged a meeting, at my residence, between him and Al Forrest. I hoped that, both being religious persons, Burg would be able to influence Forrest. Their talk was very much to the point and civilized, but Forrest continued to be hostile.

In addition to ministers Allon and Burg, the following also came to Toronto on fundraising missions: Yitzhak Rabin, when he was ambassador in Washington — on behalf of the State of Israel Bonds ("Bonds"); Foreign Minister Abba Eban — on behalf of the Weizmann Institute and the "Bonds";

minister Joseph Almogi — on behalf of the UJA; ministers Joseph Sapir and Menachem Begin — on behalf of the "Bonds"; and minister Pinhas Sapir who came on behalf of the UJA as well as of the "Bonds."

I had known Abba Eban since I worked in 1950 in the research division of the Foreign Ministry while he was ambassador in Washington.

I met Joseph Almogi for the first time in Salzburg, while I was active in the *Brichah* there. He came to Europe to visit the Jewish refugee camps. When I

Aba Gefen with Foreign Minister Abba Eban in Toronto

arrived in Israel, in February 1948, he was the head of the Haifa branch of the "Enlistment Bureau" for the Israeli army, and he accepted me for work there.

I met Pinhas Sapir in Buenos Aires when he came there during the Six-Day War for the emergency fundraising campaign. It was a really exciting experience to witness his meetings with the contributors and to see his ability to convince people to double their contribution and even triple it and more.

When Eshkol died, minister Joseph Almogi was in Toronto. I transmitted to him the news of Eshkol's death and the call to return immediately to Israel to participate in the deliberations on Eshkol's successor. When I accompanied Almogi to the airport, he told me that Sapir was the preferred candidate, but since he had refused, it would be Golda Meir.

In 1970, Prime Minister Golda Meir came to Toronto, on her way to Ottawa, where she had to fulfill a political mission to the Canadian Government.

Her stay in Toronto was for the purpose of fundraising, but it was also used for public relations. During her one-day visit she participated at a Zionist Convention, spoke at a luncheon of the UJA and a dinner of the "Bonds," and at a public meeting at Beth-Tzedek synagogue attended by 7,000 people. She also had interviews at all the television stations.

Golda Meir returned to the center of Israel's politics at the age of 72 though with a grave blood disease, and at a moment she had intended to resign from the Knesset and retire from political life. The Labor Party preferred her to the natural heirs of Eshkol — Moshe Dayan and Yigal Allon — and she was elected, in June 1969, as Prime Minister.

I knew Golda Meir from my work at the Foreign Ministry as head of the director-general's bureau and as the Foreign Ministry's spokesman. She was an intelligent woman, experienced in the political, diplomatic and social fields, and emotional, and she conducted foreign policy with vigor. When she took over the position of the prime minister, she was not popular in Israel. On her arrival in Toronto, she was at the peak of popularity after having stood firm and with dignity against the heavy pressures of the U.S. concerning the "Rogers Plan," presented by President Nixon's Secretary of State, William Rogers, for the settlement of the Middle East conflict. Its main point was the withdrawal of Israel to the June 4, 1967, borders, with slight amendments.

There were ministers in the government who warned that, if Israel would not accept the plan, the U.S. would cease its support. Golda Meir was not afraid and informed the Americans, in name of the majority in government, that Israel rejected the plan. There was no rupture, nor any crisis, in American-Israel relations.

Aba Gefen with Prime Minister Golda Meir in Toronto

When we returned to Israel in September 1971, almost a year after Golda Meir's visit to Toronto, we found Israel expanded in size from the peak of Mount Hermon, through Judea and Samaria, to the waters of the Suez Canal. The War of Attrition was over and it was for the first time since the Six-Day War that the borders of the State of Israel were quiet. A new stream of immigrants began entering from the western world as well as from the Soviet Union. The new immigrants from the Soviet Union received various benefits which aroused much anger towards the government and its policy. This was one of the factors contributing to the rise of the "Black Panthers" movement, formed by a group of youngsters from the Musrara and Katamon neighborhoods in Jerusalem.

Unfortunately, the anti-Israeli and anti-Jewish terrorist activities continued. In those days, Israelis were being killed by merciless assassins in supermarkets, apartment houses, parking lots and university cafeterias. Bombs were thrown at Israeli embassies and business premises overseas, and there were threats of kidnapping. A large number of envelopes, filled with deadly explosives, were mailed from abroad to Israeli and Jewish personalities throughout the world.

In London, Israel's agricultural attache was murdered, and an assistant military attache at the Israel embassy in Washington was shot dead outside his home. In Madrid an Israeli agent was killed; in Nicosia an Israeli merchant was shot to death and there was an attempt to kill the Israeli ambassador there and attack an Israeli plane. A Greek child was murdered at the El-Al office in Athens, an Italian employee slain at the El-Al office in Rome.

Arab terrorists were apprehended, with weapons and explosives in their possession, in England, Greece, Cyprus, Austria and Thailand. Planes were being hijacked and 47 defenseless passengers and crew were killed in a Swissair aircraft over Switzerland. At the beginning of May 1972, a team of Israel's special anti-terrorist unit, under the command of Ehud Barak and with the participation of Benjamin Netanyahu, stormed a hijacked Sabena plane at Lod airport. Two terrorists were killed, two were caught and three passengers were wounded. At the end of that month, 27 Puerto-Rican pilgrims on an Air France plane were massacred at Lod airport by three Japanese mercenaries, 71 injured. The three terrorists were members of the Japanese terror organization "The Red Star Army." Two terrorists were killed and the third, Kozo Okamoto, was caught and sentenced to life imprisonment but released from jail in the prisoners' exchange deal following the Lebanon war.

In September 1972, 11 members of Israel's team to the Olympic Games were assassinated in Munich, where the tactics and means were borrowed from the Nazis: the murderers blindfolded the helpless young sportsmen, bound them hand and foot, and after subjecting them to hours of agonizing despair, shot them down point-blank, one by one. The Arab terrorists, themselves killed in Munich, were given a state funeral by the government of Libya. Libya's President Muammar Kaddhafi bestowed upon *Fatah* an award of five million dollars for the murder of the Israeli athletes, and the terrorist broadcasting station in Syria boasted: "Congratulations to you, members of 'Black September,' on your success. Your activity in Munich is a gold medal for the Arab people."

The Kuwaiti Defense Minister declared that "the Arab brain which planned the Munich operation is a creative and inventive one." Since Israel had refused to sell Uganda's President, General Idi Amin, the Phantom planes that he wanted to use against Tanzania, Amin — ungratefully forgetful of the tremendous help extended to him by Israel — praised the bloodthirsty Arab terrorists who had murdered the Israeli team.

The entire world was privy to Amin's outrageous words, cabled openly to the secretary-general of the United Nations. The entire world kept silent. It showed tolerance towards Arab terrorism, for which violence was both a means and an end, and which threatened the fabric of international life: innocent civilians lived in fear of attack by foreign murder squads, airlines worked in a constant atmosphere of vulnerability, international mails were violated by cowards whose malice knew no restraint.

The Arab terrorists were plaguing Israel's border villages with mortar and gunfire, from bases in a complaisant Lebanon. They had moved there after King Hussein, having finally realized who his real enemy was, had liquidated the *fedayeen* activities in Jordan. The *fedayeen*, expelled or fleeing from Jordan, found refuge in southern Lebanon, where several thousand concentrated in an area that became known as "Fatahland," where they maintained training camps in which volunteers from Japan, China, Turkey, and Cyprus, as well as Arabs, were trained.

From this entrenchment they sallied forth from time to time to lay mines, dynamite Israeli houses and installations, or fire Katyusha rockets at Israeli settlements, villages or towns in the north. Children were barbarically killed in a school bus traveling along Israel's northern frontier, and Kiryat Shmona was shelled.

Arab terrorism did not emanate from the minds of deranged extremists. It did not constitute acts of despair. The Arab terror organizations could not exist were it not for the extensive support and participation of Arab governments — politically, financially, materially, militarily, overtly and covertly. Many governments found it difficult to grasp the significance of Yasser Arafat's declaration, that the aim was "the liquidation of Israel's existence," and the expressions of full support by the Arab heads of state for the program of "wiping out the Jewish State."

The concept of obliterating the identity and individuality of a sovereign state is, in general, strange. But for Jews it was nothing new. Jews judge threats against the background of another unique experience — the Holocaust — the like of which no other people has ever undergone. Experience has taught us that there are things too terrible to believe, but that, for Jews, nothing is too terrible to have happened.

In May 1973, Israel received information about the reinforcement of Syrian and Egyptian troops on the borders. The Israel reserves were immediately mobilized as a precautionary measure, but the intelligence community thought it was most unlikely war would break out. Since nothing happened, the reserves were sent home. The terrorists, however, continued their attacks, and Israel fought back by striking at their leaders and bases: seven terrorist camps in northern Lebanon were hit, and three top *Fatah* leaders were killed in the heart of Beirut, in an Israel commando attack, under the leadership of Ehud Barak.

The Syrian border continued to be comparatively quiet until September, when tension was escalated by a serious incident. An attack by Syrian aircraft on an Israel reconnaissance patrol some 30 kilometers off the Syrian coast initiated a series of clashes in which 13 Syrian fighter planes were shot down on September 13. Despite this, our intelligence people were very reassuring: it was most unlikely, they said, that there would be any major Syrian reaction. King Hussein arrived secretly in Israel by helicopter and warned Golda Meir of Egyptian and Syrian intentions to attack. General Eli Zeira, head of the Israel military intelligence, calmed Golda Meir, saying that Sadat was using Hussein to spread "bluff" about his plans for a war.

On Friday, October 5, 1973, the Israeli Government received a report that the families of the Russian advisers in Syria were packing up and leaving in a hurry. This worried Golda Meir very much, she wrote in her memoirs, since it reminded her of what had happened prior to the Six-Day War. Why the haste, she asked those surrounding her, what did those Russian families know that we don't? Was it possible that they were being evacuated? No-one around her seemed very perturbed about it, and it hadn't in any way changed the military people's assessment of the situation. Golda Meir was assured that there would be adequate warning of any real trouble, and anyway, sufficient reinforcements were being sent to the fronts to carry out any holding operation that might be required; everything necessary had been done, and the army was placed on high alert, particularly the air force and the armored corps.

The chief-of-staff, General David Elazar, was in favor of a pre-emptive strike. Golda Meir refused. She did not want Israel to appear in the eyes of the world as the one who had struck first. This was the first mistake. The second followed — she didn't order a full-scale mobilization.

The following day, the peace and calm of Yom Kippur, the Day of Atonement, was rudely shattered by the piercing sound of the air-raid alarm necessitated by the massive and unprovoked simultaneous assault by the Egyptian and Syrian armies, the outcome of a sacrilegious Arab-Soviet conspiracy. Yom Kippur is the most solemn and sacred day in the Jewish calendar. It is the one day in the year that Jews throughout the world — even those not being pious — unite in some sort of observance, totally abstaining from food, drink and work, praying and asking for atonement for sins that they may have committed. In Israel, during Yom Kippur, the country comes to a virtual standstill. There are no newspapers, no television or radio broadcasts, no public transport, and all schools, shops, restaurants, cafes, and offices are closed. The aggressors had calculated that on a day when the Israelis were fasting and worshipping, when everyday routine life in the country gave way to spiritual reflection and prayer, the Jews would not be ready to fight back.

They attacked our positions on the Suez Canal, crossed the Canal, and battered our forces in Sinai. The Syrians deeply penetrated on the Golan Heights. On both fronts, the casualties were very high. Attacked without warning, Israeli forces were fighting on two fronts simultaneously, against enemies who had prepared themselves for years to attack us. Our forces were overwhelmingly outnumbered — in guns, tanks, planes and men — and were at a severe psychological disadvantage. Israel faced the greatest threat it had known.

The shock was not only over the way in which the war had started, but also the fact that a number of Israel's basic assumptions were proven wrong: the low probability of an attack, the certainty that we would get sufficient warning before any attack took place, and the belief that we would be able to prevent the Egyptians from crossing the Suez Canal. The circumstances could not possibly have been worse. But the assault was frustrated and repelled. Golda Meir wrote: "In the first two or three days of the war, only a thin line of brave young men stood between us and disaster. And no words can ever express the indebtedness of the people of Israel to those boys on the Canal and on the Golan Heights. They fought, and fell, like lions."

On October 22, the Security Council of the U.N. adopted resolution 338 that called both sides to stop the firing. When the cease-fire officially went into force on October 24, the Arabs had been defeated again, and Israel's forces occupied some 2,600 sq. kilometers of Egyptian territory west of the Suez Canal and about 650 sq. km. of Syria east of the 1967 cease-fire line. Israel's forward positions were about 160 km. from Cairo on the Suez-Cairo road and 65 km. from Damascus. The Egyptian Third Army on the eastern bank of the Canal and the town of Suez were completely encircled. This situation was particularly intolerable for the Egyptians, whose Third Army was faced with a humiliating surrender.

The price Israel paid in the Yom Kippur War was enormous: 2,687 killed and about 7,000 injured, 508 missing and among them 293 presumed dead. The number of Israeli prisoners in the hands of the Egyptians was 213, Egyptian prisoners-of-war in Israeli hands — 8,300. The air force lost more than 180 planes and the armored corps 800 tanks. On the international scene, Israel was isolated as never before. Internally, in addition to the anguish over the loss of lives, she had to confront problems unknown after the brief wars of 1956 and 1967, arising from the prolonged mobilization of the reserves; the pay of the reservists and the care of their families; businesses abandoned at a moment's notice and threatened with ruin; and factories hampered by the absence of key technicians and managers.

Meanwhile, there was an upsurge of disquiet, soul-searching, and criticism. Public opinion was deeply disturbed over the sudden transition from confidence in Israel's military might to uncertainty and apprehension, over Arab success in taking the army by surprise, and over the indications of unpreparedness and the agonizing loss of life.

It was clear that exaggerated self-confidence had caused a refusal to believe troublesome evaluations, an abysmal disdain for the enemy, a misunderstanding of some aspects of Arab attitudes to the problems of the region, and a lack of readiness and ability to analyze the situation properly and objectively, without wishful thinking and unrealistic appraisals. That had brought about a situation in which the IDF was not prepared, was surprised by the timing of the war, plan of attack and its method of operation, and had held on to prejudices and mistaken conceptions.

Nevertheless, there is no other example in history of an army, so taken by surprise, that managed after the initial setback and the shock of the first days, to recover, hit back at the enemy and win an impressive military victory.

The Yom Kippur War reminded me personally of the surprise German attack on the Soviet Union on June 22, 1941. The difference was that in the Soviet Union there were people in the army and in the intelligence service who foresaw the German attack but were afraid to express their views which did not coincide with Stalin's. In Israel the military intelligence, responsible for the collection of information on enemy movements, as well as the government, responsible for the comprehensive appraisal of the situation, were victims of a mistaken conception. Both bodies preferred hopeful appraisals to an unpleasant reality.

Only 25 years later, General (Res.) Eli Zeira, who was head of military intelligence during the Yom Kippur War, recognized his grave errors. He said: "My biggest mistake was that I deviated from what I believed, that it was necessary to give the biggest weight to what was happening on the spot and not to the conception." He added that he trusted the conception until the last minute, while Moshe Dayan realized the mistake of the conception a day before the war, but did not act as was required.

A state inquiry commission was established for the Yom Kippur War. It was headed by the President of the Supreme Court of Israel, Shimon Agranat, and its members were: Supreme Court Justice Moshe Landau, State Comptroller Yitzhak Nebenzahl, Major-General (Res.) Chaim Laskov and Prof. Yigael Yadin. The commission placed all blame for the failures in the war on the military, with no responsibility whatsoever on the political echelon. The chief-of-staff, David Elazar, and several other senior officers had to resign while the government — which in the eyes of the public was the chief culprit — remained in office. Successes have many parents, failure is an orphan.

However, despite the fact that Golda Meir, heading the Labor Party, won the December 1973 elections to the Knesset and without difficulty formed a new government, the public would not let her be cleared by the findings of the inquiry commission. Demands were voiced in many quarters, including within her Party, for the resignation of those really responsible for the blunders and shortcomings revealed by the war. Golda Meir and Moshe Dayan had to go. Yitzhak Rabin, who was the chief-of-staff during the Six-Day War and Israel's ambassador in Washington during the Yom Kippur War, became Prime Minister in June 1974.

SADAT' S VISIT TO JERUSALEM

In November 1973, an agreement between Israel and Egypt was signed in a tent at kilometer 101 on the Suez-Cairo road. This agreement led to an exchange of prisoners-of-war and to the supply of provisions to the cut off Egyptian Third Army and to the city of Suez. In December, the opening session of the Peace Conference for the Middle East took place in Geneva, with the participation of delegations from Israel, Egypt, Jordan, the Soviet Union and the U.S. Syria was absent from the Conference because it refused stubbornly to transmit the list of Israeli prisoners-of-war in her possession to Israel and to permit Red Cross representatives to visit them. Israel considered the fulfillment of these two demands as a condition for any negotiations with Syria.

In January 1974, Israel and Egypt signed an agreement of "separation of forces," and in May 1974 a similar agreement was concluded between Israel and Syria, after Syria acceded to Israel's demands on the prisoners-of-war. After the signing of the two accords, President Richard Nixon visited Israel, followed by his Secretary of State, Henry Kissinger, who came on a "shuttle voyage."

Kissinger, considered an omnipotent secretary of state, exerted heavy pressure on Israel, among the heaviest she was ever subjected to, for the execution of a stage in Israel's unilateral withdrawal from Sinai. Yitzhak Rabin, then Prime Minister, refused to give in to pressure, mainly because the Egyptians refused to commit themselves to reciprocity. Without reciprocity, insisted Rabin, there will be no withdrawal. Kissinger's voyage was a failure. Despite the fact that the Egyptians had caused the failure of his mission, Kissinger blamed Israel for it, and the Americans announced a "re-assessment"

Prime Minister Golda Meir with President Richard Nixon

of their policy in the Middle East and delayed discussions on Israel's arms requests.

In April 1975, a group of Israeli public relations people left for the U.S., headed by Abba Eban and with the participation of Chaim Herzog. I was also part of the group. The purpose of this mission was to explain Israel's position to the American public. Each of us was assigned to a number of states. We appeared before various groups and forums, small ones and big ones, gatherings, universities and, of course, all the news media. I was sent to four states: Michigan, Wisconsin, Indiana and Ohio.

Our public relations counter-activity bore fruit, and warmth returned to American-Israeli relations, between the states as well as among the statesmen. In August, Kissinger returned to the area and this time he succeeded in effecting a reconciliation between the parties. Israel agreed to return to Egypt the oil fields at Abu Rhodes, to withdraw to the area of the Mitla and Gidi passes, and to establish bilateral warning stations.

Gerald Ford, who replaced Nixon, supported wholeheartedly Israel's existence and security, but made clear his stand that Israel's withdrawal to the passes and the return of the Abu Rhodes oil-fields to Egypt were in accordance with the best interests of the United States. On the other hand, it was President Gerald Ford who told Yitzhak Rabin, in 1976, that any peace settlement with Syria must be based on Israel's keeping the Golan Heights.

The Israeli-Egyptian Interim Agreement — achieved by means of Kissinger's shuttling back and forth between Israel and Egypt, and signed in Geneva on September 1, 1975 — established that "the Arab-Israeli conflict shall not be resolved by military force but by peaceful means," and it opened a "honeymoon" between Israel and the United States which resulted in the American supply of F-15 planes and other sophisticated weapons to Israel.

In the meantime, the Israeli fighter plane "Kfir" (Hebrew for "young lion") was exposed to the public and the television cameras.

Shimon Peres, Minister of Defense, said: "Among all the countries producing aircrafts — we are the smallest, and among all the planes being produced today in the world — the "Kfir" is one of the best." In addition to the supply of arms and the political support — to the point of using the American veto to prevent harmful anti-Israeli decisions at the United Nations — the U.S. began also a period of significant American economic aid to Israel.

Prime Minister Yitzhak Rabin with President Gerald Ford and Secretary of State Henry Kissinger

But the major significance of the Israeli-Egyptian Interim Agreement was its political nature: a contractual and public agreement between Israel and Egypt to reach a final and just peace settlement through negotiations.

This development in Israeli-Egyptian relations, however, did not change the PLO's attitude. Its terrorists continued the outrages, directed mainly against the civilian population. Intensive and prolonged efforts were made by them, mostly from bases in Lebanon and some from Syria, to attack Israeli towns and villages close to the northern frontier, firing Katyusha rockets from time to time. A group of terrorists broke into a block of apartments in Kiryat Shmona and killed 18 people, including eight children and five women. Another group broke into a house in Ma'alot, five kilometers from the Lebanese border, shot a couple and their child, and seized a school where more than a hundred children, on a school trip, were asleep. They held them, with some of their teachers, as hostages and demanded the release of 26 terrorists held in Israel. They threatened to blow up the school and kill all the children unless their demands were met. Shortly before the deadline, Israeli troops stormed the school in a last-minute attempt to save the children. The terrorists opened fire on the children and flung hand-grenades among them. 20 children were killed and about 70 wounded.

Terrorist attacks were perpetrated in the Shamir collective settlement, in the towns of Nahariyah and Beth Sh'ean, and in Jerusalem. In August 1974, Archbishop Hilarion Capucci, head of the Greek Catholic Church in Jerusalem, was arrested and charged with smuggling arms and explosives for the *Fatah* terrorist organization which were found in his official car. In Tel-Aviv, on the night of March 5-6, 1975, eight Arab terrorists occupied the small Savoy Hotel on the seafront. Just before dawn, Israeli troops attacked the hotel, but the terrorists detonated explosives, demolishing part of the building. Eight civilians, three Israeli soldiers and seven terrorists were killed. One terrorist was captured on the spot and six in a boat which had remained offshore.

On July 4, 1975, the terrorists placed a refrigerator with explosives in Zion Square in Jerusalem: 15 persons were killed, 70 wounded. At the U.N. General Assembly, a resolution, equating Zionism with racism, was adopted on November 10, 1975, the 37th anniversary of the Kristallnacht in Germany.

Israel's ambassador to the U.N., Chaim Herzog, tore up the U.N. resolution, in the presence of representatives of the entire world, and said: "Hitler would

President Chaim Herzog reciting the Kaddish at Bergen-Belsen

have felt himself at home were he present here today." By his act, Chaim Herzog repeated what his father, Chief Rabbi Isaac Herzog, had done in 1939, when he ripped up the "White Paper." Chaim Herzog was an officer in the British Army in World War II and was among the liberators of the death camp in Bergen-Belsen. He returned to Bergen-Belsen, as President of Israel, to recite the Kaddish for the victims.

The U.N. anti-Zionist resolution encouraged the Palestinian terrorists even more and they increased their activities abroad. The most famous was the hijaking in Athens, on June 27, 1976, of an Air-France plane, which was on its way from Tel-Aviv to Paris with 258 passengers — among them over a hundred Israelis — and 12 French crewmen. Seven Palestinian kidnappers took the plane to the airport of Entebbe, the capital of Uganda, whose President, Idi Amin, had been overjoyed at the murder of the Israeli athletes in Munich.

A week of almost unbearable tension followed, during which, in the director-general's office at the Ministry of Foreign Affairs in Jerusalem, was kept open around the clock a service by rotation to maintain permanent contact with the Israeli embassies abroad as well as with the foreign embassies in Israel.

My turn came the night between July 3 and 4, and it was my great privilege to send out to our embassies, scattered on five continents, the newsflash about the deliverance of the hostages, by Israel's air force, from the clutches of the Ugandian brute. I thought to myself: how different would have been the lot of the six million Jews, assassinated during World War II, had the Jewish State already been in existence.

When the good news broke, Israel was flooded with messages of jubilation and relief. It had never experienced anything of this sort. People everywhere cheered the David who had challenged Goliath; the little man who had stood up to the bully.

But the enormous success, joy and happiness of the liberation of the hostages was clouded by the grief and mourning for the death of Lieutenant-Colonel Jonathan Netanyahu who commanded the operation in Entebbe. Netanyahu directed the liquidation of the terrorists at the terminal and evacuated the hostages to the plane but was killed by a Ugandian sniper.

Except for that most daring and successful operation, the Rabin Government lacked inspiration. Many people in Israel had lost confidence and faith in the ruling Labor Party, and in the Knesset elections of May 1977, it was defeated. Menachem Begin, leader of the Likud Party, became Prime Minister, and he invited Moshe Dayan, who belonged to the Labor Party, to take up the post of Foreign Minister. Dayan accepted. The new Government, formed in June, was sharply attacked by the left-wing parties, which, during the election campaign, pictured Menachem Begin as a warmonger, who, if elected, would bring another war on Israel.

Nicolae Ceausescu, the President of Communist Romania, thought differently. Having been disappointed in his attempt in 1972, to arrange a meeting between Anwar Sadat and Golda Meir, he believed that precisely Begin would be capable of doing what Golda Meir could not, and invited him to pay an official visit to Romania. Thus, Ceausescu was the first foreign head of state to meet with Israel's new Prime Minister.

Begin arrived in Bucharest on August 25, 1977. In spite of the differences of opinion between Begin and Ceausescu about the solution of the Arab-Israeli conflict, a relationship of mutual respect and understanding arose during their long talks. Ceausescu became convinced that the new Prime Minister of Israel sincerely wanted peace, and he invited President Sadat to come to Bucharest.

Sadat arrived in October, and after a long talk with the Romanian president, asked Ceausescu whether he was really convinced that Begin wanted peace and was able to sign it. Ceausescu answered both questions affirmatively, and then

President Anwar Sadat at the Knesset, with President Ephraim Katzir and Speaker Yitzhak Shamir

Anwar Sadat with Golda Meir at the Knesset

— as Sadat himself stated publicly — while in the plane that took him from Bucharest to Teheran, he decided to go to Jerusalem. On November 19, 1977, Sadat arrived in Israel on a visit that initiated the peace process in the Middle East.

Dayan, with the previous approval of Begin, decided to appoint me ambassador to Romania. After having served for six years as Director of the Department for Cultural and Scientific Relations at our Foreign Ministry, I boarded, on January 25, 1978, together with my wife, an El-Al plane for Bucharest, leaving our two sons in the air force: Meir — as an aeronautical engineer, Yehuda — as a fighter pilot.

Before our departure, the director-general of our ministry, Ephraim Evron, stressed to me the special importance of my mission to Romania following Sadat's visit to Jerusalem. He spoke of the serious challenge facing me as Israel's ambassador in the lone Communist country which did not break diplomatic relations with us, and emphasized the delicate and sensitive relations between the two countries, with the complexities of bilateral problems in political, economic, immigration and other fields. He said that he considered Romania as "Israel's window on the Iron Curtain," a potential "bridgehead" for the renewal of relations with the countries of eastern Europe, and asked me to devote attention also to what was happening in countries surrounding Romania.

At the Bucharest airport, my wife and I were welcomed by the Romanian chief of protocol, and by members of our embassy. I was informed that my meeting with the Romanian Foreign Minister, George Macovescu, for the delivery of the copy of my credentials, had been fixed for January 30, so I prepared the text of the message I was to deliver to him, on behalf of Moshe Dayan, then Israel's Foreign Minister. At my briefing meeting with Dayan, before my departure, he spoke extensively about the visit of Sadat in Jerusalem. He considered the very presence of Sadat in Jerusalem as a major success, and said to me: "Imagine, this is the same Sadat who said, in the not too distant past, that our generation was not ready for peace, that negotiation with Israel was out of the question and that he was ready to sacrifice a million Egyptians in a war against Israel. The same Sadat who had declared that Egypt was committed to the annihilation of the Jewish State and the liberation of all of Palestine."

But Dayan was also very careful not to fall into the trap of wishful thinking.

He understood that Sadat did not see our security requirements in the same way we did. Dayan believed that Sadat had recognized the need to assure Israel's security, but he spoke in terms of guarantees and demilitarized areas, which, in his eyes, would obviate the need for occupied territories. Sadat's main goal was to get Israel out of these areas. As for his declaration that there would be no more wars, Dayan was of the opinion that Sadat could the following day declare the opposite, and a million Egyptians would acclaim him once again. Dayan asked me to inform the Romanian Foreign Minister that, in his view, the solution of the administered territories was "functional division," and not a line dividing the West Bank. Instead of division of the territories, there should be a division of the rule in the territories: a kind of federation or confederation, a condominium or an autonomy. Dayan was not in favor of annexation — as was the aspiration of the Likud — because this would transform Israel into a bi-national state, or would force the Jews to rule over another people.

Dayan was also not for the territorial compromise, as was perceived by Labor, because this would lead to the establishment of an independent Palestinian state in that part of the territories from which Israel would withdraw.

When I met Macovescu, I presented him with the copy of my credentials, expressed my appreciation for Romania's independent position and for its contribution to the initiation of the peace process in our region, and delivered to him Dayan's message. He thanked me for my warm words of appreciation for Romania's foreign policy, and said: "Peace must be achieved in the region. Peace is necessary for Israel, for the Arab countries and for Romania itself, being a close neighbor to the conflict area."

Macovescu told me that the President would receive me the next day, for the presentation of my credentials. When I met Ceausescu, I delivered a message from Israel's Prime Minister to him. Begin had asked me to transmit to Ceausescu his warmest regards and best wishes, and to thank him for his part in the opening of direct negotiations between Egypt and Israel. Begin also asked me to mention, in my conversation with the President, the Jewish community of Romania, to stress our appreciation for the good attitude of the Romanian authorities toward the community, in the fields of freedom of religion and

Jewish education, and to express hope that the process of reunification of families (emigration to Israel) would be accelerated.

The President thanked me for Begin's message and for my own words of appreciation, and said: "The relations between Romania and Israel are good — very good — and I hope that during the period of your mission, these relations become even better." Then he repeated Romania's position on the solution of the Arab-Israeli conflict, especially stressing the need for Israel's withdrawal from the occupied territories and for negotiations with the PLO about the creation of a Palestinian state at Israel's side. "Were the PLO not in existence, you would have to create it," he said.

I explained our opposition to a Palestinian state and quoted Yasser Arafat's recent declaration: "The decision in our region is in the hands of the Palestinian gun. The Palestinian state will arise by blood and fire." I concluded with quoting Prime Minister Menachem Begin who said, that "everything was negotiable, except suicide," and asked the President to distinguish between the PLO and Palestinians worthy to be partners to negotiations.

Aba Gefen in conversation with Romanian president, Nicolae Ceausescu, following the presentation of credentials

The President thought for a while, and then said to me: "Please transmit to Begin my following proposal: instead of agreeing to negotiations with the PLO, let Israel declare its readiness to negotiate with the Palestinians and with any of their organizations ready to discuss peace with her."

I promised to transmit his proposal to Begin, and with that our conversation ended. Before I said goodbye, he raised a glass of champagne and proposed a toast, wishing me success in my mission. I responded with a toast for his good health and happiness, and for the strengthening of the friendly relations existing between our countries.

Accompanying me to my home, the chief of protocol stressed the flexibility of the President in regard to the PLO issue, as expressed by him at the end of our conversation. He congratulated me on it, saying: "You started your mission on the right foot."

Ceausescu's foreign policy was considered by the West to be very positive. His "all directions policy" — which endeavored to widen and deepen his country's relations with as many countries as possible throughout the world — had reached significant achievements. The western world very much favored Ceausescu's foreign policy and his activity for peace, and on his visits to western

The diplomatic corps in Bucharest meeting with President Nicolae Ceausescu

countries, he was received like a king. When he visited the United States, he was received with the highest honors, and President Jimmy Carter called him "the architect of Sadat's visit to Jerusalem."

Romania's attitude towards Israel fell in line with her "all directions policy," but it was also very much the result of Ceausescu's being a brave man. In regard to Israel, he proved to be very courageous vis-à-vis the Soviets. Already in 1967, he was the only Communist leader who refused Moscow's demand, following the Six-Day War, to break off relations with Israel. A year later, he agreed to raise the status of the diplomatic representations in Israel and in Romania to that of embassies. In 1998, Israel and Romania marked 50 years of uninterrupted diplomatic relations.

On September 18, 1978, at a solemn ceremony at the White House, the President of the United States Jimmy Carter, the President of Egypt Anwar Sadat, and Israel's Prime Minister Menachem Begin signed the Camp David agreements: for a peace treaty with Egypt and negotiations for the solution of the Palestinian problem. In the Knesset, 84 voted in favor of the Camp David agreements, 19 voted against and 17 abstained.

On October 11, I received a message from Menachem Begin for Ceausescu. In it, Begin reported to Ceausescu about the talks and discussions to reach the agreements, and thanked Ceausescu for his efforts. Ceausescu was very pleased with the message. When he was invited a month later to Moscow for a meeting of the seven heads of state of the Soviet Bloc, to condemn the agreements, he went there but didn't sign the condemnation. It was published with the signatures of six countries only: the Soviet Union, Poland, Czechoslovakia, Hungary, Bulgaria, and East Germany. Ceausescu's not signing the condemnation was a brave deed on his part which merits praise.

On March 16, 1979, I received a message from Begin for Ceausescu on the successful results of the negotiations towards the peace treaty with Egypt to be signed on March 26, according to which Israel was to withdraw from the entire Sinai peninsula. Begin again thanked Ceausescu for his significant contribution to the historic peace process, and concluded his message with expressions of appreciation and friendship. Ceausescu asked me to transmit to Begin his congratulations on the signing of the peace treaty, and welcomed it publicly, in spite of the Arab and Soviet condemnations. On December 10, 1979, Anwar Sadat and Menachem Begin were awarded the Nobel Prize for Peace.

When on June 7, 1981, Israel's air force destroyed the Iraqi atomic reactor, the Romanians published a statement in which they expressed deep concern and rage for the "aggressive attack," in their view, and called it a "dangerous precedent which should not be tolerated." But when I met Ceausescu, on October 6, to report to him about Shamir's conversation in New York with Andrei Gromyko on Israel's relations with the Soviet Union, he was very cordial and did not mention the Iraqi affair at all. We discussed the ways to advance the peace process in the Middle East, at the precise moment when in Cairo, Anwar Sadat was being assassinated.

The PLO spokesman declared that he embraced the man who shot Sadat. In Damascus, Tripoli and Beirut there was dancing in the streets, and shots of joy were fired into the air. Ceausescu sent a cable of condolences to Egypt, and went to the Egyptian embassy in Bucharest to sign the book of condolences, never having made a similar gesture before.

Egypt's Vice President, Hosni Mubarak, succeeded Sadat and promised that

Sadat, Carter and Begin shaking hands at the signing of the Egyptian-Israeli Peace Treaty

President Yitzhak Navon with President Hosni Mubarak

Egypt would continue on the road of peace and would fulfill all its international commitments, especially the Camp David agreements.

Ceausescu's friendly attitude towards Israel found expression also in regard to the emigration of Romanian Jews to Israel. Since the re-establishment of the Jewish State, Romanian Jews had been permitted to leave for Israel, although there was a certain quota. For instance, during my five years of service in Romania, about 1,000 Jews could leave every year, in the framework of "reunification of families." Before World War II, the Romanian Jewish community counted more than 800,000 souls. Approximately 400,000 of them were killed during the war — in death camps and in the camps of Transnistria (a German-occupied area of the U.S.S.R. across the Dniester River), to which a quarter of a million of Jews were deported and where they subsisted in sub-human conditions of hunger and diseases.

Most of the Jewish Romanian survivors emigrated to Israel, and those who remained there, felt that if they so wished, they could preserve the Jewish religion, its customs and tradition, to fulfill their cultural hetritage and give expression to their national desires.

During our stay in Romania, there were about 20,000 Jews in the country. In addition to the Jewish community of the capital, there were another 63 organized communities — with a synagogue and a community office.

My wife and I visited all the 63 Jewish communities of Romania. I was the first Israeli ambassador to visit all of them, and our meetings with the Jews were a very emotional experience for us. Pre-war, Romania was considered a reservoir of Jewish national creative forces, but the Holocaust put an end to that.

During these tours, my wife and I traveled thousands of kilometers, and the trips were sometimes very tiring, but the glow of pride in the eyes of our fellow Jews when they saw the Israeli ambassador and the Israeli flag, the great cordiality and affection they bestowed upon us and the happiness seen in their faces — made the visits to those communities an unforgettable experience. The Jews would circle our car, fondly touch the flag and say: "When we see this flag, our hearts warm up."

They would make the benediction of "*Shehechiyanu*" (having been sustained in life), for having lived to see the moment that an Israeli ambassador finally came to their community, and would recite a prayer for the State of Israel.

A shocking experience for us was the visit to Iasi, the capital of Moldavia, known as "Jerusalem of Romania's Jews." Before the war, there were 55,000 Jews out of a total population of 100,000 there, and now we found only 3,000 Jews in a population of 320,000. The synagogue where we prayed had been built 330 years ago and was in a street in which before the Holocaust there were 117 synagogues. Now only three remained.

From the synagogue we went, accompanied by the leaders of the Jewish community, to the common grave, at the Jewish cemetery, of those murdered in the great pogrom, on June 28, 1941. The "Iron Guard" on that day brutally slaughtered 11,000 people. We said Kaddish there and a survivor from the train, which transported the Jews on that day to their death, recited the El Male Rachamim memorial prayer.

When Shimon Peres, as leader of the Labor Party in Israel, visited Bucharest, the Choral synagogue was filled to capacity. The Rabbi invited Peres and myself to open the Holy Ark and he blessed the State of Israel. The choir sang "We brought you peace," "*Hava Naguila*" (Let us be joyful) and "Jerusalem the Golden."

The reception for Peres at the community restaurant was also attended by some of the Romanian hosts. After they heard the speeches and saw the enthusiastic crowd, one of them came to me and said: "You are very privileged, as an ambassador, to have such a community." It was the first time an Israeli ambassador had heard this kind of expression in a Communist country. Israel's ambassadors were used to hearing that only in the Western countries. This special situation of the Jews in Romania was, no doubt, largely because of Ceausescu's positive attitude towards the Jews and Israel. Of course, not only this: the Romanians also had concrete economic interests in the development of relations with Israel.

Part of these was the emigration of Jews to Israel. This was linked to Romania's status as Most Favored Nation (MFN), granted to her by the United

Aba Gefen with Shimon Peres and Chief Rabbi Moshe David Rosen at the Choral synagogue

Foreign Minister Moshe Dayan and his wife Rachel at an artistic evening, organized in their honor by the Jewish youth of Bucharest

States. This status had to be renewed every year by the Senate, and towards this end, a Senate sub-committee discussed the matter with the American administration, and examined the problems of emigration from Romania to Israel, Germany and the United States.

When Moshe Dayan, as Foreign Minister, visited Bucharest in April 1978, Ceausescu asked him whether he could put in a good word for Romania in regard to the MFN. Dayan replied: "I will talk to our ambassador in Washington and I promise you, Mr. President, that we will do everything we can."

LEBANON WAR

Ceausescu also maintained close contacts with us in all the stages of the war in Lebanon, which was the fruit of the PLO's renewed wave of terrorist activities. It killed the Israeli diplomat Yaacov Bar-Simantov, in Paris, at the beginning of April 1982, and — after the failure of its attack, in November 1979, against our ambassador in Lisbon (one guard was killed and three wounded) — it carried out an attack on our ambassador in London, Shlomo Argov. Argov was wounded in his head, on June 3, 1982, after leaving a diplomatic dinner at the Dorchester Hotel.

At that time, Israel's Defense Minister General Ariel Sharon was on a private jaunt in the Carpathian mountains. He returned to Israel on Saturday, June 5, 1982, at lunch time, and the next day began Israel's operation "Peace for Galilee," to free the settlements of Galilee from the terrorist threats and liquidate the organization which had fixed as its goal the destruction of the State of Israel.

Israel's defense forces crossed Lebanon's border, advanced along the coastal road to Tyre, passed Nabatiyeh and moved into the PLO stronghold called "Fatahland." The Israeli navy landed tanks and infantry north of Sidon, and IDF units reached the Beirut-Damascus road. Continuing the advance, the IDF clashed with the Syrian army: 41 Syrian planes were downed by the Israeli air force, 19 Syrian ground to air missile batteries were destroyed, and the IDF reached the vicinity of Beirut's international airport.

On his return to Israel, Sharon informed the news media that he had been "on a secret mission overseas," and it was soon leaked to the press that he had been in Romania. This news reached Bucharest, and provoked a series of rumors about the purpose of his Romanian visit on the eve of the war in Lebanon.

My fellow ambassadors contacted me, and the Soviet military attache told me there was a rumor that I had arranged a meeting between Sharon and the Soviet chief-of-staff. He said: "I know nothing about it. Tell me whether there is anything true in this story." When I told him that I, too, knew nothing about the visit of his chief-of-staff, and said that Sharon was in Romania on a private visit, he replied: "From a military point of view, it is simply impossible that on the eve of launching a major campaign your Defense Minister was on a private excursion in the Carpathian mountains, but I believe you."

Sharon's predecessor, Defense Minister Ezer Weizman, too, caused embarrassment to Israeli diplomatic representatives abroad. During the Camp David talks, Weizman established a special relationship with President Sadat, and following the peace treaty with Egypt, he — a former hawk — became a dove. One day, he entered the office of the Prime Minister in Jerusalem, tore off the poster "*Shalom*" (peace) hanging on the wall, and said to reporters present: "A government that doesn't want peace has no right to hang such posters. I am going to prepare the army for the next war."

Moshe Dayan, too, supplied "merchandise" to those who criticized Israel. When my wife and I arrived in Israel in October 1979, for the wedding of our son Yehuda to Nurit (the daughter of Dani and Yehudit Ilovitch), meetings were set up for me with Prime Minister Begin and Foreign Minister Dayan. My meeting with Begin took place, but the meeting with Dayan was canceled because of his resignation, accompanied by a statement that he did not want to continue "eating bitterness": to speak of autonomy and mean annexation. Israeli ambassadors in various parts of the world were asked to explain the meanings of those statements.

In the middle of April 1981, the Romanian Deputy Foreign Minister, Aurel Duma, suggested to me, that if we agreed to an international conference on the Middle East, the Soviet Union would renew diplomatic relations with Israel, and the renewal would precede the convening of the conference. The Romanian proposal seemed to me worth the price and I suggested to Jerusalem to accede to it. But the government in Jerusalem rejected any idea of an international conference, and I had to continue and defend this position despite not agreeing to it.

On one occasion, I succeeded in changing Prime Minister Menachem Begin's decision. When the Knesset adopted the Law of Jerusalem, declaring it as Israel's sovereign, undivided, eternal capital, the Romanians published a condemnation of the law in which they proclaimed their non-recognition of Israel's sovereignty over the entire city. I was presented with the condemnation which they requested me to transmit, in Ceausescu's name, to Begin. I transmitted it and within 48 hours I received Begin's reply. He rejected the condemnation, and inter alia, asked me to tell the Romanian president that nobody could expect us to have less feelings towards Jerusalem than the Romanians towards Bucharest, and to remind Ceausescu of the fact that Romania was holding on to Transylvania which the Hungarians claimed for themselves.

I cabled back to Begin that only Hungary objects to Romania's holding Transylvania, while the entire world objects to our sovereignty in Jerusalem. I added that there was no need to do something, which would be interpreted by the Romanians as a provocation, especially since Romania was the only Communist country with diplomatic relations with Israel, whereas Hungary was part of the camp hostile to Israel. I asked Begin to delete from his reply the reference to Transylvania, and he agreed.

On August 23, 1982, Bashir Gemayel, the leader of the Phalangist forces, was elected President of Lebanon, and on August 30, the Lebanese army entered into West Beirut, for the first time in seven years. After Syria, Jordan and Saudi Arabia had agreed to absorb the thousands of PLO terrorists, Arafat left Beirut for Greece. Years later, it was published that senior IDF officers were watching Arafat's evacuation from a roof nearby, at a distance of not more than 200 meters. Arafat's head, wearing a kaffiyeh, was seen in the center of the pointing sight of the gun held by one of the snipers. But Begin gave an order not to shoot at him.

On September 1, Prime Minister Begin held talks with Bashir Gemayel in the northern Israeli town of Nahariyah. However, two weeks later, Bashir Gemayel was murdered. The IDF was ordered to take control of key positions in West Beirut. IDF units seized West Beirut and surrounded the Palestinian refugee camps Sabra, Shatila and Fakahani without entering them. During the days of September 16-18, the Phalangist forces of Bashir Gemayel carried out massacres in the Sabra and Shatila camps, killing hundreds of civilians. When the IDF found out about it, it removed the Phalangists from the camps and from Beirut airport and thus prevented more massacres.

On the day Begin met with Gemayel, Israel radio announced that Begin had received a letter from President Ronald Reagan about the autonomy talks. In his letter, President Reagan expressed his opposition to the establishment of an independent Palestinian state on the one hand, and to the annexation of the territories by Israel on the other. He supported the freezing of the settlements during the envisioned period of autonomy and suggested that, after five years of full autonomy, the Palestinians be granted self-government, in a federation or confederation with Jordan. "Jerusalem has to remain united," wrote Reagan, "but its final status will be decided in negotiations." He added that in his view, his plan was in line with the Camp David agreements and the United States did not intend to demand from Israel a return to the pre Six-Day War fragile borders.

When the American ambassador to Israel, Samuel Lewis, delivered the letter to Begin, the latter said it was his saddest day since becoming Prime Minister. Begin was hurt by the plan itself and by the fact that the kings of Jordan and Saudi Arabia were among the addressees of the letter. At the Israeli cabinet meeting on September 2, Reagan's plan was defined as a "grave deviation from the Camp David agreements." Begin said the plan was even worse than the Rogers Plan and quoted Golda Meir's statement that whoever will adopt the Rogers Plan will be considered a traitor. The government decided unanimously to reject the Reagan Plan and Begin sent a reply to President Reagan. President Reagan soon realized his error and quietly withdrew from his plan.

On May 17, 1983, an Israel-Lebanon agreement was signed, which proclaimed the termination of war between Israel and Lebanon and established the formation of a security zone. The two countries committed themselves to signing a peace treaty which would ensure lasting security for both of them. Both Israeli and Lebanese parliaments ratified the agreement. 1,217 Israeli soldiers were killed in the "Peace for Galilee" operation.

On March 5, 1984, Lebanon unilaterally abrogated the agreement. It represented a capitulation to Syrian dictates and a death sentence for Lebanese independence and sovereignty. Israel implemented a redeployment of its forces in the north, with peace being maintained by the IDF with the help of the South Lebanon Army, whose first commander was Major Haddad. After his death, General Antoine Lahad was appointed, and given the mandate for maintaining the security and safety of the residents of the area.

In June 1984, Israel and Syria exchanged prisoners: Israel returned 291 soldiers and 72 coffins, Syria returned three soldiers, three civilians, and five coffins. Earlier, Israel and the PLO had exchanged prisoners: Israel received six IDF soldiers in return for 4,700 terrorists. Ceausescu tried to bring about an exchange of prisoners with Syria and the PLO two years earlier. I met with him on July 15, 1982, and delivered to him an urgent personal request from Begin. Begin asked Ceausescu to address, in Israel's name, President Assad of Syria and to propose to him the exchange of prisoners.

Israel would transfer to Syria all the Syrian prisoners in her hands — soldiers and officers — and the thousands of terrorists who were taken prisoners by the IDF. In exchange, Assad would return to us all the Israelis in the hands of Syria and the PLO. Ceausescu promised to transmit our proposal immediately to President Assad. On various occasions, I inquired about Assad's reaction, and was told that Ceausescu never received an answer from the Syrian president. On May 20, 1985, the Israeli Government decided to release 1,200 Palestinian prisoners, among them cruel murderers sentenced to life imprisonment, in exchange for three Israeli prisoners held by the extremist terrorist Ahmed Jibril organization. This exchange of prisoners was sharply criticized by many, and demonstrating bereaved families waved banners saying "this was a black day for the State of Israel."

Through the good offices of Ceausescu, Arafat and Begin exchanged messages on the Beirut crisis, and a couple of times during the war, Ceausescu sent his special political adviser, Vasile Pungan, with messages to Prime Minister Begin.

On November 13, 1982, I went to see Ceausescu for my farewell meeting. Most ambassadors met with Ceausescu only twice during their term of service: to present their credentials and to say goodbye. As a result of the exchange of messages between him and Begin, I had held 10 meetings with Ceausescu. The

President thanked me and expressed his appreciation for my activity during the five years of my service in Bucharest which — he said — contributed much to the development of relations between our two countries. He expressed his opinion, that there was now a majority among the Palestinians in favor of a peaceful agreement and understanding with Israel. He said: "As long as the Palestinian problem remains unsolved, danger will constantly threaten Israel's existence, and if Israel depends on the amount of arms she has, the Arabs, with all their money, will be able to buy any arms that they wish."

The President argued, that Sadat, too, had said years ago publicly, like Arafat now, that his aspiration was the destruction of Israel, but in 1977 he had changed his mind, and a peace treaty was signed between Egypt and Israel. Ceausescu said he was convinced that a similar development would take place in the positions of Assad and the PLO. He asked me to transmit to Begin, Shamir and Peres his feeling that Jerusalem did not give enough consideration to his evaluations, did not respond to his proposals, clung to wishful thinking and set patterns of thought, and thus missed opportunites for a peaceful solution of the Arab-Israeli conflict.

On my return to Jerusalem, I did transmit Ceausescu's message to Begin, Peres and Shamir. A year later, Begin resigned from the prime ministership. Observers mentioned as reasons for his resignation his delicate state of health, the death of his wife, the needless involvement in the Lebanon war and the large number of killed and wounded.

Begin secluded himself at his home, made no more public appearances and avoided visitors. He refused categorically to explain the factors which made him retire from political life. All the attempts to have him return to his office were in vain. When my book "Window on the Iron Curtain," on my five years of service in Romania, was published, he received me at his home and I presented him with the first copy of the book. I spent an hour with him and we had a very friendly and interesting conversation. He looked at his picture with Ceausescu walking and conversing in the President's garden and related to me in detail (I was amazed by his memory) the contents of that conversation. Inter alia, he said to me: "For seven consecutive hours, Ceausescu tried to convince me to agree to a Palestinian state."

After I had already retired, Shamir visited Romania twice — first as Foreign

Minister and then as Prime Minister. It was the period of the National Unity Government, formed in September 1984 on the basis of rotation: during the first two years Shimon Peres was Prime Minister and Yitzhak Shamir Foreign Minister, and after two years Shamir became Prime Minister, and Peres Foreign Minister.

Prime Minister Shimon Peres and Foreign Minister Yitzhak Shamir with President Ronald Reagan

SOVIET MANEUVERING

Ceausescu did not limit himself to a friendly political dialogue with Israel, and to contributing to the peace process in the area. When the Chinese leader, Huah-Kuo-Fen, visited Bucharest, Ceausescu received me, at Begin's request, and promised he would use his good offices for the normalization of the relations between Israel and China. Ceausescu raised the question with Huah-Kuo-Fen, first in Bucharest and later during his visit in Beijing, but the Chinese were not yet ready for it. Though we were among the first nations to recognize Communist China, the Chinese were not at all interested in having an Israeli embassy in Beijing.

On various occasions, I also discussed with Ceausescu and with his Foreign Minister our relations with Moscow. They told me they were constantly trying to convince the Russians to re-establish relations with us. In October 1978, when I asked to see Ceausescu to deliver Begin's message, he was very busy with Soviet Foreign Minister Andrei Gromyko, who had then arrived in Bucharest. But Ceausescu received me the same day, just before his meeting with Gromyko. Ceausescu promised me he would discuss with Gromyko the renewal of our relations. When I left his office, Gromyko entered it. When Gromyko insisted the Camp David agreements should be rejected, Ceausescu explained to him the importance of those agreements for the Arabs. "Sadat already got back part of the territories and will get the rest," Ceausescu argued, and asked Gromyko: "Should Sadat abolish the agreements and return the territories to Israel?" Gromyko remained silent.

In those days, I was maintaining a friendly dialogue with the Soviet ambassador in Bucharest, as well as with almost all the other ambassadors from the Communist countries. The Soviet Ambassador, Vasili Drozdenko, was the dean of the diplomatic corps in Bucharest, and I asked to see him in this capacity.

It was the first time, since the breaking of relations between the two countries in 1967, that an Israeli ambassador was paying an official visit to a Soviet embassy, and it was at a time that relations between Jerusalem and Moscow were tense because of the Jewish problem. On the one hand, the Soviets were well aware of its existence and made efforts to solve it within the Soviet regime. On the other hand, there was their frustration and disappointment in face of their failure to achieve a solution.

The existence of the Jewish problem in the Soviet Union was well realized by the Soviets when Golda Meir arrived, in 1948, as Israel's Minister in Moscow, and 50,000 Jews assembled near the synagogue when she came there for the New Year prayers. The event was photographed by an anonymous Russian Jew and the picture delivered to an official of the Israeli legation in Moscow, on the street. In her memoirs, *'My Life,'* Golda Meir writes that the picture with the 50,000 Jews surrounding her was printed in thousands of copies, and when she met Jews on the street, they would whisper into her ear that they had it. Even many years later, new immigrants from the Soviet Union brought her copies of the picture.

I arrived at the Soviet embassy in Bucharest in my official car, where the Soviet ambassador received me very cordially. We spoke Russian and English (through an interpreter).

The ambassador spoke extensively about the Soviet Union's role in destroying Fascism in World War ll, about 20 million Soviet citizens — among them many Jews — killed, and mentioned that every year, on May 9, ceremonies were held in Bucharest to mark the end of the war and the victory over Nazism. Wreaths of flowers were placed in memory of the Unknown Soldier: at four places, including the statue for the Unknown Soldier of the Red Army. He expressed his hope that I would attend these ceremonies, including the one at their statue.

I responded affirmatively and explained to him, that in addition to doing so in capacity as Israel's ambassador, I had two good personal reasons for it. First, I was liberated from Nazi oppression by the Red Army, on July 29, 1944. A Jewish Red Army Captain was the first person to embrace me and kiss me as a free man.

Second, when I was active in the *Brichah* organization in Austria, in the transporting of Jewish Holocaust survivors on their way to the Land of Israel, I encountered a warm and supportive attitude on the part of Soviet soldiers and

Golda Meir surrounded by 50,000 Jews near the Moscow synagogue

officers we met while crossing the borders. Then, I mentioned to the ambassador the Soviet Union's role in the creation of Israel, and quoted Andrei Gromyko's speech, at the U.N. in favor of the Jewish State, which the Jewish people will never forget.

I added, that his country had thus contributed to the change in my personal life: on November 29, 1947, I was a refugee; now — I am an ambassador of the independent Jewish State. With the help of the Soviet Union, I said, we, the survivors of the Holocaust, have lived to behold the miraculous realization of a restored Jewish Commonwealth prayed for through two millennia — a privilege tragically denied to the lost millions of our brothers and sisters, mothers and fathers, assassinated by the Nazis.

The ambassador reacted: "We both belong to the same generation, and certain events are part of ourselves, too deep in our hearts to be forgotten." He added that he was acquainted with the history of the illegal transports of Jewish Holocaust survivors across the European frontiers, on their way to Palestine. He knew it from personal experience, having in those days been a general in the Red Army which refrained from interfering in the *Brichah* activities.

During my conversation with the ambassador, I did not know what I later found out when I worked at Israel's State Archives on an Israeli-Russian project to publish books containing documents of both Israeli and Russian foreign ministries. Among the Russian documents, I found a circular of September 17, 1946, from the Soviet Foreign Ministry to the Soviet embassies in Poland, Romania, Czechoslovakia, Bulgaria and Hungary, with information on the *Brichah* and an instruction not to interfere with nor to hinder the passage of Jewish refugees on their way to Palestine.

When we parted, he said he would be happy to continue conversing with me, and expressed his hope that we would have many opportunities to meet.

When the Egyptian, Israeli and American delegations convened in Camp David, I met the Soviet military attache, General Kociumov, at a reception at the Portuguese Embassy, and he asked me what were, in my opinion, the chances at Camp David. I replied that I was very optimistic, and added: "The Soviet Union could make my optimism come true." "How?" — asked the general, and I said: "As long as the Soviet Union plays an anti-Israel role in our area, she cannot be a partner in the negotiations on the solution of the Arab-Israeli conflict. But if the

Soviet Union renews its diplomatic relations with us, she will then become a partner to the discussions and could make a constructive contribution. This would be to the benefit of all the peoples of the Middle East as well as to the benefit of the Soviet Union herself."

He responded: "The policy of the Soviet Union has always been that Israel has the right to exist as an independent and sovereign state, but you must understand, that the Soviet Union has interests in Syria, Algeria, Iraq, and other Arab countries, and therefore, the problem is not simple. I will, however, report on our conversation to the High Command."

On July 14, 1980, at a cocktail reception at the French embassy, on the occasion of the French National Day, I met, for the first time, the new Soviet military attache, Commodore Terentiev, who had replaced Kociumov. He was very cordial and said that Kociumov had informed him about his talks with me, had told him that I was sincere and frank, and that I had good personal feelings towards the Soviet Union, being a Holocaust survivor who had been liberated by the Red Army. Terentiev expressed his hope that friendly relations would also prevail between us, and he immediately passed on to business.

He said he was not a political person, but a military one, and therefore, whatever he would say to me, would be his personal view. In his opinion, Moscow's breaking off diplomatic relations with Israel was a mistake. He felt these relations should be renewed, convinced that they would be, because only by maintaining relations with us, would the Soviet Union be able to negotiate and have discussions with us. "It's not in the Soviet Union's interest to remain outside the peace process," he added. I replied that the Soviet Union was the one to break off the relations, and the initiative for their renewal would have to come from her. Terentiev then asked whether he could consider our conversation as the first contact towards negotiations on the renewal of diplomatic relations between us. I replied affirmatively, and at that point, the American military attache, Colonel Womak, approached us. Terentiev said to him: "I am talking with the Israeli ambassador about the renewal of diplomatic relations." "If it will happen — it will be wonderful," Womak replied.

My cable on my conversation with Terentiev reached Prime Minister Menachem Begin when he was on his sick bed. Begin replied to my cable from the hospital and asked me, when I would next see the Russian commodore, to emphasize Israel's permanent interest in the maintaining of normal relations with the Soviet Union and the other Soviet Bloc countries, as he, Begin, had noted publicly on June 20, 1977, and repeated in a public speech on July 7, 1980.

The Prime Minister also proposed that I remind the Soviet military attache that Lenin had recognized Jewish nationality while the Soviet Union recognized the Jewish State when it was established. It therefore made sense that the Soviet Union should permit children of Jewish nationality to emigrate to the Jewish State. I transmitted Begin's reply to Terentiev on August 19, at a reception given by the Liberian embassy. Terentiev thanked me and said he would report to his superiors that Israel was ready to renew the diplomatic relations. I agreed. However, on January 22, 1981, the East German ambassador, Dr. Sigfried Bock, told me that no East European country would renew its diplomatic relations with Israel as long as it knew that Moscow was against it, and, to the best of his knowledge, Moscow was still holding to that position.

On November 30, 1981, a Memorandum of Understanding for Strategic Co-operation was signed between Israel and the United States, and Radio Moscow came out with an attack against Israel. The same day, I met the East German ambassador again, and he told me that the Israel-American Memorandum of Understanding had complicated the situation: this step will increase Israel's dependence on the United States, and it will make it more difficult to advance towards the normalization of Soviet-Israel relations. I told him that, unfortunately, all our efforts to get closer to the Soviet Union had failed: the Soviet Union has remained hostile to Israel and is acting in a way that imperils Israel's security, having transformed Syria and Libya into dangerous arms arsenals. "Moscow is ready" — I said — "to supply arms to anyone who proclaims a holy war against us, and I consider that behavior as an expression of anti-Semitism."

He replied: "How could you say such a thing, in view of your contacts and conversations with me and with my colleagues from the other Socialist countries?" I answered that the Holocaust taught us something, and we separated with a warm hand-shake.

A week later, on December 7, 1981, I received an invitation from the Bulgarian ambassador, Pitar Danailov, to a reception he was to host on December 10, for the diplomatic corps and the Romanian authorities, on the occasion of his departure from Bucharest. It was the custom that invitations to such events were sent a fortnight in advance. The invitation to me, at the last moment, must have been sent as a result of a consideration which did not exist when the other invitations had been sent out.

In spite of the fact that on the invitation was explicitly written "Aba Gefen and wife," and on the envelope "Aba Gefen, Ambassador Extraordinary and Plenipotentiary of Israel," I could not exclude the possibility of a mistake by a Bulgarian secretary. We checked with the Bulgarian embassy. There was no mistake.

It had not happened since 1967 that an Israeli ambassador was officially invited to a reception at an embassy of a Communist country which had broken off relations with us. I sent a cable to Jerusalem asking for permission to accept the invitation, and permission was granted.

During the two days until the reception, we were full of excitement: to go to the Bulgarian embassy in the official car, with the Israeli flag, was not a small thing. What would my colleagues say? What would the Arabs say? From my personal point of view, our visit to the Bulgarian embassy was to be the climax of my contacts with the diplomats from the Soviet Bloc countries.

On December 10, I arrived with my wife at the Bulgarian embassy. When we entered the big hall, the Bulgarian ambassador and his wife welcomed us with a smile, shook our hands, and expressed their pleasure at our having come. The Soviet ambassador was standing close to the Bulgarian hosts, not surprised at all to see us. We shook hands warmly, and for an hour and a half we were the focus of the reception, the sensation of the evening. Ambassadors from the West and from the East approached us: some of them to greet us, others to express their opinion about our very presence there. The Romanian Deputy Foreign Minister, Constantin Oancha, said to me: "Your presence here is a significant step forward towards the renewal of your relations with Moscow."

Moscow, however, didn't renew the relations. The Russians turned this way and that with all kinds of maneuvers and excuses: the Camp David agreements, the peace treaty with Egypt, the Jerusalem law, the Golan Heights law, the international conference, the destruction of the Iraqi atomic reactor by our air force, the Memorandum of Understanding, our world campaign for the right of the Soviet Jews to emigrate to Israel, or increased Arab pressure on them not to permit emigration. They always found a reason that it wasn't the appropriate moment for the renewal of relations, but never interrupted the contacts and relations with me.

When I concluded my mission in Bucharest, on November 16, 1982, and my wife and I arrived at the airport to depart for Israel, all the members of our embassy came to bid us farewell, in addition to the Romanian chief of protocol and a group of colleagues from the diplomatic corps and their wives. To the astonishment of all, the wife of the East German ambassador, Mrs. Siegfried Bock, was there as well.

She said I surely understood that her husband couldn't come due to the absence of diplomatic relations between our countries, but she could not miss it. Her husband asked her to tell me that he always enjoyed talking to me and he appreciated me and our contacts, from which he had learned very much, in particular one important thing: it is possible to discuss and understand each other even without diplomatic relations between the countries. Her coming to the airport was a nice gesture, which added to the warm and cordial atmosphere of the emotional farewell.

In December 1989, Nicolae Ceausescu was overthrown and executed together with his wife Elena.

PART FIVE

INTIFADA

UNHOLY ALLIANCE

With the establishment of the State of Israel, the gates of the country became wide open to receive every Jew who wanted to come, but the three million Jews of the Soviet Union were not permitted to leave. Any attempt by a Jew to leave the Soviet Union was considered illegal and severely punishable. It was after the death of Stalin, and the twentieth Congress of the Communist Party in 1956, that the truth of the persecution of Soviet Jewry became widely known. Only then, did awareness of the Jewish problem in the USSR spread throughout the West.

Shaul Avigur, who, before the founding of the Jewish State, was the head of the "Mossad Le'aliyah Beth" (the institution for the "illegal" immigration), established the organization "Nativ," Israel's secret arm for activities among the Jews living behind the Iron Curtain. In parallel, he formed the organiztion "Bar," whose task was to divulge the truth about the situation of the Soviet Jews, and the global cry "Let my people go!" began to be heard.

Shaul Avigur, head of the "Mossad Le'Aliyah Beth"

The main focus for the work of "Nativ" was the Soviet Union, and the second was Romania. The "Nativ" people served as ordinary diplomats within Israel's diplomatic missions there. Their task was to establish contacts with the Jews and lift their morale as well as to provide them with information on Israel, Judaism and Zionism. The principal places of contact were the few still existing synagogues. In the main synagogue in Moscow, there was always a presence of representatives of the Israeli embassy, and on Sabbath and holidays, they were surrounded by thousands of Jews. The "Nativ" people also attended the few Yiddish concerts that still took place from time to time.

As diplomats, the "Nativ" people traveled throughout the Soviet Union and met Jews, including young people, at any place. Throughout the years, the embassy people distributed to the Jews tens of thousands of copies of the Bible, prayer books, Russian-Hebrew dictionaries, calendars, history books and all kinds of "souvenirs": records, stamps, coins and so on. They also helped financially needy communities.

"Bar" had special representatives in the main Jewish centers: New York, London, Paris and Buenos Aires. In other places, one of the members of the embassy was entrusted with these tasks. I, for instance, was responsible for "Bar" activities when I served in Lima and Toronto, and in Buenos Aires I helped the special "Bar" representative there. When I was ambassador in Bucharest, all my visits to the Jewish communities throughout the country were organized in full coordination with the "Nativ" representatives and with their tours of the country.

"Nativ" activity in the Soviet Union brought about a renewed Jewish and Zionist awakening and young Jews began to organize in clandestine cells. Israel's victory in the Six-Day War emboldened Soviet Jews. Many of them, the younger generation in particular, literally risking their lives, began courageously to demand the right to depart for Israel, whether under the family reunion scheme or as repatriation to the historical national homeland of the Jewish people. In the Leningrad trial, in December 1970, Jews were convicted for trying to hijack a Russian plane and escape to Israel. Two of the convicted hijackers, Mark Dimshitz and Edward Kuznetzov, were sentenced to death and nine others to prolonged years of imprisonment with hard labor. Under international protests, the Soviet authorities did not execute the death verdict.

The courage of the Soviet Jews, the activity of "Nativ," the prolonged and tenacious efforts by Israel's envoys on every continent, at the United Nations and in other international forums, as well as the intervention of Jewish organizations, intellectual personalities in many lands, parliaments and governments, drove the Soviet Union into a defensive moral quandary. In spite of strong Arab opposition, Moscow began to answer the call to let the Jews go.

While in 1945 I was "repatriated" from Russia on false papers and under a false name, in the 1970's large numbers of Jews could leave Russia legally. I had not dared to envision that in my wildest dreams. The Arabs declared war on that *aliyah*, and when with the parting of the Iron Curtain the blessed massive *aliyah* from the Soviet Union increased, the Arabs launched a propaganda and political campaign sending letters, exerting pressure, and making threatening statements directed not only against the *aliyah* and Israel, but also against the Soviet Union for opening its gates and the United States for demanding that opening. The big stream of *aliyah* began in 1989, when the Soviet Union's government was headed by President Mikhail Gorbachev, and the Foreign Minister was Edward Shevardnadze (later, President of Georgia) with whom Israel's Foreign Minister, Moshe Arens, met in Cairo.

The flow of the *aliyah* continued during the years 1990 and 1991, and brought to Israel about 300,000 Soviet Jews. It highlighted Israel's historic role

Foreign Minister Moshe Arens with Soviet Foreign Minister Edward Shevardnadze

as the homeland for the Jewish people, but also presented the Jewish State with a very serious challenge. In the former Soviet Union, there were more than two million Jews, many of whom were waiting to emigrate to Israel. A large number had in the meantime postponed their departure because of the not very encouraging reports reaching them from relatives and friends about the enormous absorption difficulties in Israel — tens of thousands of new immigrants were unemployed, other tens of thousands did not work in their professions, and there was a housing problem.

Israel's main challenge was to absorb successfully the Russian immigrants already in Israel and thus speed the *aliyah* of those who hesitated to take the plunge *aliyah* lying at the very roots of Jewish existence in the Land of Israel and being the raison d'être of the State of Israel. The longing for *aliyah* kept the Jewish people alive during nearly 2,000 years of exile. Thanks to *aliyah,* the independent Jewish State has been re-established. The state was to grow and develop following *aliyah.* A constant *aliyah* was to secure the very existence of Israel — politically, militarily, economically and demographically — and give the Jewish people the possibility to develop to the maximum of its capacity and creativity.

In July 1950, the Law of Return was adopted unanimously by the Knesset, giving every Jew the right to immigrate to Israel and to receive its citizenship. Thus was incorporated into law the Zionist goal according to which the State of Israel was to serve as a home for all Jews wherever they may be. In February 1954, an amendment to the Law was adopted that a Jew with a criminal past, who might endanger public safety, would not be permitted to immigrate to Israel.

While the Law established that every Jew is entitled to immigrate to Israel, it did not deal with the question of "Who is a Jew?" This question constitutes an issue of dispute between secular and religious Jews, has caused government crises and was discussed more than once before the Supreme Court of Justice.

By historic coincidence, the opening of the gates of the Soviet Union was followed by the end of the tragedy of Ethiopian Jewry. After years of alienation, Ethiopia resumed full diplomatic relations with Israel and permitted the remaining Jews there to emigrate to Israel. Thanks to the intervention of the American president, George Bush, with the authorities in Addis Ababa, 14,000

Ethiopian Jews were flown to Israel within 36 hours. While the *aliyah* of Soviet Jews presents Israel with the need of providing them with new homes and employment, the problem of the Ethiopian *aliyah* goes far beyond that. It is literally a question of rebuilding their lives in every sense of the word. The absorption of all those new immigrants requires much imagination, vision and dedication.

While "Glasnost" and "Perestroika" made mass emigration of Soviet Jews to Israel possible, it also opened all the anti-Semitic faucets. True, institutionalized governmental anti-Semitism is no longer Russian policy, but there is a considerable increase in anti-Semitic manifestations on the public and grass-roots levels. The President of the Russian Federation, Boris Yeltsin, condemned the increase of anti-Semitism in Russia when he attended, in August 1998, the inaugural ceremony of the first synagogue established in Moscow since the Communist Revolution in 1917. On the eve of the second millennium, Boris Yeltsin resigned and was replaced by Vladimir Putin. On January 5, 2000, Yeltsin

From left to right: Naina and Boris Yeltsin with Israel's President, Ezer Weizman and his wife Reuma

arrived in Israel to attend the Christmas Eve Midnight Mass according to the Julian calendar followed by the Orthodox Churches.

Dormant racial factors woke up and new ones arose in East and West and this led to an increasing number of circles joining the organized mendacious and hateful campaign to deny the reality of the Nazi regime's systematic murder of six million Jews in Europe during World War II. These deniers claim that the Holocaust never happened and that in Auschwitz there never were gas chambers — "they were constructed after the war as a means to draw tourists," it is claimed.

The denial of the Holocaust filled the vacant space of the ideologies of the extreme groups, from the left and from the right. The deniers of the Holocaust succeeded in attracting to their ranks academics who provide "credibility" for their terrible lies. 50 years after Hitler's death he has heirs in various corners of the world.

Anti-Semitism was not eradicated by emancipation, atheism, liberalism, socialism and communism, nor by the Holocaust and the establishment of the Jewish State. When the term anti-Semitism seemed to be unpopular, the enemies of Israel invented a new term — anti-Zionism. The same old anti-Semitism undergoing various metamorphoses according to circumstances and time: religious fanaticism in the Middle Ages, economic accusations in the 19th century, transformed by Hitler into an ideology. The war against Zionism is in our days directed against this century's greatest creation by the Jewish national movement — the State of Israel.

During my years of service in various countries I realized that anti-Zionism was an unholy alliance of factors diametrically opposed to one another but united in their opposition to the State of Israel and the Jews. What else was common to Old Leftists in Russia or China and Neo-Nazis in England, South Africa or the United States; to new Leftists and "Skinheads" in Germany and Neo-Fascists in Italy; to a black general in Uganda, a "Tacuara" racist in Argentina and Arab "Black September" terrorists; to an avowed anti-ecumenical Vatican spokesman, a nationalist Socialist bigot in Quebec and a liberal United Church editor in Toronto? All that held them together was hatred of the Jews.

In its struggle against the anti-Zionist unholy alliance, Israel has a blessed partner in the United States — the Anti-Defamation League of B'nai B'rith (ADL), which, from its creation in 1913, has been committed to fighting anti-Semitism and working for the security of the Jewish people.

In its early decades, the League devoted itself to anti-Semitism in the United States. After the destruction of European Jewry, ADL concluded that it must concern itself with Jews in danger beyond the American scene. When, with the creation of the State of Israel, it became clear that anti-Semitism had again reared its ugly head and that the ultimate manifestation of anti-Semitism in the post-Holocaust world would be the destruction of Israel, ADL became an ardent, devoted and consistent supporter of the Jewish State.

Brichah *people in Austria. Left to right: Standing — Dr. Boris Roisin, Joseph Weinstein — Aba Gefen's brother, Zvika Pines — soldier from the Jewish Brigade, Aba Gefen. Sitting — Joseph Foxman, Kleist, Moritz Aizikovitch.*

Abraham Foxman (center) with ADL National Chair Howard Berkowicz (right) and Israel's Prime Minister Benjamin Netanyahu

Throughout the decades, ADL has carried out a vast array of programs and advocacy efforts, and has issued publications to counteract a myriad of Arab threats against Israel's security and well-being in the form of boycott, terror, anti-Semitic incitement, denial of the Holocaust and anti-Israel hostility in the international community. ADL has helped Israel in its peace process with the Arabs and the campaign for a united Jerusalem.

While ambassador in Bucharest, I was pleased to meet the National Director of ADL, Abraham Foxman, the son of the late Joseph Foxman, a Holocaust survivor, who in 1945, when I was in Salzburg, was the leader of the Zionist Revisionist movement in Austria. Joseph Foxman was a very good friend of mine and we collaborated closely in the *Brichah*.

Now, I found his son Abraham dedicated to the advocacy for the State of Israel and to the struggle against today's promoters of the ideology which caused the genocide of six million Jews.

However, not only the Jews — whose number is today estimated 13 and a half million (five and a half million in the United States, five million in Israel, and the rest in 100 countries scattered throughout the world) — should worry about the activities of those enemies of Israel. These activities should be a source of serious concern for democracy as a whole, because they are to be found in the United States and in England and other countries of Europe; in Russia and in the other countries of Eastern Europe; in Latin America, in South Africa and in the Arab and Islamic countries; and on the Internet. Those groups have collaborated closely with the *"Hizbullah"* in southern Lebanon and with the Palestinian terrorists in the territories and have contributed to the outburst, in December 1987, of the *intifada*.

Since 1967, there have been demonstrations, strikes and violent anti-Israeli riots in the West Bank and Gaza Strip. But they never reached such an all-out intensive and continuous outburst as occurred in December 1987.

At the beginning of the *intifada*, IDF did not attribute much importance to the demonstrations and disturbances and believed that, as in the past, it would be able to subdue them in a short time. Very soon it became clear that this time there was much more readiness on the part of the Palestinian population to bear the confrontation with the Israeli soldiers. After Israel's response with live fire caused numerous Palestinian fatalities, the live bullets were replaced by plastic ones. Then followed rubber and paint bullets and the IDF was compelled to bring in larger forces into the territories. Nevertheless, it did not succeed in subduing the riots, and the *intifada*, which started in Gaza, spread to all the cities and villages of the West Bank.

The *intifada* continued in 1988. The disturbances in the territories increased and became more violent. The number of the Palestinians killed by IDF soldiers reached dozens every month. The international media reported the events widely and the organizers of the demonstrations exploited well the power of film and pictures. They supplied the international television networks "hot" material on their confrontations with the Israeli soldiers. For the purpose of achieving public relations gains, and in order to provide avid representatives of foreign media with juicy and sensational scenes, the terrorist ringleaders hid behind a human wall of children and old women, unashamedly pushing them into the front line.

As a result of the elections in Israel, in November 1988 a National Unity

Government was formed: Yitzhak Shamir — Prime Minister, Moshe Arens — Foreign Minister, Yitzhak Rabin — Defense Minister and Shimon Peres — Finance Minister. The government decided to adopt a hard line against the *intifada*. Defense Minister Yitzhak Rabin declared: "We will enforce order in the territories even if it will hurt."

But the disturbances increased in frequency and the territories continued to be in turmoil. The population in the territories responded to the call of the Palestinian leadership to participate in violent activities against Israel's domination by the throwing of stones and Molotov cocktails, the setting up of barriers, the burning of tires, the use of knives and axes, clashes with IDF soldiers and acts against Palestinians who collaborated with the Israeli authorities. And so, PLO henchmen perpetrated numerous savage assassinations of local Palestinians — men and women alike. Arafat himself has publicly justified such killings.

In February 1989, soldiers Avi Sasportas and Ilan Saadon were murdered. That same year, the violent activity of the "*Hamas*" escalated to a degree never seen before. In May, the Israeli authorities arrested the founder and head of *Hamas*, Sheikh Ahmed Yassin, and other leaders of that movement. Yassin was sentenced to life imprisonment for incitement to murderous acts against Jews. But the violent activities continued. In July, a terrorist commandeered an "Egged" bus on line 405 between Tel Aviv and Jerusalem and caused it to overturn and fall into an abyss. 17 persons were killed and 27 injured.

Navigator Ron Arad
before falling into captivity

On August 8, 1989, a PLO resolution was adopted calling for "the continuation, intensification and escalation of the armed struggle in order to liquidate the occupation of the Palestinian land." The IDF was compelled to allocate more forces, and in South Lebanon, Sheikh Abd El-Karim Obeid, the commander of *Hizbullah* there, was abducted and brought to Israel to serve as a bargaining chip for the exchange of Israeli prisoners, and foremost among them was navigator Ron Arad who had disappeared in October 1986. During an attack on terrorist targets south of Sidon by Israel planes, one Phantom plane was hit. The two crew members abandoned the plane and parachuted to earth safely. The pilot was rescued by a quick action of combat planes. The navigator, Ron Arad, looked for a place to hide and disappeared. It was impossible to rescue him and he was captured by the *Shi'ite* "Amal" organization.

During the first two years of his captivity, contact was kept with Arad through letters and mediators trying to negotiate his release. But there were no results. On the contrary, Ron Arad was transferred to the *Hizbullah*, and since then nothing has been heard from him or about him.

Since Arad fell into captivity, Israeli governments have been making enormous efforts for his return home, but without results.

Israel is using all means to obtain any information on the fate of Arad, including — as mentioned — the abduction of Sheikh Obeid as well as later, the abduction of Mustafa Dirani, commander of the "Amal" unit responsible for holding Arad, and who transferred Arad to the Iranians. Israel continues to consider Iran responsible for Arad's fate. On the anniversary of 12 years since Arad's falling into captivity, 100,000 Internet surfers, from all over the world, signed a petition to Iran's President Muhamad Hatemi for his release.

When Hatemi visited the Vatican, in March 1999, he was the most senior Moslem personality to go there. Pope John Paul II transmitted to him a message from Ron Arad's mother asking him for help in obtaining information about his fate.

The *intifada*, backed by Iran, which cost Israel 278 killed and 1,259 injured, committed cruel acts that shocked the world, but also caused the world, including Israel, to pay more attention to the Palestinian struggle for self-determination.

The *intifada* grew out of the refusal of 2.5 million Palestinians to bear the Israeli occupation. While their yearning for national independence gained even greater momentum as well as encouragement from the international

Palestinians throwing stones against the IDF soldiers

community, it was becoming evident to Israel that it would not be able to subdue the *intifada* by force. The necessity to separate in a peaceful manner brought, eventually, both parties to Oslo.

GULF WAR

When Iraq's dictator Saddam Hussein, invaded Kuwait and threatened Israel with annihilation, Yasser Arafat rushed to Baghdad to embrace Saddam, whom President George Bush had called another Hitler. After the demise of Hitler, most people believed he was unique, one of a kind, never to be equalled. It looked as if there could be no comparison between Hitler and any other totalitarian tyrant in history. With the advent of Saddam, this view proved to be a delusion. The analogy between Saddam and Hitler was not a journalistic metaphor or a propagandistic hyperbole, but based on their characters and deeds. The main drive of both was constant aggressiveness, both made territorial demands, and to both the Jews were not the only enemy.

Hitler considered as his enemies the Czechs and Poles, the British, French, Dutch, Belgians and Scandinavians, the Balkan nations and Russians, as well as the Americans. Likewise for Saddam — the Iranians, the Saudis, the Kuwaitis, the Egyptians, the Syrians and all the other "infidels," as he calls them.

Both had a limitless capacity for cruelty, slew their own colleagues, were ready to sacrifice millions of their people to satisfy their ego, and considered themselves to be deserving of that sacrifice. On one occasion, Hitler made a remark that "the German people wasn't worthy to survive." Saddam on his part, used civilians to shield military targets by purposely placing military installations, tanks, planes and command-and-control centers in residential areas and villages and at archeological sites.

Exactly as Hitler in 1939 held negotiations with the British for the solution of the Polish crisis and at the same time sent his army to the Polish border with explicit instructions when to start the war, so Saddam in his day, cheated the entire world. He promised Egyptian President Mubarak that he wanted to solve the problem in a friendly manner, held negotiations also with other Arab countries, and at the same time sent his soldiers to attack Kuwait.

Hitler attacked Poland only after he signed an agreement of friendship with his enemy number one, Stalin. Similarly, Saddam, so that he could take on the Americans, offered his enemy number one, Iran, everything it wanted; thus he could divert 100,000 soldiers from the Iranian border.

Hitler occupied Austria under the guise of a request by the Austrian traitor, Seyss Inquart, the leader of the Austrian Nazi Party. Saddam annexed Kuwait "at the request of the temporary Kuwaiti government," headed by Saddam's son-in-law.

Hitler destroyed millions of people in concentration camps. Saddam forcibly concentrated thousands of foreign citizens in camps.

Hitler and Saddam used the same belligerent terminology promising to "fight to the very end," and created special elitist army units of their fanatic followers: Hitler — the SS, Saddam — the Republican Guard.

Both developed an extreme personality cult. In Germany, the slogan was "Hitler is Germany and Germany is Hitler." In Iraq, it was "Saddam is the second Nebuchadnezzar," "the rising sun on both rivers" (the Euphrates and the Tigris).

Finally, the common Jewish denominator. For both, the hatred of the Jews served as the most ideal instrument to achieve their goals. In his book "My Struggle" ("Mein Kampf" in German), Hitler "prophesied" that a new world war would lead to the extermination of the Jewish race in Europe. Saddam, in his book "Our Struggle" ("Unser Kampf," the German edition, published in 1977) — asserted that there must be a war in the Middle East to drive the Jews from Israel. Hitler used chemical means in order to liquidate the Jewish people, and Saddam threatened to liquidate the Jewish State with chemical means produced with the help of German experts.

When, some time before invading Kuwait, Saddam declared, "In the name of Allah, we shall cause fire to devour half of Israel," the world reacted with the same indifference it had shown to Hitler's rise to power, so long as the Jews were the only ones affected. When at last the global perils were recognized, for six million Jews the hour of doom had already struck.

So long as the Iraqi Hitler threatened only Israel, everybody sneered that Israel was exaggerating. There were even those who unashamedly insinuated that its warnings were designed to push aside "the main issue — the solution of the Palestinian problem," in their words. Despite all Israel's warnings, in the course of a decade, against the danger of selling sophisticated weapon systems and instruments of mass destruction to a monstrous dictator, East and West persisted in doing so, building up Saddam's arsenal of deadly weapons.

Various companies — from Germany, France, Britain, Austria, Italy, Switzerland, Belgium, Spain, and even the United States — supplied Iraq with conventional and non-conventional military equipment, and helped her to produce chemical, biological and nuclear weapons. The Soviets supplied Iraq with armaments, ranging from battle tanks and supersonic fighters to Scud missiles. Western know-how enabled Iraq to improve the Soviet-made missiles.

In 1988, an International Technological Fair took place in Iraq, and among the foreign participants were many American companies. They came to the fair on the warm recommendation of the American administration, including the president himself, since White House and State Department advisers held Saddam to be a reasonable, Western-oriented Arab leader. What absolute blindness!

On August 2, 1990, Saddam invaded Kuwait, using American technology to fight the Americans.

The United Nations condemned the invasion of Kuwait, and an anti-Iraqi coalition of 28 countries was formed. But Yasser Arafat, the leader of the PLO, who had, on an earlier occasion, received a standing ovation from the representatives of 153 nations when he addressed the United Nations General Assembly, stated: "We declare our support for Iraq...to achieve liberation from Baghdad to Jerusalem." The Palestinians — for whom reality and fantasy intertwine — supported Saddam, and the whole world witnessed the Saddam-PLO alliance against the U.N. and against the U.S.-led coalition.

When in the night between January 16 and 17, 1991, the Gulf War broke out, the West faced the tough task to crack British designed "super bunkers" protecting Iraqi warplanes. Those bunkers, made of reinforced steel and concrete and partly buried in sand, had been built in Iraq with western engineering skills to NATO specifications, to absorb any blast and to withstand perhaps even a nuclear attack. In spite of Israel's not being part of the war coalition, Saddam launched — before dawn on January 18 — the first salvo of eight deadly missiles against Israel.

Sirens sounding throughout the country sent residents scurrying to hermetically sealed rooms, for fear of a chemical attack. Israelis, across the nation, clung to their gas masks day and night, and rows of water hoses were placed outside hospitals to wash down victims.

Holocaust survivors who had managed to evade the German gas-chambers were watching, with tears in their eyes, their Israeli-born grandchildren donning masks in fear of German-made poison gas. For them, every air-raid siren, each exploding missile, and every mention of the word "gas" brought back their private nightmare, and they were forced to relive their past struggles for survival. Innocent civilians were killed and wounded, and enormous damage was inflicted on property.

The reaction of the world to the unprovoked criminal attacks against Israel, was the same as 50 years earlier. When millions of Jews were being tortured, maimed and murdered by the Nazis in installations, Jewish communities which were not under the Nazi jackboot were entreated not to raise their voices too high, "lest supreme interests be harmed." Now, the Jewish State was entreated not to react, "lest supreme interests of the coalition be harmed!" Exactly the same excuse! Even the Vatican, which did not condemn the missile attacks on Israel, called on her not to react.

But the Jews are not the same as those of 50 years ago — Jewish statehood and sovereignty were the catalyst in this transformation — and Israel decided to retaliate. The U.S. insisted on Israel's restraint, committing itself publicly to making the destruction of the Scud missiles the highest priority of its war effort. Therefore, the American efforts in the search-and-destroy mission against the Soviet-made missiles were significantly increased.

In Israel, a narrow majority Likud Government headed by Yitzhak Shamir, with David Levy as Foreign Minister and Moshe Arens as Defense Minister, was in power. Shamir showed maximum ability of restraint in face of a natural impulse to react and demands from the public for immediate military action. He decided to let the Americans and the anti-Saddam coalition members attack Iraq while a U.S. aircraft carrier was sent to the eastern Mediterranean off the coast of Israel, to help preserve the safety of the Jewish State, and an emergency shipment of American "Patriot" anti-missile batteries was airlifted to Israel. American crews were brought in from U.S. military installations in Europe to man the "Patriots."

Throughout the world, people meanwhile realized how truly dangerous the situation of the entire world would have been, had Israel not destroyed Saddam's nuclear threat in 1981. Voices of repentance began to be heard all over the world for having condemned, ten years earlier, Israel's destruction of the Iraqi atomic reactor.

However, the real trauma for the Israelis was the thought of what might have happened had Saddam not invaded Kuwait but decided to act against Israel as he had threatened. King Hussein of Jordan's unconditional support of Saddam made plausible a situation in which Israel could have suddenly found itself facing, along the Jordan River, the Iraqi military monster — with all its chemical, biological and nuclear weaponry, hundreds of missiles and thousands of tanks — a frightening force that stood up against all the armies of the West.

President Bush called the war against Saddam a war to uphold fundamental principles of justice, and sent 500,000 Americans to fight against unmitigated evil. At the same time, the agents of that evil, the PLO followers, stood on the roofs of their houses in Israel and applauded the falling of the Scud missiles on Tel-Aviv and Haifa, while the *Hamas* terrorist movement stated: "All of Palestine is ours and we want to liberate it from the river to the sea in one fell swoop. But the PLO feels that a phased plan must be pursued. Both sides agree on the final objective. The difference between them is the way there."

George Habash, leader of the "Popular Front for the Liberation of Palestine," added: "I come from Lod. My fight and struggle will not cease until I return to Lod... We seek to establish a state which we can use in order to liberate the other parts of Palestine..."

They mean what they say: they don't want peace with Israel, they want Israel piece by piece. But we continue to hope the Arabs will finally realize that the State of Israel is here to stay and is not, as so many of them wishfully think, a temporary phenomenon. They will understand that Israel has not emerged only as a result of Nazi persecution, that Jews have not just found a refuge, but have come home, clinging to the historical roots and gathering the contemporary strength which will assure the permanence of this state. They will have to recognize — in all its millennial depth — the reality of Israel: it is the only state in the world which speaks the same language, upholds the same faith and inhabits the same land it did 3,000 years ago. And if Israel will be strong, they will make peace with it. No-one will make peace with a weak Israel.

Following Saddam's attacks on Israel, we witnessed encouraging developments. Resolutions were passed in the U.S. Congress extolling the Jewish State. The American military aid to Israel was increased and the strategic cooperation between the two countries became much closer. A significant rapprochement took place between Israel and the European Community, and the Germans, conscious of the damage done by their sale of poison gas and other deadly weapons to Iraq, offered Israel military and financial assistance. Relations with the Soviet Union also improved, and there were manifestations of sympathy and support for Israel throughout the world. The display of good will, the rhetoric and the gestures were extremely impressive.

On February 22, 1991, President Bush gave Saddam an ultimatum to withdraw unconditionally from Kuwait within 24 hours. When the ultimatum deadline expired, President Bush ordered a ground offensive and — to use the President's own words — "swiftly and decisively to eject the Iraqis out of Kuwait." Within hours, the allied forces struck deep into southern Iraq. Thousands of hungry and thirsty Iraqi troops began surrendering without a fight, and General Norman Schwartzkopf declared that "the ground, sea and air operation had met only light opposition and the offensive was progressing with dramatic success."

At the end of the first day's fighting, the Iraqis delivered their deadliest missile attack. A single Scud missile demolished — in the outskirts of Dhahran, site of the main U.S. military base for the Gulf War — a barrack housing American soldiers, killing 28 American servicemen and wounding 98.

This painful event made perceptible to the entire world the enormous casualties Israel would have suffered had the 39 missiles launched on her been direct hits. As for the Americans, it provided the final momentum for the White House to take a hard-line stance regarding continued military pressure on Iraqi forces, and this attack proved to be Iraq's costliest error of the war.

Already on February 25, Kuwait's Day of Independence, Kuwaiti soldiers were dancing in the outskirts of their capital. The allies liberated the whole of Kuwait, and continued to crush the encircled elite divisions of the Republican Guards, Saddam's main supporters. The Iraqi forces began to retreat. 4,000 Iraqi tanks had been destroyed, as were over 2,000 artillery pieces; 42 army divisions — amounting to over 400,000 soldiers — were crushed. The allies turned the Iraqi retreat into a total rout, and — according to military sources — there were between 50,000 and 75,000 Iraqi prisoners, and between 100,000 and 150,000 Iraqi soldiers died. "A very, very large number of Iraqis had been killed" — said General Schwartzkopf. There were 126 allied soldiers who lost their lives in the fighting.

After the routed Iraqis accepted all U.N. Security Council resolutions on Kuwait, President Bush announced the allies' stunning victory, and suspended offensive combat operations, declaring: "Kuwait is liberated, Iraq's army is defeated, and our military objectives are met. The war is now behind us."

With the liberation of Kuwait, the world became aware of the long nightmare of its occupation by Saddam. Over and again, liberated Kuwaitis spoke of murder, rape and pillage by the occupiers. The tales of horror came unsolicited, volunteered in a rush to anyone who paused to listen, ghastly words tumbling over each other.

A Kuwaiti minister said that 33,000 of his people had been killed, taken hostage or had gone missing since Iraq's invasion. Kuwaiti officials showed reporters mass graves of civilians killed by Iraqi occupation forces. Reporters saw bodies of murdered Kuwaitis, most badly mutilated, in a hospital morgue. Others visited a cemetery with the graves of 5,000 Kuwaitis shot or hanged by Iraqi soldiers. Another cemetery was the burial place of 135 murdered babies and 200 premature babies who had been removed from incubators at maternity hospitals.

Britain's Prime Minister, John Major, declared that Iraq should be treated as an international pariah as long as Saddam remained in power.

The evidence emerging from the emirate about the kind of tortures to which innocent Kuwaitis had been subjected by the Iraqis and their enthusiastic, merciless Palestinian collaborators was hair-raising, and no Arab country had supported the PLO more generously than Kuwait. It had given Arafat billions of dollars over the years, and the Kuwaiti Defense Minister applauded, in September 1972, the brutal PLO murder of the eleven Israeli athletes in Munich.

For Israel, it was symbolic that Saddam — who had threatened the "mother of all battles" — collapsed in the "mother of all defeats" on Adar 14, the day on which the Jewish people celebrates Purim, the Feast of Lots. Purim commemorates the occasion when the Jews of the Persian empire were saved — through the influence of Queen Esther and her uncle Mordechai — from destruction, planned by their enemy, King Ahasuerus' senior minister Haman. And thus, Saddam, called a new Hitler, acquired an additional title — a new, modern Haman. However, only one of Israel's sworn enemies was subdued in the Gulf War. It was certain that no coalition would be assembled to protect Israel from its remaining enemies, as it would never have been assembled had Saddam invaded Israel instead of Kuwait. Unfortunately, nine years after the Gulf War, Iraq is back in the business of making weapons of mass destruction: biological, chemical and nuclear.

Jonathan Pollard, who in the early 1980's worked in the Intelligence Unit of

Prime Minister Yitzhak Shamir with President George Bush

the American Navy, realized that certain information on Iraqi preparations in the field of nuclear weapons was not being transmitted to Jerusalem by the American intelligence services as was supposed to be done.

Pollard must have known, like many others did from publications in the press, about the vital material which Israel had transmitted to the American intelligence on Soviet ground-to-air missiles "Sam-6," on their war planes "Mig-21" and "Mig-23," on their satellites and on other kinds of Soviet weapons. This material the Americans had not previously received from any other source.

Thanks to Israel, the Americans could present to the entire world one of the most important achievements in the intelligence field. After the death of Joseph Stalin, in 1953, he was succeeded by Nikita Khrushchev and a collective leadership. At the 20th Congress of the Communist Party, in Moscow, in February 1956, Khrushchev delivered a speech, behind closed doors, the contents of which was not published by the Soviet press. Crumbs of information leaked out to the West. In June 1956, the Americans published Khrushchev's entire speech in all the news media. The publication of the speech was like a bombshell announcing to the world the process of de-Stalinization. In his speech, Khrushchev defined Stalin's deeds as "mass terror" and said that "Stalin murdered many thousands of honest and innocent Communists, in his attempt to become a superman." It was the Israeli *Mossad* which obtained the speech and transferred it to the C.I.A.

When Jonathan Pollard saw in his unit material that should have been transmitted to Israel within the framework of the agreement on cooperation and information exchange, but was not, he concluded that his Government was not fulfilling its promises and obligations towards Israel. Therefore, he decided to transmit the material to Israel on his own, and did not consider it a betrayal of his American motherland.

When suspicion arose among Pollard's colleagues, and Pollard felt that he might be in serious trouble, he tried to escape into the Israeli embassy. But the Israeli security man at the embassy in Washington didn't let Pollard enter the embassy. On November 21, 1985, he was arrested. Jonathan Pollard was sentenced to life imprisonment.

Since relations between Israel and the United States are not based on equality of obligations and commitments, the Israeli government had to deny having carried out espionage activities in the United States. What is permitted to the big brother — and the C.I.A. does carry out intelligence activities in Israel — is not allowed to the little one. Israel's spokesmen were compelled to declare: "If anything of this kind was done, it was somebody's private initiative."

In face of great pressure by the public committee for Pollard's release, the Israeli Ministry of the Interior granted Pollard Israeli citizenship, the Israeli Finance Ministry allocated money to the public committee — for its activities as well as for the needs of the Pollard couple — and the government proclaimed Pollard as "an Israeli agent" and asked for his release. Even at the Wye Plantation Summit, in October 1998, Prime Minister Benjamin Netanyahu asked President Clinton to release Pollard in the framework of the Israeli-Palestinian agreement, and President Clinton referred to it in his speech at the signing of that agreement.

When he visited Israel in December 1998, Clinton said that he is again reviewing the issue, but on January 20, 2001, he concluded his term of office in the White House without releasing Pollard.

MADRID

Washington was convinced that Saddam's collapse caused changes in the Middle East and created new opportunities; a short while after the end of the Gulf War, American Secretary of State James Baker began his shuttle diplomacy towards convening an Arab-Israeli peace conference. At the 1991 U.N. General Assembly, President Bush demanded the repeal of the 1975 U.N. resolution equating Zionism with racism. The President declared: "This world body will never be viewed as a peace-seeking organization until the resolution is eliminated. By repealing this resolution unconditionally, the United Nations will enhance its credibility and serve the cause of peace."

Spokesmen of many other nations came out in support of President Bush's demand to repeal the resolution. Among them were also the representatives of the countries of Eastern Europe, where the dramatic developments led to the resumption of their full diplomatic relations with Israel. Thus came to an end an era of bitter enmity between Moscow and Jerusalem.

The Soviet Union restored full diplomatic relations with Israel 24 years after severing them. The signing ceremony in Jerusalem confirming the renewal of the ties, on October 18, 1991, came just an hour before Soviet Foreign Minister Boris Pankin joined American Secretary of State James Baker in formally issuing invitations — on behalf of the presidents of the United States and the Soviet Union — to the Middle East conference.

Israel's willingness to participate at a regional peace conference was based on the understanding with the United States that the PLO would not be a party to the process, directly or indirectly.

The historic peace conference convened in Madrid, Spain, on October 30,

1991, under the co-chairmanship of President George Bush and President Mikhail Gorbachev. Over 7,000 journalists came to Madrid to report on the proceedings. The Jews came to Spain — from where they were expelled 500 years before — to negotiate peaceful co-existence with the Arabs. But violence hung like a cloud over what should have been a more triumphant arrival by the Israeli delegation, headed by Prime Minister Yitzhak Shamir.

In two attacks in southern Lebanon, Arab terrorists killed three Israeli soldiers and wounded six. In an attack between Ramallah and Nablus, Arab gunmen killed two Jewish civilians and wounded six others, five of them children. One of the dead was a mother of seven, and the other — a father of four. "Some might have expected that in the face of this terror Israel would not attend the conference," Shamir said, and added: "But, despite this violence, our quest for peace is unrelenting."

Presidents Bush and Gorbachev made efforts to appear as honest brokers and assured the parties — Israel, Lebanon, Syria, Jordan and the Palestinians — that the co-sponsors intended to act as no more than catalysts, since any attempt by the United States or the Soviet Union to impose a solution, or in any way to interfere in the process, could only guarantee failure.

In his opening address, Prime Minister Shamir invited the Arab delegations to break taboos and barriers, declare an end to war and to belligerency; and to conduct the direct bilateral and multilateral talks with the purpose of reaching a peace based on the mutual interests of Arabs and Israelis that would stand the test of time.

After three days of formal speeches and responses, the moment Israel had been waiting for since the birth of the state — arrived. For the first time, all the country's neighbors, including its most implacable enemy, Syria, had agreed to conduct direct, bilateral, independent negotiations without pre-conditions. Shamir was the first Israeli Prime Minister to speak face-to-face even with the Syrians, and there is no doubt that the Madrid Conference was a turning point in the history of the Middle East conflict.

In Madrid was created a framework for additional meetings of those involved in the conflict. It was a landmark achievement and it was historic not only because direct negotiations were, in fact, recognized as the only way to peace, but because they implied Arab recognition of Israel's sovereignty and legitimacy. It is the absence of such recognition that has been the root cause of the Arab-Israel conflict. In the initial bilateral negotiations, in Madrid, between Israel and each of its Arab neighbors, no agreement was reached — neither on the venue of the next negotiations nor on the date of the next meeting. The feeling was that there was a long way to go. The Americans, however, were determined to build on the momentum reached at the first ever face-to-face bilateral peace talks between Israel and all its immediate Arab neighbors. After a series of contacts between the U.S. Secretary of State, James Baker, and the various governments, the delegations met in Washington on December 10, 1991.

On December 18, the talks recessed. They were renewed on March 2, 1992, and again produced no results. It became clear that no serious progress could be achieved before the parliamentary elections in Israel, scheduled for June 23, 1992. On January 28, 1992, the multilateral talks opened in Moscow. They were aimed to promote progress between Israel and her neighbors on water, the environment, economic development, refugees, security and arms control. Five committees were established, and they all convened for the first time during the month of May: in Vienna — on water, in Brussels — on economic development, in Ottawa — on refugees, near Tokyo — on the environment, and in Washington — on security and arms control.

Syria refused to participate in the multilateral talks unless any progress was made in the bilateral negotiations. Israel refused to participate in the discussions of the committee on refugees because it objected to the participation of Palestinians living outside the administered territories.

At the same time, President Bush personally continued the world-wide campaign to repeal the United Nations resolution equating Zionism with racism, and it was overwhelmingly abrogated on December 17, 1991, by the General Assembly of the United Nations.

Out of the 165 member-states of the United Nations, 111 voted for the repeal, 25 voted against, 13 abstained and 16 were absent. Thus ended 16 years of what Israelis termed their country's "delegitimization" by the world body. It was also the end of Israel's diplomatic isolation, and even China and India established diplomatic relations with her.

The New York cardinal, John O'Connor, declared that the Vatican, too, was considering a "historic shift" in its attitude towards Israel, including the issue of Jerusalem. The cardinal visited Israel in January and met officially for the first time with President Chaim Herzog and Prime Minister Yitzhak Shamir. Following his visit, a joint Vatican-Israeli commission was formed to discuss matters of common interest. At the Vatican, Pope John Paul II said at a meeting with the diplomats accredited to the Vatican: "I hope that circumstances will make it possible for additional states to join those represented here today. I have in mind, among others, China, Vietnam, Israel and Jordan."

This time, the Pope mentioned Israel. In January 1964, during the 12-hour stay in Israel of Pope Paul VI, he deliberately refrained from uttering the words "State of Israel." He only said that "he prays to God for the children of the people of the Testament whose part in the history of the religions will never be forgotten."

The Vatican's refusal to normalize its relations with Israel stemmed from the fact that Christianity's attitude towards Judaism is theological, and Israel is the only country in the world that, in the eyes of the Catholic Church, is different

President Zalman Shazar welcomes to Israel Pope Paul VI

Israel's Deputy Foreign Minister, Yossi Beilin, and the Vatican's Deputy Foreign Minister, Monsignor Claudio Celli, exchange copies of the basic agreement between Israel and the Holy See

from any other state. As long as the Jews were a "despised and humiliated" people, scattered among the nations of the world, their very inferior existence was proof of the superiority of Christianity over Judaism.

At the moment that the Jews joined the family of nations as equals, it was as if Judaism had overcome Chistianity, and this is problematic in Catholic thought.

It was, therefore, not by accident that it took the Vatican 44 years until in July 1992 it opened official talks with Israel on the normalization of relations. Only in December 1993, did the Vatican yield to advantage and advisability considerations and signed with Israel the basic document on the establishment of diplomatic relations.

It is doubtful whether these developments in Israel's position among the nations would have occurred without the demise of the Soviet empire. After years in the throes of terminal disease, the USSR was finally pronounced as non existing — neither as a geopolitical fact nor as an entity recognized by international law. The Soviet Union formally ceased to exist on January 1, 1992, and was replaced by a "Commonwealth of Independent States." The red flag was lowered from above the Kremlin on New Year's eve. Gorbachev was replaced by Boris Yeltsin as President of Russia.

But Gorbachev will always be recorded in the annals of mankind for his dedication and courage to uplift the peoples of the Soviet Union to democracy and freedom, and as one who brought humanity closer to peace and a better future. His personal attitude and policy towards the Jews in the Soviet Union will always be remembered by us. As a result of Gorbachev's understanding and actions, the Jews were given the freedom to return to their ancient homeland where they are able to resume their national life. Israel and the Jews will also remember his decisive role in facilitating the process of normalization of Soviet relations with Israel.

The parliamentary elections in Israel brought about a political upheaval. The Likud lost and Labor won. Yitzhak Rabin, Labor's leader, became the new Prime Minister of Israel.

The Likud had not expected such a defeat. In most countries, when the standard of living is on the rise, a large majority of the population is

Foreign Minister David Levy with Soviet president Mikhail Gorbachev

economically comfortable, the country's status in the world is dramatically improved, the incumbent government is rewarded with reelection. However, although its achievements were remarkable in many areas, the majority of voters perceived the government as a failure, and the Likud lost the confidence of one-third of its voters. Partly, it was a result of a media blitz in Israel and abroad because of the government's failure to absorb the new immigrants, and the serious rise in the number of unemployed. But what diminished the Likud's image more than anything else was the impression of disarray, contentiousness and political corruption perceived by the public.

GOLAN HEIGHTS

After the elections in Israel, Prime Minister Yitzhak Rabin received President Bush's invitation to come to the United States. It was clear that Bush wanted to meet with him before the Republican National Convention. Not that Bush and Baker could be expected to approve building in "security settlements" or give official recognition to Israeli sovereignty in Jerusalem. But Rabin believed that the administration was ready to approve the promised 400 million dollars in loan guarantees for Soviet Jewish immigrants' housing, with the understanding that no new settlements would be established, and that only buildings in the administered territories already begun would be completed.

It was also evident that, with November approaching, Bush's interest in the American Jewish community grew, and it seemed clear that the President would have made a pronounced pro-Israel gesture even if Yitzhak Shamir had been reelected. The Labor victory made such a gesture easier and more natural. Not only did the lack of personal "chemistry" between Bush and Shamir cease to play a role; the accession of a dovish, more flexible new government invited, from the U.S. point of view, reward and encouragement.

As for the American Jews, it was encouraging to them to again be the focus of political attention. Until less than a year earlier, when President Bush seemed invincible and the election little more than a formality, he had permitted himself to show less interest in wooing the Jews. In the meantime, his popularity plummeted, the promised economic recovery was slow, and the much-touted "new world order" looked like a mixed bag of embryonic democracies plagued with xenophobic, belligerent chauvinism. Instead of basking in its position as the world's only superpower, the U.S. was confronted with international situations about which it could do little. It was not surprising that Americans were dissatisfied and both parties were after the votes of the Jewish population, which — concentrated in large, electoral-vote-rich states — was now potentially more pivotal than ever. Even a slight shift in its voting patterns could determine who would be occupying the White House the following year.

Rabin on his part did not allow the improvement in U.S.-Israel relations to obscure the harsh facts of life. Expressions of friendship must never divert attention from the dangerous area in which Israel is situated. With commendable bluntness, Rabin reminded his Washington audience of hard reality by opposing the sale by the U.S. of 72 F-15E jet fighters to Saudi Arabia.

Rabin said: "I don't believe any responsible politician in Israel can but oppose the sale of arms to an Arab country that continues to stress that it is in a state of war with Israel. We are told that Saudi Arabia is an American ally. But before the invasion of Kuwait we heard the same thing about Saddam Hussein."

Rabin stressed that the arms sales should not take place if the United States is committed to maintaining Israel's qualitative edge, and he recalled the sale of tanks to the Jordanians in 1965, adding: "They were tanks President Lyndon Johnson promised would never cross the Jordan river. In 1967 they crossed it. We have proof. We destroyed them all."

Rabin also mentioned Syria's purchasing vast quantities of arms from Russia, the Ukraine, China and North Korea, and said that the Syrians now possessed a Scud-C missile which could hit any target in Israel with double the accuracy of the older Scud-Bs. Rabin made it clear that the most important front was Syria, with whom Israel shares a border, and because Syria has the ability to start a war against Israel, one including the use of planes and missiles.

Rabin informed his American counterparts that since 1975, the Syrians had been deploying surface-to-surface Scud missiles, which enabled them to hit the Israeli home front sidestepping the need to cross the border and jeopardize pilots and planes. Since 1980, Syria had also been systematically deploying missiles with a shorter range (90 kilometers), which are far more accurate and capable of hitting Israel's military targets such as army bases and airstrips. Over the years, the Syrians have continually improved their missile deployments, adding chemical warheads, and they possessed missile attack capabilities several times more dangerous than those of Iraq.

Rabin stressed that it was our power of deterrence that had until now prevented Syria from initiating a war against us, and it would not dare to attack us as long as Israel had the ability to roll back the war into Syrian territory and retaliate devastatingly. Israel must therefore, keep its army ready to deter any Arab country from going on the offensive against her and, should the deterrent factor fail, defeat the enemy quickly. Quickly — in order to secure the home front from being hit by the launching of surface-to-surface missiles.

In Rabin's view, the weakening of the Iraqi military in the Gulf War and the work of the U.N. inspection teams had postponed the threat to Israel, at least from Iraq. But following developments in Iran, Israel might find itself in the future in even greater danger, and this was not the kind of rosy picture of the post-Gulf War Middle East that the Bush administration liked to paint. Nor was it a scenario in which Israel could take many risks for peace. Nevertheless, Israel was ready to make far-reaching proposals to Lebanon, with whom the bilateral talks were quite friendly: to withdraw from all of southern Lebanon, once Syria did the same from other Lebanese territories.

The Syrians, however, insisted that they would discuss peace with Israel only after an Israeli withdrawal from every inch of the Golan Heights, and even rejected Israel's proposals to discuss the definition of the peace process objectives, or the issue of recognition of Israel, or their readiness to negotiate without threats and terror. Nevertheless, even after having been appalled at President Bush's public commitment to help maintain Israel's strategic edge, they arrived — on August 24, 1992 — in Washington, to participate in the renewed Arab-Israeli talks.

On the eve of the renewal of those talks, the Israeli government published a series of measures taken to contribute to some kind of confidence-building: 600 political prisoners were ordered released; the expulsion order handed down in January to 11 Palestinians was rescinded, and orders were given to permit free access to Israel to all Palestinians more than 50 years of age. Israel also declared that the "land for peace" principle applied to the Golan Heights too. Rabin stated that Israel's security does not require holding on "to every single centimeter of land on the Heights," promising, however, that in any case, a referendum would be held before any withdrawal from the Golan Heights.

In this context, Rabin recalled that the National Unity Government of 1967 (the Eshkol-Begin Government) recognized Syria's sovereignty over the Golan Heights and peace based on the international frontier, subject to Israel's security needs. He quoted Menachem Begin having said in the Knesset, in 1981, before the approval of the Golan Heights Law, that "as soon as the Syrian President says that he is ready to negotiate a peace treaty with Israel, and such negotiations begin, nothing will stand in our way."

However, Israel was not ready to define exactly the perimeter of its eventual withdrawal from the Golan before the Syrians clarify that peace with Israel, although part of a comprehensive Middle East peace would also stand independently on its own. Israel also demanded from the Syrians a commitment to honor the security arrangements which would be agreed upon and whose goal would be: prevention of a surprise attack on Israel, the lowering to a minimum of the temptation for war, avoidance of border incidents which might deteriorate into serious clashes. Israel also insisted that, for the talks to succeed, the Syrians should give public expression to their peaceful intentions in order to prove to the Syrian public, as well as to the Israeli public, that they have crossed the Rubicon and really want peace. But the Syrians were not swayed by Rabin's gestures, did not respond to Israel's demands, and even tried to dictate their intransigence also to the other participants in the talks.

The talks with the Jordanians, however, in spite of occasional ups and downs, were quite cordial and a certain amount of progress was made. It was agreed that resolutions 242 and 338 of the Security Council would be the basis for the negotiations and that the issues to be discussed should be: the achievement of peace, refugees, borders, and collaboration in the fields of water, energy, environment, tourism, and security arrangements.

As for the Palestinians, they refused to stop killing Israelis while negotiating peace, and considered the talks a propaganda tool by presenting lists of claims for an independent Palestinian state. They arrived for the renewal of the peace talks without having altered their positions. In their proposals on the interim agreement they referred to a state, while Israel proposed setting up commissions to discuss only interim arrangements in various spheres. During the talks, Prime Minister Rabin — having imposed curbs on the kind of Jewish settlement that flourished in the territories under Shamir — urged Israelis to abandon any hopes of controlling all biblical Israel, and to try to reach peace with the Arabs before the balance of power in the region had shifted against Israel.

The Israeli delegation to the Washington talks outlined a timetable for the election of an administrative council for self-rule which would give the Palestinians the possibility to be in charge of day-to-day life on the West Bank and Gaza, while Israel would continue to maintain responsibility for defense and security, for the Jewish settlers in the territories, and for foreign affairs.

After 10 days of talks, a 10-day break was taken, the Israelis being convinced that the Americans fully supported the interim arrangements proposed by Israel, in view of the pro-Israeli Middle East paragraph of both parties in their election platforms. Both parties stressed the importance of Israel as the only American democratic ally in the Middle East and its strategic value. They supported economic assistance to Israel, the preservation of its qualitative military edge, and the preservation of Jerusalem as an undivided city. They called for the end of the Arab boycott against Israel and opposed an independent Palestinian state or any political entity that would jeopardize Israel's security.

President Bush, at his meeting with Rabin, said: "The relationship between the USA and Israel is based on a shared commitment to democracy and to common values, as well as a solid commitment to Israel's security, including its qualitative military edge, and this is a special relationship, one that is built to endure."

He continued: "Literally hundreds of thousands of Jews from Ethiopia, from the former Soviet Union now make their homes in Israel, and in this regard, I am extremely pleased to announce that we were able to reach agreement on the basic principles to govern our granting of up to 10 billion dollars in loan guarantees."

On his part, the Democratic presidential candidate, Governor Bill Clinton, pledged, in his meeting with Rabin, that he was fully resolved to continue his commitment to the security interests of Israel and his support for the loan guarantees. He made it clear that he was utterly determined to make progress in the peace process, and that there would be complete continuity in that process after the election if he won in November.

In November, Bill Clinton won, and in January 1993 he began his first term as President of the United States. Four years later he was reelected.

The Jewish people have an incomparable historical memory: they remember their persecutors and never forget their friends. George Bush, who lost the elections, did some very positive things for Israel: the immigration of the Jews from the Soviet Union and from Ethiopia, the 10 billion dollars in loan guarantees for the absorption of the immigrants, the repeal of the U.N. resolution equating Zionism with racism, the elimination of the danger by Saddam Hussein and the Madrid Conference.

President Clinton kept his promise to Rabin and acted for the continuation of the peace process. Warren Christopher, appointed secretary of state in place of James Baker, continued his predecessor's efforts. Christopher appointed Ambassador Dennis Ross as American coordinator for the peace talks, and Ross began a "shuttle voyage" between Israel and the Arab states.

In March 1993, Yitzhak Rabin visited Washington. At a joint press conference with Bill Clinton, the American president stressed the special relationship between the two countries and repeated the American commitment to Israel's qualitative military edge.

In 1993, a new president was elected in Israel: Ezer Weizman. His predecessors were: Chaim Weizmann, Yitzhak Ben-Zvi, Zalman Shazar, Ephraim Katzir, Yitzhak Navon and Chaim Herzog. After five years, Ezer Weizman was reelected for another term.

PART SIX

MUTUAL RECOGNITION

OSLO

Unlike the Shamir Government, Rabin's Government factually recognized the role of the PLO in the peace process. Palestinian delegates went openly to Tunisia to consult with PLO leader, Yasser Arafat, and it became most evident to the Israelis, that the only Palestinian authority to take decisions was the PLO headquarters in Tunisia.

It was possible to cling to the understandings reached with the Americans on the eve of the Madrid Conference that in no way would the PLO be party to the process, either directly or indirectly. One could continue to cover one's head in the sand and claim that Faisal Husseini and Hannan Ashrawi represent the inhabitants in the territories and that we don't know, or don't want to know, who is behind them. Morally, Israel was entitled not to sit at the same table with the PLO, a merciless terror and sabotage organization, which had sent its members to murder the children of Avivim and Ma'alot, to kill guests at the Savoy Hotel and innocent travelers on the bus along the coastal highway, and had carried out hundreds of other acts of terror, sabotage and murder. Israel didn't want to shake hands with one who had wielded the knife or pressed the trigger.

However, Yitzhak Rabin held the view that we cannot choose either our neighbors or our enemies, and we therefore, have to negotiate with those who are available.

Following Rabin's victory in the 1992 elections and after the Knesset amended the law prohibiting contacts with the PLO, official secret negotiations between representatives of Israel and the PLO began in Oslo, the capital of Norway, on May 20, 1993. These negotiations were official in the sense that they were not low-level, for the purpose of "feeling out," but talks authorized by the Prime Minister. These negotiations were concluded on August 20, 1993, with an agreement between the parties and, on September 9 of that year, an exchange of letters between Yasser Arafat and Yitzhak Rabin on the mutual recognition of Israel and the PLO took place.

The exchange comprised letters from Arafat to Rabin and to the Foreign Minister of Norway, Johan Jurgen Holst, under whose mediation and auspices the secret talks were held, and Rabin's reply to Arafat. In his letter to Rabin, Arafat stated that he recognized Israel's right to exist in peace and security, accepted United Nations Security Council Resolutions 242 and 338, and committed himself to a peaceful resolution of the conflict.

Arafat further declared that all outstanding issues relating to permanent status would be resolved by negotiation, renounced the use of terrorism and other acts of violence in Israel, in the territories and elsewhere, and assumed responsibility over all PLO elements and personnel in order to ensure their compliance, prevent violations and discipline violators.

Arafat also affirmed that those articles of the Palestinian Covenant denying Israel's right to exist, and the provisions of the Covenant inconsistent with the commitments of this letter would henceforth be inoperative and invalid. Consequently, the PLO undertook to submit to the Palestinian National Council for formal approval the necessary changes in regard to the Palestinian Covenant.

In his letter to Holst, Arafat undertook that, by signing the Declaration of Principles with Israel, the PLO encourages and calls upon the Palestinian people in the West Bank and Gaza Strip to take part in the steps leading to the normalization of life, rejecting violence and terrorism, contributing to peace and stability and participating actively in shaping reconstruction, economic development and cooperation. In his reply to Arafat, Yitzhak Rabin confirmed that the Government of Israel had decided to recognize the PLO as the representative of the Palestinian people and to commence negotiations with the PLO within the Middle East peace process.

On September 13, on the lawn of the White House in Washington, under the auspices of the U.S. and the Russian Federation, the Declaration of Principles between Israel and the PLO was signed on the establishment of an Interim Palestinian Self-Government Authority in the West Bank and Gaza Strip, for a transitional period not exceeding five years, leading to a permanent settlement based on Security Council Resolutions 242 and 338. It was agreed in the Declaration that permanent status negotiations would commence between the Government of Israel and the Palestinian people's representatives as soon as possible, but not later than the beginning of the third year of the interim period. Yitzhak Rabin and Yasser Arafat shook hands and, in addition to them, speeches were delivered at the signing ceremony by Foreign Minister Shimon Peres, member of the PLO Executive Committee Abu Mazen (Mahmud Abbas), the President of the United States Bill Clinton, Secretary of State Warren Christopher, and Soviet Foreign Minister Andrei Kozyrev.

A week later, Yitzhak Rabin brought the Declaration of Principles for the approval of the Knesset and he opened his address as follows: "In three days, every Jew, everywhere, will wrap himself with the holiness of Yom Kippur, with its attendant national and personal soul-searching... On the eve of Yom Kippur of the year 5754, the Government of Israel presents to the people of Israel a chance for peace, and maybe for the end of the wars, the violence and terror..."

Rabin-Clinton-Arafat handshake

In a nominal vote, the Declaration of Principles was approved by 61 members of the Knesset. 50 members voted against, eight abstained and one was absent.

The President of the United States, Bill Clinton, expressed in his address at the signing ceremony, as well as in a letter to Yitzhak Rabin, admiration and respect for the courage and leadership Rabin had shown for peace. Clinton promised that, while Israel was taking risks for peace, the United States would stand at her side to reduce those risks. He repeated his commitment to maintain and amplify Israel's qualitative military superiority.

It was agreed in the Declaration of Principles that in the first phase the Interim Agreement would apply to the entire Gaza Strip and to a defined area around the city of Jericho. Israel considered this phase as a kind of test of the capability of the Palestinians to implement the Declaration of Principles.

The agreement on "Gaza-Jericho First" was signed on May 4, 1994, in Cairo. With the signing of the agreement, Israel's army began to evacuate its forces

Signing of the Israeli-Jordanian Peace Treaty.
From left to right: Prime Minister Yitzhak Rabin, President Bill Clinton, King Hussein, President Ezer Weizman

from the territory of the autonomy in the Gaza Strip and the Jericho area, and an agreement was signed on the arrangements to transfer the powers and responsibilities in the West Bank from Israel to the Palestinian Authority. On October 26, 1994, the Israeli-Jordanian Peace Treaty was signed in the Arava desert under the auspices of President Clinton, who visited Israel the next day. The Knesset approved the Peace Treaty between Israel and the Hashemite Kingdom of Jordan by 105 votes. Three voted against, six abstained and six were absent.

The journey to this peace between Jordan and Israel began formally at the Madrid Conference. But the dialogue between Jordan and Israel had taken various forms and had been carried on on both sides of the Jordan river since the establishment of Israel. King Hussein confirmed publicly that he had secret meetings with most of Israel's prime ministers. On October 30, 1994, Hassan II, the King of Morocco, convened in Casablanca the first Economic Summit of the Middle East/North Africa. The presidents of the United States and Russia took it under their wings and there were those who perceived it as the beginning of the development of a new Middle East. On December 10, 1994, the Nobel Prize for Peace was awarded in Oslo jointly to Rabin, Peres and Arafat.

These developments gave an additional push to the renewal of diplomatic relations between Israel and a number of countries which had severed them and to the establishment of relations with other countries. Kings, presidents, prime ministers and foreign ministers from all the continents began to come to Israel. The relations between the United States and Israel had never been better. Clinton continued the magnificent tradition of his predecessors to protect in every way the existence and vital interests of Israel. The two houses of Congress approved, by a great majority, a bill requiring the transfer, by May 1999, of the American embassy from Tel-Aviv to Jerusalem.

The situation was marred by continuous acts of terrorism. Arafat committed himself to restraining violence and terror by the Palestinians. This commitment was not fulfilled. The wave of terror continued in Israel's towns and in the territories, carried out by the *Hamas* and the *"Islamic Jihad"* against Israelis as well as against Palestinians suspected of collaboration with the Israeli authorities, causing many casualties, even more than before the mutual recognition between Israel and the PLO. On the other hand, in February 1994, a

Jew carried out an abominable act in the Cave of the Patriarchs in Hebron: Dr. Baruch Goldstein, a physician from Kiryat Arba, killed 29 Palestinians in the Cave, who were praying during the Fast of Ramadan, and wounded 134.

In October of the same year, Nachshon Waxman was kidnapped by the *Hamas* while he was standing at the crossroads of Bnei Atarot, on his way to a friend in Ramle. The terrorists murdered Waxman when IDF soldiers broke into the place where he was being held, in an attempt to free him. In the rescue attempt, Israeli Captain Nir Poraz was also slain and 11 soldiers were wounded. Three terrorists were killed, a fourth terrorist and one who helped them were captured.

Near Dizzengoff Square in Tel-Aviv, a bus was blown up by a suicidal terrorist and 21 Israeli civilians and one Dutch citizen were killed. 48 persons were wounded. In January 1995, 20 Israeli soldiers and one civilian were killed in two explosions, with an interval of a few minutes, at the Beit Lid junction. The booby traps were activated by suicide bombers, disguised as soldiers. 52 soldiers and eight civilians were wounded. Most of the casualties were soldiers and civilians assisting those injured in the first explosion.

An inspector and a staff sergeant were killed when a Palestinian driver clashed intentionally with a border police jeep which accompanied an Israeli convoy near Netzarim. A booby-trapped transporter, driven by a suicidal terrorist, clashed on April 9, 1995, at 12:00 noon, with a public transportation bus near Kfar Darom in the Gaza Strip. The bus, arriving from Ashkelon, was loaded with soldiers and a few civilians. Six soldiers and two civilians were killed and 36 persons wounded. After two hours, a second attack occurred at the Netzarim junction. A booby-trapped car, driven by a suicidal terrorist, blew up close to a border police jeep and nine soldiers were injured. Two Jewish youngsters, walking in Wadi Kelt, near Jerusalem, were shot to death by terrorists.

A settler of Maaleh Michmash was stabbed to death by a terrorist who broke into his house at night; his pregnant wife was stabbed, too, was wounded and lost her unborn child. Six civilians were killed in July by a suicidal terrorist in a bus in Ramat-Gan and 30 persons were wounded. A month later, a suicidal terrorist blew up a bus at the Eshkol junction in Jerusalem: three civilians and a police officer were killed, 107 persons were injured. Disturbances by

Palestinians continued at the Netzarim junction, in Hebron, Jenin, Tul Karem, Nablus, Kalkilya and Ramallah.

After every explosion closure was imposed on the territories, then removed a few days later. Once, the government interrupted the negotiations on the release of Palestinian prisoners and President Ezer Weizman called on the government to postpone the negotiations with the PLO. But it continued with its policy and, on September 28, 1995, the Israeli-Palestinian Interim Agreement was signed in Washington and approved by the Knesset on October 5 by 61 votes in favor, 59 against. In accordance with this agreement, 1,000 Palestinian prisoners were released from jail.

Tens of thousands of Israelis demonstrated — in the cities of Israel, in front of the prime minister's home in Jerusalem and at the Western Wall — against the government's policy which continued despite the large number of terrorist incidents in the territories and within the green line itself. Thousands of Jews gathered in Hebron to protest the signing of the agreement. All the Jewish settlements in the Jordan Valley declared a strike in protest against the agreement, claiming that it extended the autonomy area of Jericho. They also claimed that the agreement contradicted Prime Minister Rabin's commitment to keep the Jordan Valley as the Eastern security belt of the State of Israel.

About 100,000 people demonstrated in Jerusalem against Arafat's visit to Gaza. In Tel-Aviv, demonstrations were held for the agreement and against it. Protests against the agreement were organized also by Palestinians in the refugee camps in Lebanon and by Jews in Washington.

The situation caused an even deeper polarization between the left and right in Israel, a sharpening of the differences of opinion between the political camps and a split in the nation. While the government continued with the acceleration of the peace process and the implementation of the accords with the PLO, the incitement against the government grew to fever pitch, especially against the prime minister and the foreign minister. A rabbinical edict was published calling on soldiers to refuse orders instructing them to remove settlements in Judea and Samaria. The demonstrations in front of Yitzhak Rabin's house increased and on the other side of the street demonstrators were shouting "Murderer." Anti-Rabin stickers appeared on cars and blaspheming signs on the streets.

The contemptible calls were endlessly repeated. Their climax was at the demonstration on Zion Square in Jerusalem. There, a poster was shown with Rabin in the uniform of a Nazi soldier with his eyes extracted, while in the background were heard calls: "Rabin is a Nazi! Rabin is a traitor!"

After Yona Avrushmi, a Jerusalem youngster, murdered Emil Grinzweig — a member of the "Shalom Achshav" (Peace Now) movement — who attended a demonstration of his movement on February 10, 1983, in front of the prime minister's office, he claimed that he was influenced by the propaganda of the right against the left. The unrestrained incitement of the extreme right against Yitzhak Rabin was intended to distort Rabin's image, to defame his character and finally to call for his blood, as could be understood from the words of Rabbi Moshe Bentov, called "the reader of the *Mezuzot*" (door-posts).

This rabbi said in a sermon in 1995 that the name Pharaoh is composed, in Hebrew, of the initials of Peres, Rabin, Arafat and Hitler. He expressed the hope that Rabin, Peres and Arafat would die as Hitler and Pharaoh had died. And from a rightist crazy man to a leftist insane one. Prof. Chaim Gordon, of Ben-Gurion University, anticipated Rabbi Bentov with similar blasphemy: in 1987, he expressed the hope that Ariel Sharon would die, and said that he would rejoice if Sharon were to suffer a heart attack.

ASSASSINATION OF YITZHAK RABIN

Saturday night, November 4, 1995, Yitzhak Rabin, Prime Minister of Israel, was murdered during a peace assembly at "Malchei Israel Square" in Tel-Aviv. Shortly before his assassination, Rabin had said at the assembly: "This Government, that I have the privilege to head, decided to give peace a chance...I always believed that the majority of our people wants peace and is ready to accept risks for peace...The nation really wishes for peace and is opposed to violence. Violence is the gnawing at the basis of Israeli democracy, it is necessary to condemn it, to denounce it, to isolate it."

120,000 people attended the gathering which concluded with all the participants singing together the "Song of Peace." Yigal Amir, aged 25, student of law at Bar-Ilan University, murdered the Prime Minister of Israel and wounded one of his security men. Amir shot the Prime Minister at zero range, before Rabin managed to enter his car.

Three bullets, which will be remembered with shame by generations of the Jewish people and of the State of Israel, hit the back of the Prime Minister. Rabin died on the operating table. Two leaders, who had chosen to work for peace, Anwar Sadat and Yitzhak Rabin, paid for it with their lives.

The government held a bereavement session and determined the arrangements for the funeral and for the period of national public mourning for the late Prime Minister. Hundreds of thousands passed by the coffin wrapped in the national flag, on view in the Knesset Plaza. Amid a sea of flowers, wreaths, flickering candles; among the thousands of letters expressing love and yearning for Rabin, a signpost with the two holy tablets of the Decalogue was placed emphasizing the commandment "Thou shalt not kill," the most Jewish and most human words — a command for soul-searching, repentance and warning. Tens of thousands stood in front of Rabin's home and returned to the square where he was assassinated, the name of which was changed from "Malchei Israel Square" to "Yitzhak Rabin Square," and others sat down around the memorial candles. Never have Israel's young mourned as they did after the death of Yitzhak Rabin.

The young generation had lost a captain who conquered its heart, a leader with whom they could identify. All mourned for him: Jews and Arabs, Druze and Circassians, secular people and religious ones, members of all religious denominations and faiths, from cities, towns and villages, from the "Kibbutzim," "Moshavim," and development towns, oldtimers and new immigrants.

Yitzhak Rabin belonged to the generation of 1948, the year of the establishment of the State of Israel. He was born in 1922 in Jerusalem during the British Mandate. The trajectory of his life was marked by fighting and sacrifices since before the creation of the state.

Rabin enlisted in the *Palmach*, participated in the incursion of the *Palmach* units into Syria at the side of the Allied forces. He was among the commanders of the action to free *Ma'apilim* (illegal immigrants) from the detainees' camp in Atlit and was imprisoned in 1946 on the "black Sabbath." Rabin fought as a commander in the War of Independence, was responsible for the supply of convoys to besieged Jerusalem, was head of the "Harel" Brigade and commanded the battles for the liberation of Jerusalem and of its access route. He was the operation's officer of the southern front and one of the commanders of the battles for the liberation of the Negev and Eilat. He was the youngest ever major general and was head of the Training Division as well as of the Operations Division, head of the Northern Command, deputy chief-of-staff and finally the chief-of-staff who led the IDF to glorious victory in the Six-Day War, liberated Jerusalem and united it as Israel's eternal capital.

After his retirement from the army, he was appointed Israel's ambassador in Washington, and after the resignation of Golda Meir as Prime Minister, following the Yom Kippur War, he was elected leader of the Labor Party and

Prime Minister of Israel. He served as Prime Minister during the most difficult period that followed the Yom Kippur War.

During his term in office, the IDF was rehabilitated and its military strength restored. His government negotiated the Interim Agreement with Egypt. As Prime Minister, he opted for an adamant struggle against terror instead of yielding to it, and he took the momentous decision to extricate the hostages of the Air France plane in Entebbe. This was one of the most difficult decisions by an Israeli Prime Minister. The success of this daring and brave operation presented to the entire world a model of uncompromising struggle against terror and raised the status of every Jew in the world.

In April 1977, Rabin resigned and the turnaround occurred — the Likud leader, Menachem Begin, became Prime Minister. Rabin was elected to the Knesset.

In 1984, with the formation of the National Unity Government, Rabin became Defense Minister and had to develop methods of fighting against the *intifada* — a new and unfathomable situation.

In 1992, he was elected Prime Minister and assumed also the post of Defense Minister. Rabin excelled in both war and peace. On the happiest day of his life, when tens of thousands expressed their support for his policy and their admiration for his personality, he was assassinated, and his last day turned out to be a great tragedy in the life of the Jewish people and of the State of Israel. During the last three years of his premiership, Rabin produced a turnaround in the entire Middle East. He did not leave a testament but left a path to follow, and the last song he sang was the "Song of Peace." He received a copy of the song's lyrics and put them into his pocket. When he was shot, the assassin's bullet pierced him and the song.

The peace process was the unique expression of Rabin's Government and he was assassinated on the altar of this process. With his assassination, deep grief descended on the Israeli people who were shocked, angry, pained, alarmed and refused to stop crying. 101 delegations arrived from abroad for Rabin's funeral; all the diplomatic representatives in Israel attended it, and there were delegations from Jewish communities and organizations from all over the world. All those who participated — kings, counts, heads of state, ministers — from all parts of the world, came to honor the memory of this glorious son of Israel, the

A group of foreign dignitaries at the funeral of Yitzhak Rabin
From left to right: Jacques Chirac, French president; John Major, British prime minister; Prince Charles; Felipe Gonzales, Spanish prime minister and President of the European Union; Helmut Kohl, German chancellor; Victor Chernomirdin, Russian prime minister, Boutros Boutros-Ghali, secretary-general of the United Nations; Hosni Mubarak, Egyptian president; Mrs. Hillary Clinton and Bill Clinton, U.S. President

statesman, politician, leader, commander, fighter and friend. At his fresh grave stood the leaders of the United States and of Europe, of Asia and of Africa, of Australia and of our region. They came first of all to honor Yitzhak Rabin, but also to honor the State of Israel which changed under Rabin's leadership and gained much appreciation throughout the world.

On November 6, 1995, I attended the funeral of Yitzhak Rabin on Mount Herzl in Jerusalem. The eulogies were by: Ezer Weizman, President of Israel; Shimon Peres, acting Prime Minister of Israel; Bill Clinton, President of the United States; King Hussein of Jordan; Hosni Mubarak, President of Egypt; Victor Chernomirdin, the Prime Minister of the Russian Federation; Boutros Boutros-Ghali, secretary-general of the United Nations; Felipe Gonzales, Prime Minister of Spain and President of the European Union; Shimon Sheves, former director-general of the prime minister's office; Noah Ben-Artzi-Philosoph, Yitzhak Rabin's granddaughter; Eitan Haber, director of Yitzhak Rabin's bureau and his adviser. All those who eulogized him, expressed deep admiration for him.

Peres called him at the grave "My older brother, hero of peace." President Clinton eulogized Rabin with emotion and said: "The world has lost one of its great men, a fighter for the freedom of his people and for peace." He quoted from the Bible and said: "When our father Abraham was to sacrifice his son Yitzhak, God saved his life. This time, God took Yitzhak from us." He concluded his eulogy with the Hebrew words: "Shalom, Chaver." (Goodbye, friend). Thousands visited Rabin's grave and 250,000 persons participated at a gathering in Tel-Aviv in his memory.

The Government established a state inquiry commission on the Rabin assassination. The commission was composed of: Meir Shamgar, former president of the Supreme Court — Chairman; Zvi Zamir, former head of the *Mossad*, and Ariel Rosen-Zvi, the dean of the Law Faculty at Tel-Aviv University — members.

The President of the state, Ezer Weizman, empowered Shimon Peres to form a new government which Peres presented to the Knesset on November 22: himself — Prime Minister and Defense Minister, and Ehud Barak — Foreign Minister. 62 members of the Knesset voted for the new Government, eight against, 38 — abstained, 12 were absent.

On December 5, indictments were presented in court against Yigal Amir, his brother Chagai Amir and Dror Adani for the assassination of Yitzhak Rabin. On December 19, the trial opened. Yigal Amir was found guilty and sentenced to life imprisonment, and in addition, six years in prison for the wounding of the security man. Chagai Amir and Dror Adani were also found guilty of conspiracy to murder the prime minister. Chagai Amir was sentenced to 12 years and Dror Adani to seven years.

In the meantime, on January 20, 1996, elections took place in the West Bank: Yasser Arafat was elected president of the Palestinian Authority and a Palestinian Council was elected.

On February 25, 1996, a suicide bomber blew up a bus at the junction of the Yafo and Sarei Israel streets, near the central bus station in Jerusalem: 25

persons were killed in the attack — nine soldiers and 16 civilians. 48 were wounded: 35 civilians and 13 soldiers.

One hour after the attack in Jerusalem, another occurred at the soldiers' hitchhiking stop at the Ashkelon crossroads. A terrorist, wearing a soldier's uniform, blew up explosives, hidden on his body, among a group of soldiers waiting at the stop. A female sergeant was killed and 29 persons injured — 17 soldiers and 12 civilians. A week later, another suicide bomber exploded a bomb in Jerusalem in a bus at the junction of Yafo and Shlomzion Hamalka streets in Jerusalem: 18 persons were killed — 16 civilians and two soldiers, seven were injured. The following day, a Palestinian terrorist killed himself at a crossing passage at the junction of the Dizengoff and King George streets in Tel-Aviv: 14 were killed — 13 civilians and one soldier. 179 were injured, three of them soldiers.

Since the signing of the Declaration of Principles with the PLO on September 13, 1993, until March 1996, 27 civilians and 28 soldiers were murdered in Judea, Samaria and Gaza, and 107 civilians and 39 soldiers within Israel itself.

On March 13, 1996, a conference to fight terrorism was convened in Sharm el-Sheikh, at the initiative of President Clinton. The host of the conference was Hosni Mubarak, President of Egypt. Heads of State from 29 countries attended, among them Presidents Clinton, Chirac and Mubarak, King Hussein, Chancellor Kohl and Prime Ministers Chernomirdin, Major and Peres. 13 Arab states were represented at the conference. Syria refused to participate.

A new atmosphere of fear was created on the Israeli street. The feeling of personal security was, without precedent, at its nadir, and the elections for the Knesset were set for May 29, 1996. It was the first time direct elections for prime minister, separate from those for the Knesset, were to take place in Israel. The two candidates for prime minister were Shimon Peres, the leader of the Labor Party, and Benjamin Netanyahu, elected in 1993 as leader of the Likud Party.

Netanyahu exploited to its maximum the new sense of insecurity and adopted the election slogans "Secure peace," and "an all out fight against terrorism," adding to it the rallying cry: "Peres will divide Jerusalem." Despite Peres' vigorous denials, Netanyahu's messages struck roots. The great majority of the Jewish population was not ready for a situation in which, despite receiving territories from Israel, the Palestinians were blowing up buses and murdering innocent people on city streets. The attacks, which occurred after the Oslo Agreements, influenced the elections, and Netanyahu won with 1,501,023 votes, against 1,471,566 votes received by Peres. A very small difference, but in a democracy one vote, too, determines.

On June 17, 1996, the 14th Knesset convened and next day, the new government was sworn in: Benjamin Netanyahu — Prime Minster, David Levy — Foreign Minister, Yitzhak Mordechai — Defense Minister. The new Government had the support of a coalition of political parties with a majority of 62 Knesset members out of 120.

TREMENDOUS ACHIEVEMENTS AND DISTURBING PHENOMENA

In the political field, the Likud Government inherited the Oslo Agreement. In the security domain, it was faced with continual acts of terror. In general, the new government received a state in which Israelis and Jews everywhere could be proud. Despite the wars and terror, political and economic boycotts, the State of Israel has to its credit tremendous achievements and great successes in all fields, more than many countries that are bigger, stronger, richer and older than Israel, and which are eager to learn from its experiences.

Israel is proud of a wonderful army — the IDF is still considered the strongest army in our region and among the best in the world. But 20,333 men and women have been killed since the struggle for its independence.

1,592 persons were killed in the struggle for the establishment of the State. 4,783 lost their lives in Israel's War of Independence — from November 29, 1947, when the U.N. Partition Resolution was adopted, until July 20, 1949, when the last armistice agreement was signed. 1,151 were killed until the Sinai campaign in October 1956, and 231 in the campaign itself. After that, 1,001 were killed until the Six-Day War in June 1967, and 776 in the war itself. 2,069 were killed until the Yom Kippur War in October 1973, and 2,687 during the war. 2,020 were killed until the Lebanon War (Peace of Galilee operation) in June 1982, and 1,217 during the war. 2,806 soldiers on active service, in the reserves and regular army as well as members of the security forces were killed since the end of the Lebanon War until March 31, 1998.

Israel is among the eight states which have a satellite in the orbit, and is considered as one of the nine states with nuclear capabilities. In spite of Israel not yet having permanent borders and being still in a state of war with two of her neighbors, and despite the existing danger to the lives of Israelis as a result of the continuous terror and the suffering it causes to many families, Israel's security apparatus has the situation under control and there is no danger to the existence of the state or to its citizens as a collective.

Israel was admitted to the family of nations and, celebrating its 50th anniversary, maintained diplomatic relations with 163 states on all the continents, among them seven Arab countries — Egypt, Jordan, Mauritania, Morocco, Oman, Qatar and Tunisia — and was in a peace process with the Palestinians.

Israel is one of ten states (out of the 189 U.N. members) that is a focus of international attention. It is recognized as one of the states best organized to extend help quickly and efficiently to countries affected by disaster — such as extrication and rescue operations, supply of food and medicines, and the setting up of field hospitals (by the IDF).

Israel's economic growth is unceasing. The desert has flourished; a wonderful modern agricultural development has been reached, envied in the entire world; a magnificent, sophisticated and prosperous industry has been set up; and an exemplary high-tech economy has been developed. By means of heavy investment, hundreds of thousands of working places have been created. Productivity has been increased and industrial exports have risen; the annual per capita national product in Israel is $US 18,000. Israel is considered among the 20 leading states in the world for standard-of-living and quality of life of her citizens.

Israel ensures its citizens full democracy, a developed judicial system, a lively religious life and advanced health services. Life expectancy is among the highest in the world. The country has reached enormous achievements in the fields of education, culture and science. Israel has a well developed traffic system and the tourism rises and falls with the barometer of the peace process.

Despite economic and social difficulties, the population of Israel grew from 806,000 in 1948 to 6.4 million in 2000. The Jewish population in Israel has grown from 650,000 on the day of the state's establishment to over five million. The State of Israel has offered a national home and security to hundreds of thousands of Holocaust survivors, to Jews from lands of hardship and from totalitarian states, and to new immigrants from the free world. 2.7 million immigrants have arrived in Israel. According to statistical data published by Israel, the immigration, since the establishment of the State in 1948, consisted of: 59% from European countries, 19% from Africa, 15% from Asia, 7% from the United States and Oceania. The absorption of the immigrants from over a hundred countries has in general been an unprecedented success.

Despite Israel's extraordinary accomplishments, disturbing phenomena cannot be ignored. Somewhere, in the course of time, in the euphoria of our marvelous deeds, seeds of trouble were sown; together with moments of heroism, victories and achievements, we experienced also a reduction in motivation and a lowering of moral standards.

There exists a wild chase after materialistic values and private gains. The old modest pioneer conduct of life has disappeared and cleared the way for ostentation. Too many pursue a life of pomp and luxury from which many "white collar" offenses derive.

The newspapers and electronic news media are full of information about "Pandora's boxes" in governmental and public corporations and companies, about the closing of enterprises and plants which were once profitable and supplied work and sustenance to tens of thousands of workers. Daily we are shocked by stories on the rise in delinquency and crime, bribes and corruption, assaults on elderly people and violence within family — murder of women by their husbands, and abuse of children. In addition, we are witness to tensions between rich and poor, left and right and cultural conflicts between religious and secular people.

The high unemployment affects the social fabric. According to the data of the Central Bureau of Statistics, in 2000 the number of unemployed was higher than at any time since 1948 — 223,000, in a country where a quarter of a million foreign workers are employed. Parallel to the increasing abundance in the country, there is real hardship: in 1999, 1,133,900 persons, among them 509,700 children, lived below the poverty line.

The struggle to climb up the ladder is, unfortunately, conducted first of all on the backs of the ordinary citizens: whoever flouts more the public order and the laws of the state, is more admired as a "proletarian leader."

A general strike of the entire public sector, ignoring a court order, caused the state 200 million shekels worth of damage. In the enlightened world, a general strike of the whole public service, and especially a strike causing such grave damage, is a last resort, after an impasse in negotiations and all measures having been exhausted. In Israel, a general strike is often the first step, the opening in a struggle.

Injustice in the social domain, corruption in the economic field, moral degradation, political chicanery and missed opportunities in foreign policy — are irritating and angering. A failure in the security field is burning and painful.

In an exercise at the training base in Tze'elim, on November 5, 1992, five soldiers were killed and six injured. According to the London "Sunday Times," this was a top secret exercise, in preparation for an operation to liquidate Saddam Hussein. A largely publicized affair was also the one related to the killing, in 1984, of two Palestinian terrorists, captured alive, by Israel's security services. Embarrassing mistakes and operational failures also occurred in the *Mossad.*

After the murder of the Israeli sportsmen at the Olympics in Munich, in 1972, by the Palestinian "Black September" terrorist organization, the Israeli Government decided to liquidate those involved in the criminal attack. A chase after Ali Hassan Salameh, the "Red Prince" — who was among those who had planned the slaughter — led to the Norwegian village of Lillehammer. In July 1973, a Moroccan waiter, Ahmed Bushiki, was shot there and killed by mistake. Six Israeli agents were caught and brought to trial. Three of them were found guilty.

In April 1991 in Cyprus, an elderly policeman arrested four Israeli agents who had tapped in to a telephone line of the Iranian embassy in Nicosia, and seven years later, a woman — unable to sleep one night — brought about the capture of five Israeli agents who tried to install a wiretap in a building near Bern, Switzerland, where a senior *Hizbullah* activist was living.

Then came the attempt, in September 1997, by two *Mossad* agents, bearing false Canadian passports, to kill in Amman, Jordan, the head of the political bureau of the *Hamas,* Haled Mashal. They tried to poison him and were caught. It was really foolish of the higher echelons to approve this act. After it failed, Israel was compelled — in order to put an end to the affair — to help save

Mashal's life by supplying an antidote to the lethal venom, that had been injected into his body. Israel also had to comply with King Hussein's demand to free from jail in Israel Sheikh Yassin, the founder, spiritual leader and military commander of the *Hamas* movement. Together with him other Palestinian prisoners were also freed.

From the prime minister's bureau it was leaked that Sheikh Yassin was in any case gravely ill. But when Yassin arrived in Gaza, the "gravely ill" Sheikh suddenly recuperated, took the command of the *Hamas* and began to travel to Arab capitals to raise funds and call for *Jihad* against Israel. In order to restore Israeli-Jordanian relations to normal, Dani Yatom, head of the *Mossad,* was compelled to resign, and he was replaced by Ephraim Halevy, a step welcomed by King Hussein.

As a former member of the *Mossad,* I was especially shocked by the Yehuda Gil affair. Gil had worked at the *Mossad* since 1970 and retired in 1989. A year later, he was again employed, on a special contract, and produced information which — he claimed — was received from a Syrian agent. It turned out to be false. Its contents had been invented in the feverish mind of their author. Gil's trial opened on December 17, 1997, behind closed doors, and in March 1999, he was convicted of delivering false information to his commanders in the *Mossad* on Syria, and for theft of *Mossad* money, and was sentenced to five years of imprisonment.

However, all the failures — though very painful — are dwarfed by the tremendous successes of the *Mossad,* which brought it the reputation of being the "best intelligence service in the world," even if it is not quite so. I will mention a few of its major achievements: obtaining a copy of Nikita Khrushchev's speech at the 20th Congress of the Soviet Communist Party in Moscow at which he denounced Joseph Stalin's crimes; the defection to Israel of an Iraqi pilot with a Mig-21 plane; locating Adolf Eichmann in Argentina and his abduction; the infiltration of the Israeli spy, Eli Cohen, into Syria's top leadership; the intelligence assistance that enabled "Operation Jonathan" to free the hijacked passengers on the Air France plane to Entebbe, Uganda; the secret transfer to Israel of the Ethiopian Jews; the success of the operation to liquidate all the terrorists responsible for the slaughter of the sportsmen in Munich; and so on.

Abu-Jihad, Arafat's deputy for military affairs and head of operations of *Fatah*, was liquidated in Tunisia. Fathi Shkaki, the leader of the *Islamic Jihad*, was shot dead in Malta. In the Gaza Strip, Yihye Ayash, nicknamed the "engineer," was killed by an exploding cellular phone. Ayash had produced many of the bombs used by Palestinian terrorists in attacks against Israelis, killing at least 51 persons and injuring 300.

A survey, performed three days before the 50th anniversary of Israel, showed that 49% of the interviewed replied that their mood on the eve of the 50th Independence Day was "very good" and 35% replied "good enough." 46% were of the opinion that Israel's achievements during the 50 years of its existence were "very good" and 49% — "good enough." It meant that the great majority of the people was very satisfied with the state's achievements, and the country prepared to celebrate the 50th Independence Day with the slogan: "together with pride, together with hope." This was the feeling on the national level; on the personal level this day will remain engraved in my memory as a very sad one.

My younger brother, Joseph, together with whom I survived the Holocaust, had fallen ill with cancer three years earlier. He underwent surgery and received chemotherapy treatments. He fought his illness heroically and was always optimistic — while reminding me from time to time that every day we have lived since the Holocaust was given to us as a gift from heaven. On the 50th Independence Day, when I asked him how he was feeling, his mood was different. For the first time he said: "I feel a deterioration." Three days later he passed away and I dedicate this book to his memory and to that of my parents and brothers murdered in the Holocaust. May their memory be for a blessing!

The late Joseph Weinstein, Aba Gefen's brother

My brother Joseph arrived in Palestine as a lad of 19, in 1946. He joined the "Irgun Zva'i Leumi" (the Zionist Revisionist underground military group) and later served in the IDF as an officer in the navy. He concluded his military service as a major in an anti-aircraft unit.

He completed his studies that had been interrupted by the Holocaust. He succeeded as a lawyer, opened a well-respected office and raised a beautiful family. He was a man with a very good heart and personal charm. He loved people and was concerned with the welfare of others. Everything he did, he did with sincerity, devotion and loyalty. He was a serious person, intelligent, modest, gentle and pleasant. He was a noble person who combined the human spirit with the spirit of law and was exemplary in human relations. He was not granted to celebrate joyfully the 50th anniversary of the state on which the national mood was defined by some as exalted.

As a Holocaust survivor, I was fortunate to live in the State of Israel whose 50-year history is no doubt the most dramatic, exciting and thrilling one of the

Aba Gefen and his wife Frida with their entire family:
Daughter Ruhama, her husband Sol Goldstein and their children: Benjamin, Rachel, David.
Son Meir, his wife Shelli, born Kochav, and their children: Michal, Sharon, Ido.
Son Yehuda, his wife Nurit, born Ilovitch, and their children: Jonathan, Lyn, Ophir.

20th century. I was privileged to act in this state, in its name and on its behalf, and to raise a beautiful family which fills me with great pride and joy.

On the national level, my dream is that the tremendous forces be reinvigorated within us to give the state a new momentum and to return to it the image it had when it came into being.

In his speech during the celebrations of the 50th anniversary, the President of the State, Ezer Weizman, stressed the need for unity and national soul-searching. Such an Israel will again be a center of attraction for the Jews of the Diaspora and a source of pride and inspiration. Israel, living in peace, security and unity will also be the best guarantee that Auschwitz, Treblinka and Majdanek will remain only terrible memories of the past, never to be repeated.

WYE PLANTATION

With the election of Benjamin Netanyahu as Prime Minister, the attacks against IDF soldiers and officers in southern Lebanon continued, from ambushes of the *Hizbullah*, in coordination with Syria. The next day after the elections, four soldiers were killed and seven injured. Ten days later, five more IDF soldiers were killed in an ambush and eight injured. One more week passed, three soldiers were killed, two injured.

In August 1998, revealing superior intelligence and operational skill, the IDF succeeded in killing, from a helicopter, Hassam Al-Amin, the chief of operations of the "Amal" movement in the western sector of the security zone. But this did not deter "Amal" from continuing terror acts, just as the liquidation from a helicopter in 1992, of Abbas Mosawi, the secretary-general of the *Hizbullah*, had not deterred that organiztion. They were also not discouraged by the expulsion from Israel of the 415 *Hamas* and *Islamic Jihad* activists to Lebanon in December 1992, by the IDF's "Operation Accountability" in July 1993 and "Operation Grapes of Wrath" in April 1996.

In the West Bank, too, the wave of terror by the *Hamas* and the *Islamic Jihad* continued, presumably in coordination with the Palestinian Authority. Netanyahu hesitated three months until he met Yasser Arafat. When they met on September 4, 1996, at the Erez checkpoint, they declared, at a joint press conference, their commitment to the Israeli-Palestinian Interim Agreement and their decision to implement it.

At the end of September, a second entrance to the Western Wall tunnel was opened in the Islamic quarter of Jerusalem. In response, there were demonstrations and disturbances on the part of Palestinians and Israeli leftists.

Dozens of Palestinians were killed and hundreds injured. 12 Israeli soldiers and one civilian were killed, 58 injured, in exchanges of fire with Palestinians, including their policemen. The Israeli patrons of the Oslo Accord did not expect that the thousands of guns, delivered by Israel to the Palestinians, would be used against IDF soldiers. Yitzhak Rabin had warned that the whole peace process would collapse the moment those guns were turned against us. Nevertheless, the peace process continued even under the Likud Government.

At the beginning of December, Madeleine Albright was appointed Secretary of State of the United States and, on December 13, Netanyahu spoke on the telephone with Arafat and repeated his commitment to the signed agreements.

On January 5, 1997, Netanyahu met with Arafat and again ten days later when they initialled the "Hebron Protocol." The same day, the Israeli Government approved the Protocol: 11 ministers voted in favor and seven against. The Knesset approved it next day by a majority of 87 votes, with 17 votes against and one abstention. Next day, on January 17, the Protocol was signed. The Protocol determined the evacuation of Hebron, the redeployment of the IDF in the city, and reciprocity in the implementation of commitments.

On March 13, a Jordanian soldier shot to death seven school girls from Beit Shemesh and injured a teacher and five pupils who had come to visit the Naharayim enclave under Jordanian rule. The soldier was sentenced to life imprisonment. King Hussein did not limit himself to condemning the act: in an extraordinary gesture, he traveled to Israel for a condolence visit with the bereaved families.

Around that time, the government decided to build a Jewish neighborhood at "Har-Homa" (Jebel Abu Ghneim) south of East Jerusalem, and next to it a residential neighborhood for young Arab couples. This decision raised much anger in the world, particularly in the Arab states. The reaction of the Palestinians was restrained but they interrupted the talks with Israel.

On March 20, there was an explosion at Cafe Apropos in Tel-Aviv: three women were killed and six people injured. Four months later, on July 30, two suicide bombers blew themselves up at the Mahane Yehuda market place in Jerusalem: 16 people were killed, 178 injured. The Mahane Yehuda market had long been a terror target. Already in November 1968, a booby-trapped vehicle placed there blew up, killing 12 persons and injuring 70. In June 1978, explosives blew up in a shopping basket causing two deaths; 37 were injured. A similar explosion killed one person and injured 15 in May 1990. In January 1997, a 16-year-old boy deliberately drove a car into a store in the market, killing one person and injuring six. On September 4, 1997, three suicidal terrorists killed five people at the Ben Yehuda mall in Jerusalem.

The government approved a series of decisions for dealing with terrorism, but the first stage of the IDF's redeployment was executed, with international presence, in Hebron. Towards the execution of the second stage of withdrawal, Israel drew up a detailed list of demands for implementation by the Palestinians, in the framework of the "Hebron Protocol." At the top of its demands was the convening of the Palestinian National Council (PNC) to ratify the abolition of the paragraphs in the Palestinian Covenant calling for the destruction of Israel.

In addition, Israel demanded from the Palestinian Authority to wage war against the terrorist infrastructure; to extradite wanted terrorists to Israel; not to free the murderers being detained by the Palestinian Authority, usually brought to a quick field trial but released with the same speed; to collect illegal arms and to punish those carrying them; and to detain the *Hamas* activists.

Israel also demanded from the Palestinians to reduce the number of policemen which had reached that of 38,000, instead of 24,000 as stipulated in the Interim Agreement; to present to Israel, for examination and approval, the complete rosters of those enlisted into the Palestinian police; to stop any activity by the Palestinian Authority in Jerusalem, both political and security; to put an end to the incitement to violence against Israel in the Palestinian official news media (including radio and television) and educational institutions; to dismiss employees of the Palestinian Authority, mosque preachers and others inciting to violence against Israel, to put them on trial and punish them.

Despite the gap between the positions of Israel and the Palestinian Authority, discussions began within the Government of Israel on the principles of the permanent settlement from which the perimeter of the second withdrawal would derive.

Madeleine Albright met with Netanyahu in Paris and Arafat in London, and made it clear to them that she expected a serious second withdrawal from Netanyahu, and from Arafat the fulfillment of his commitments.

In Netanyahu's talks with President Clinton, on January 20, 1998,

Netanyahu told the President that Israel's withdrawal could only be 9% and it would begin after the Palestinians had fulfilled their security commitments. Clinton agreed to the IDF's withdrawal in stages, parallel to the gradual implementation of the Palestinian commitments in the Oslo and Hebron agreements, but expressed the American view that the second withdrawal should be 13% and that there should also be a third withdrawal from the West Bank, divided — according to the Interim Agreement — into three areas:

Area A — to be the municipal area of six cities: Jenin, Nablus, Tul Karem, Kalkiliya, Ramallah and Bethlehem. The civil and security authority in this area to be in the hands of the Palestinian Authority.

Area B — to comprise almost all the 450 towns and villages where Palestinians live. In this area, there would be a separation of authorities: The Palestinians would have the authority to run their lives while Israel would have the security authority which comprises the security of the Israelis and the war against terror. IDF forces and the various Israeli security arms would be entitled to enter at any time in any place in this area.

Area C — to comprise all the areas not included in areas A and B, which amount to about 70% of the West Bank. In this area are included all the Jewish settlements, all the IDF installations and the areas bordering with Jordan.

Netanyahu met with King Hussein in Eilat and with President Mubarak in Cairo, and on May 4 he met in London with Madeleine Albright and Yasser Arafat, who declared that exactly a year from that date, on May 4, 1999, he would proclaim the establishment of an independent Palestinian state, with East Jerusalem as its capital. The London meeting did not advance the peace process and the contacts continued in Washington and New York.

In New York, Netanyahu participated in the "Salute to Israel" march on Israel's 50th anniversary and, in his address, he stated that the Israelis alone would decide on their security, hinting at the letter he received from Secretary of State Warren Christopher, on the day the "Hebron Protocol" was signed. In his letter, Christopher promised to take into account, in the framework of the IDF redeployment, the security needs of Israel. In Israel's interpretation, she alone would determine the perimeter of her withdrawals in accordance with her security needs.

A disagreement with the Americans, or a warning by them of an eventual "re-assessment" of policy, need not frighten or worry, and a withdrawal should not be a result of American pressure, but only the product of a clear Israeli interest. Israel had already in the past had disagreements with American administrations: on the "Rogers Plan," the "re-assessment" of Richard Nixon and the "Reagan Plan." When Israel stood firm on its vital interests, the Americans finally accepted her position and the friendship between the countries and its leaders continued to be strong.

Whether as a result of American security interests or deriving from the strength of the American Jewish community, Israel enjoys a deep support by the American population. The United States stands at Israel's side as a friend and supporter, and this is one of Israel's important assets, a source of strength and inspiration. The United States knows that the security interests dictate Israel's borders to be beyond the frontier she had before the Six-Day War. It also understands well Israel's refusal to hand over to the Palestinian Authority additional territories as long as the Authority does not fight terror.

On August 20, 1998, it was published that Israel presented the Palestinians with an official document on a second withdrawal of 13%. The same day, Rabbi Shlomo Ra'anan was murdered in the neighborhood of Tel Rumeida in Hebron. After two months, a Palestinian murdered Corporal Michal Adato in the village of Tomer in the Jordan Valley when she got off the bus for a Sabbath leave from her officers course, and a few days later, two Palestinians murdered Itamar Doron from the village of Ora, near Jerusalem, and gravely injured Ilan Mazon from Aminadav while they were bathing in the Ora well. The peace process, however, continued, and President Clinton announced that at the beginning of October, Madeleine Albright would arrive in the region, and in the middle of October, Netanyahu and Arafat would arrive in Washington, together with their teams, for intensive negotiations, Camp David style, with the purpose of achieving an agreement on the second withdrawal.

Albright arrived in Israel on October 6. The next day, she met at the Erez checkpoint with Netanyahu and Arafat. During that meeting, Netanyahu came to Arafat's bureau for lunch. It was the first time that an Israeli prime minister entered into the area of the autonomy and had lunch at the table of the chairman of the Palestinian Authority. After lunch, Albright held a press conference, with Netanyahu and Arafat at her sides. She spoke of a new atmosphere of collaboration in the talks and said she was more than satisfied. She announced that on October 15, a triple Summit meeting, Clinton-Netanyahu-Arafat, would take place at Wye Plantation, near Washington.

During the very days of discussions at Wye Plantation, a Palestinian terrorist, Salem Sarsur, threw two grenades at the central bus station in Beer Sheva, injuring 64 persons. It wasn't the first terrorist attack by Sarsur: he murdered Rabbi Ra'anan in Tel Rumeida and injured in Hebron, on Yom Kippur, 14 soldiers and border guards.

Towards the end of the Summit at Wye Plantation, King Hussein — who was in hospital for treatment of his cancer illness — arrived there, at the request of the Americans, and met separately with Netanyahu and Arafat to convince them to reach an agreement. At the end of the Summit, on October 23, the Wye

Signing of the Wye Plantation Summit Agreement.
From left to right: Yasser Arafat, King Hussein, Bill Clinton, Benjamin Netanyahu

Plantation agreement was signed in Washington by Clinton, Netanyahu and Arafat, in the presence of King Hussein.

In this agreement, Israel agreed to a second withdrawal of 13%, and the transfer of the land by Israel was to be in stages, parallel to the implementation of the Palestinian commitments. It was agreed that an Israeli-Palestinian committee would discuss the perimeters of a third withdrawal, while Israel insisted on 1% only.

The Palestinians, on their part, promised to collect the illegal arms in the territories and not to tolerate any terror ("zero terror," in the words of the agreement). They committed themselves to an efficient security collaboration in the framework of the struggle against terrorism and for the crystallization of a detailed program on this subject to be presented to the Americans. They also agreed to a control system for the execution of their commitments.

A day after Netanyahu returned to Israel from the Summit, a new round of bloodshed erupted in the territories: Daniel Vargas of Kiryat Arba was murdered as well as Muhamad Zelmut of the village of Beit Purik. Not much time passed before in the neighborhood of Abu Tor in Jerusalem, another Palestinian, Osama Natche, was murdered. The Palestinian police caught the murderers of Daniel Vargas, who confessed to having also assassinated Itamar Doron at the Ora well.

A suicidal terrorist tried to blow himself up in a booby-trapped car next to a bus with 35 children from Kfar Darom. He crashed into a military jeep and Sergeant Alexei Neikov was killed. The jeep's driver, Ziv Chazanovsky, whose quick move away from the booby-trapped car saved the children, was injured. This time, the Palestinian police reacted vigorously: it detained tens of *Hamas* members, put Sheikh Yassin under house arrest and carried out a search at his home. When released, Yassin declared at a crowded gathering: "We will continue the armed struggle until we establish the Palestinian state with its capital in Jerusalem."

In Jerusalem, two suicide bombers of the *Islamic Jihad* tried to carry out an attack in the Mahane Yehuda market. The two were killed. 28 persons were injured. Only by miracle were no Israelis killed. Abu Mazen, on his part, expressed support for the violent protest acts which broke out in the territories to demand the release by Israel of the Palestinian prisoners.

At Wye Plantation, it was agreed that Israel would release 750 Palestinian prisoners who took part in terrorist activities but did not have blood on their hands. The Palestinians, on their part, promised to reduce the number of policemen, which had been agreed on at 24,000. The Palestinians promised to put in jail 30 out of 36 Palestinians wanted by Israel as suspected in murder of Israelis — all then at liberty, some even serving in the police. Israel, on its part, renounced its demand to arrest the commander of the Palestinian police, Colonel Razi Jabali, suspected of having ordered terror acts in Israel. But it insisted in its demand for the arrest of head-terrorist Muhamad Def, the commander of the military arm of the *Hamas*, who had masterminded the attack on the bus with the children from Kfar Darom.

At Wye Plantation, the two parties confirmed again their commitment to deepening their economic relations, and it was agreed to set up a joint industrial park at the Karni checkpoint. Israel agreed to implement a previous agreement to create two corridors for free safe passage between the Gaza Strip and the West Bank: one — from Gaza to Hebron, the other — from Gaza to Ramallah. Israel confirmed its commitment to make possible the opening of a maritime port in Gaza, and both sides reached an agreement on the conditions of inaugurating a Palestinian airport in Gaza. One month later, the airport was inaugurated under Israeli security supervision. The Palestinians considered the opening of their international airport as a first step on the way to sovereignty. It was also decided to form a joint Israel-Palestinian-American committee to examine the phenomenon of anti-Israeli incitement in the Palestinian educational system and in the news media. Another committee would be activated to advance contacts between the Israeli and Palestinian societies.

It was agreed to refrain from unilateral steps to change the status of the West Bank and the Gaza Strip. The Palestinians' interpretation of this paragraph was that Israel would postpone projects for the enlarging of the settlements. In Israel's interpretation, the Palestinians would postpone steps for the unilateral proclamation of an independent Palestinian state. Another paragraph in the agreement established that both parties would begin accelerated negotiations on the permanent status and would make a supreme effort to achieve an agreement until May 4, 1999.

As for the abolition of the paragraphs in the Palestinian Covenant which call for the destruction of Israel, it was agreed that the Executive Committee of the

PLO and the Palestinian Central Council would reaffirm it, in the presence of President Clinton, at a special assembly in Gaza, to be convened by the PLO Chairman and by the speaker of the Palestinian National Council.

The Israeli Government approved the Wye Plantation agreement on November 11, 1998, by a majority of eight ministers, four against and five abstaining. Netanyahu's opponents criticized him of having yielded on the reconvening of the Palestinian National Council (PNC), the extradition of the wanted terrorists and the enlargement of the settlements. The settlers in Judea, Samaria and Gaza felt they had been abandoned and exposed to a noose tightening around their neck, in exchange of promises which could be violated at any moment, while Israel's withdrawal from 42% of the homeland is irreversible. The leaders of the settlers defined the Wye Plantation agreement as "treason." Demonstrations were organized near the home of the Minister of Defense, Yitzhak Mordechai, and his life was threatened, as was the life of President Weizman.

Photo-montage placards were pasted on the advertisement boards in Jerusalem and Beer Sheva with Netanyahu wearing a kaffiyeh and the inscription "liar." In demonstrations near his home, Netanyahu was called a "traitor" and accused of having become a partner of Arafat, handing over to the enemy part of the homeland. In a Jerusalem Post Office an envelope was found, and in it a bullet of a gun and a letter threatening the life of the prime minister.

At the funeral of Daniel Vargas, the accusation was heard that "Netanyahu abandons the Jews, and it is necessary to bring him down by any means."

When General (Res.) Amnon Lipkin-Shahak, former chief-of-staff and one of the leaders of the newly formed Central Party, visited the Hatikvah neighborhood in Tel-Aviv, somebody shouted at him: "The next bullet will be in your head." In reaction to this, somebody screamed in Kiryat Shmona that "it would be better to murder Ehud Barak." The casualness with which incitements and threats to kill a public figure are uttered is terrible, and it has already caused the murder, by a Jew, of a Jewish prime minister who wished to bring peace. It seems that the soul-searching — national as well as personal — for this abhorrent deed has not yet been completed if after only three years that horrible murder had become a potential precedent, and 60% of the public feared an eventual possible attempt to assassinate Benjamin Netanyahu.

Netanyahu rejected all the arguments against him and presented the Wye Plantation agreement as a most important result that no other Israeli government would have achieved. He, undoubtedly, exaggerated when describing the agreement as an "enormous achievement" and a "victory." The main importance of the agreement was in its being signed and its test would be in its execution. Netanyahu also claimed that the agreement gives Israel the possibility to advance towards a permanent settlement with the Palestinians which will ensure her peace with security. The question is how do the Palestinians see the peace with security for Israel?

On May 14, 1998, the day on which Netanyahu discussed in Washington the perimeters of the second withdrawal, the Palestinians marked — as they do each year — the day of Israel's establishment as the day of "Nakbah" or "day of their disaster."

Throughout the West Bank and the Gaza Strip, including East Jerusalem, mass processions took place to mark 50 years of "the 1948 disaster." A prolonged siren was heard, and Yasser Arafat's pronouncement was broadcast on "the Voice of Palestine" and over loudspeakers. Yasser Abed Rabu, the Palestine Authority's Minister of Information and Culture, announced that a million Palestinians would take part in the parade and added: "The parade of this million is a turning point in the struggle of the Palestinian people which declares by this that it is adamant in its view to realize its rights whatever be the difficulties." The "rights" being nurtured by the term "Nakbah" is the dream of the "return" of the Palestinians to the towns and villages within the State of Israel.

The dream of return is fostered by the Palestinians not only by means of speeches and declarations, but mainly in textbooks in the schools, in the educational system and in summer camps for children for youth. In his address at the U.N. General Assembly, Netanyahu related that the Palestinians continue their hate propaganda against Israel, on television, in programs for children who are called on to become suicidal terrorists.

Even after our peace treaties with Egypt and Jordan and our agreements with the Palestinians, there is still no acceptance of Israel in Arab education. To quote Netanyahu: "No map with the name of Israel, no textbook referring to Israel as a legitimate state, no child is taught that Israel is a permanent neighbor, no Arab

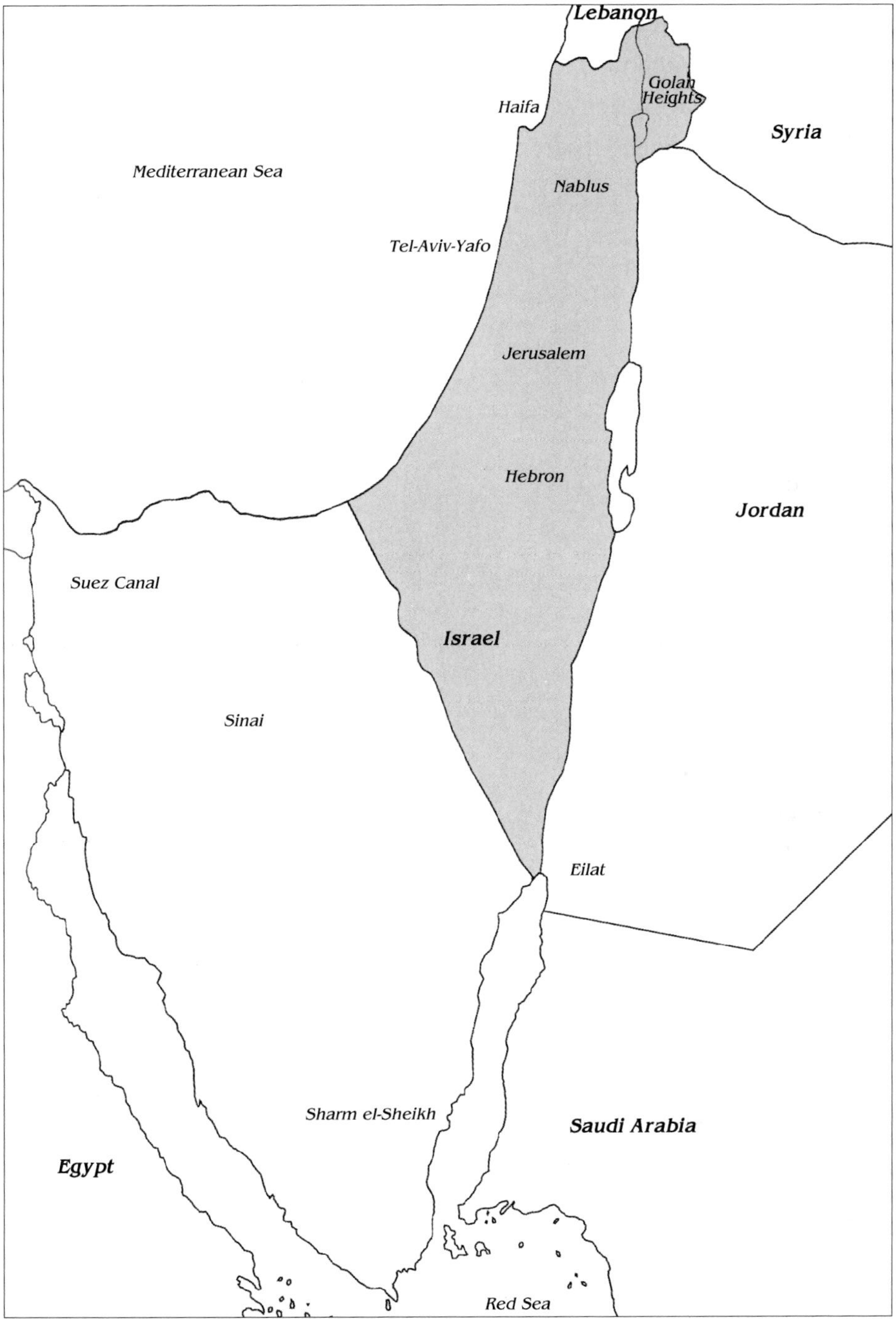

Present map of Israel, since it signed the Peace Treaty with Egypt, in March 1979, and withdrew from the whole Sinai peninsula

religious leader preaches tolerance for the Jewish State, and no newspaper avoids the most venomous incitement against Israel and the Jews."

Even after an Israeli rightist-religious government gave up the dream of the "whole of Eretz Israel," there is no certainty that the Palestinians have renounced their aspiration for the "Whole of Palestine," as envisaged in their Covenant.

YEARNING FOR AN OUTSTANDING LEADER

With the confidence in Netanayhu's ability to lead the country diminishing, the number of those supporting new elections grew, and, in a preliminary vote, 60 members of the Knesset approved, with six voting against, a law to disperse the Knesset. The traditional political frameworks seemed to many as obsolete and crumbling. The existing parties have lost their individuality, they have become similar to each other and there is no essential difference between the traditional right and the classic left. Ideology has come to an end and has been replaced by "chairology," the dream of obtaining a seat [in the Knesset]. The dissatisfaction with both major parties resulted in an impulse to find a third option, on the eve of the 1999 elections — the party called "Center."

Foreign Minister David Levy resigned from the Netanyahu Government and called it a government that is flying nowhere. He finally joined an alignment with the Labor Party and "Meimad," a moderate religious party, and was granted the third place in that alignment, headed by Ehud Barak. Shimon Peres was given second place. As head of the "Peres Peace Center," Peres succeeded in bringing to a gathering in Israel hundreds of guests from around the world, among them heads of state and foreign ministers, past and present, Nobel Prize laureates and heads of economic corporations. All came to Israel to express support for peace.

Netanyahu was accused of cynicism. In the beginning, his position on the withdrawal was of 1%; it went up to 3% and 6% and then came his statement that there wouldn't be a withdrawal of more than 9%. At the same time he presented to Arafat a written document on 13%.

Ehud Barak was Netanyahu's principal rival for the premiership and he had difficulties getting started despite the public's disappointment in Netanyahu; not even after his meeting with Bill Clinton at the White House at a time when the American president refrained from inviting Benjamin Netanyahu to the White House during his visit in the United States.

Over the head of Barak hovered the accusation by the Minister of Justice, Tzahi Hanegbi, accompanied by the slogan "Ehud ran," that he had abandoned the wounded in the disaster during the secret exercise in the training base of Tze'elim. Only with the publication of the report by State Comptroller Eliezer Goldberg, the accusation was revealed as being a calumny.

When Netanyahu returned to Israel with the Wye Plantation agreement, he invited Barak to join a National Unity Government. Barak rejected the proposal, and it was difficult to understand why he did so, in face of the tough negotiations awaiting Israel on the permanent settlement, after Netanyahu gave

Labor Party leader, Ehud Barak, with President Bill Clinton

up at Wye Plantation the dream of the "whole of Eretz Israel." Barak, however, fulfilled his promise to grant the government a "security net" in the Knesset for the approval of the Wye Plantation agreement.

The agreement was approved by a majority of 75 Knesset members, most of them from the Labor opposition, 19 members of the coalition parties voting against, nine abstaining and 17 being absent, among them five coalition ministers.

After Netanyahu achieved the approval of the agreement with the help of the opposition, Barak began to act in anticipation of the Knesset elections, instead of openly questioning the seriousness and sincerity of the Prime Minister. Barak had to limit himself to a statement that, if Netanyahu would act for the implementation of the agreement, he would merit the Labor Party's unreserved support. But while Netanyahu was compelled to swallow the bitter pill of the Oslo agreement signed by a Labor government, then face the accusation that he will be engraved in the history of the Palestinians as the "Ben Gurion of their state," and absorb daily poisoned bullets of hatred and the shouts of "traitor" by a nationalistic crowd besieging his residence, politicians of the Labor Party, supposed to represent peace, hurried, in collaboration with extreme rightists, to prepare for elections.

The government approved (by twelve votes in favor, five against and one abstention) the beginning of the withdrawal according to the Wye Plantation agreement and carried out the first stage, but repeated its demand for reciprocity and decided, with the abstention of one minister, to freeze the implementation of the continuation of the withdrawal until the Palestinians implemented their commitments.

It is to be noted that the demand for reciprocity by the Palestinians was not an invention by Netanyahu concerning the Palestinians. When the Americans exerted pressure on Israel for the unilateral implementation of one of the withdrawal stages from Sinai — in January 1974, following the Yom Kippur War — the then Prime Minister, Yitzhak Rabin, refused to give in to pressure because the Egyptians refused reciprocity. Only seven months later did Henry Kissinger succeed in achieving an agreement by the parties and Israel withdrew to the area of the passes.

Netanyahu demanded from the Palestinians the implementation of their commitments on the collection of the illegal arms, the reduction of the number of their policemen, the stoppage of the incitement and violence against Israel, full collaboration with Israel in the war against terror, and the giving up of their intention to proclaim unilaterally the establishment of a Palestinian state with Jerusalem as its capital.

Netanyahu tried to avoid early elections by a last moment repeat of the proposal to form a national unity government, but Barak again rejected the offer. In order to avoid a no-confidence vote, the Likud decided to vote for new elections. The final vote was: 85 in favor, 27 against, one abstention. The prime minister was absent. May 17, 1999, was fixed as the day of elections for prime minister and the Knesset.

Whoever would be elected prime minister, would be faced with crucial issues on three fronts: Palestinian, Lebanese and Syrian.

On the Palestinian front — the permanent borders, the distribution of the water resources, the settlements in Judea, Samaria and Gaza, the problem of the 1948 refugees and the issue of Jerusalem which — according to U.N. resolution 181 of November 29, 1947 — should be a corpus separatum. It was Arab aggression in 1948 that prevented its realization, and today, Jerusalem is, and will remain, an open city, under the authority of a single administration, which is indigenous, not foreign. Israel is deeply sensitive to universal interests and does not claim exclusive jurisdiction over the holy places of Christianity and Islam. It is Israel's policy that the Moslem and Christian holy places always be under the responsibility of those who hold them sacred.

Jerusalem is today a city where complete religious freedom and protection of holy places are guaranteed, a city where there is freedom of movement within it, to it and from it, for members of all faiths, including nationals of countries still claiming to be at war with Israel.

In the course of history, Jerusalem has known many rulers. But only for the Jews, three times in history, has it been the capital of the nation living in this land. Until the destruction of the First Temple it was the capital of the kingdom of David and his successors. Until the destruction of the Second Temple it was again the capital of the Jewish people. In 1948, it became once more the capital of a Jewish State. At all other times, Jerusalem was ruled by foreigners, who treated it as a provincial town: Babylonians, Greeks, Romans, Byzantines,

Persians, Arabs, Crusaders, Ayyubids and Mamluks, Ottomans and British, and, between 1948 and 1967, as I have alreday mentioned, a part of the city was ruled by Jordan from the Hashemite capital in Amman.

The Jews of Jerusalem of today are the inhabitants with the longest unbroken historical association with it. Their memory of it is recorded in the Bible, the Mishnah (collection of laws) and the Talmud (the Amoraic discussions on the Mishnah), in prayer and poetry. Once every year, on the ninth day of the month of Av, the Jewish people fast and mourn the destruction of Jerusalem. On the Seder night and on other festivals they greet one another with: "Next year in Jerusalem!"

The Psalmist sang: "If I forget thee, O Jerusalem, let my right hand wither! Let my tongue cleave to my mouth if I remember thee not, if I prize not Jerusalem above all my joys," and these words of the psalmist are no empty verbiage for the Jewish people, but a living reality, an actual part of their daily awareness.

All the milestones in life, of rejoicing no less than of sorrow, are marked by the anguish of the destruction of Jerusalem. No joy is ever total. Even a wedding ends with the groom breaking a goblet of glass underfoot, to remind him that no Jewish bliss can be perfect because of the ruin of Jerusalem. That ruin was more than the devastation of the holiest of holy places of Judaism, of the national capital. It struck at the very existence of the people.

This bond of Jewish memory of Jerusalem is engraved upon the ancient stones of Jerusalem and structures now being uncovered by archaeologists. Remnants have been revealed of the City of David and of the First and Second Temple periods. The Western Wall of the Second Temple still stands as a focus of Jewish longings for nineteen centuries. The story of Jewish attachment to Jerusalem under alien dominion is of an unremitting struggle to preserve a Jewish presence in it, never allowing the link to be broken.

The Babylonians destroyed the city — 70 years later the Jews were rebuilding it. The Romans destroyed it and changed its name to Aelia Capitolina. The Bar-Kochba revolt, which cost half a million Jewish lives, was a last desperate attempt to oust the Romans and free Jerusalem. The Byzantines denied Jews the right to live in Jerusalem. The Crusaders massacred the Jewish population of the city. Yet, despite embargoes and constraints, Jews maintained a continuous presence in Jerusalem.

The Christian link with Jerusalem is the traditional association of many places with the story of the life and death of Jesus of Nazareth. But for no Church, does Jerusalem represent its world center. Churches with a world center have established it anywhere but in Jerusalem — for instance, the Catholic Church in Rome.

As for Islam, Jerusalem's first encounter with it was in the seventh century and it was also its first encounter with the Arabs who were Islam's apostles and, under its banner, acquired a vast empire from the Persian Gulf to the Atlantic Ocean. Arab Moslems refer to Jerusalem as Al-Quds — the Holy. It is not the holiest of Moslem cities; Mecca and Medina outrank it. But since the Dome of the Rock was built there, it became centrally associated with the developing Islamic tradition in the Holy Land.

But, for the Jews, Jerusalem is the place where the Lord has chosen to establish His Name. It is here that His eyes and heart dwell eternally. Therefore, for three thousand years, Jerusalem has been, and still everlastingly is, for the Jewish people and for no other, the focus of their faith and nationhood, and now has been the center of government of its state for over 50 years.

When the Israeli cabinet decided to close two offices of the Palestinian Authority in the "Orient House" in East Jerusalem, and to transfer them to Abu Dis, east of Jerusalem, this decision by Netanyahu was considered by observers as a sign of pragmatism on his part. At a meeting with the leaders of the American Jewish Committee, Netanyahu said that even on Jerusalem there exists a solution — that the Palestinian capital will be in the neighborhood of Abu Dis where the Palestinian parliament is being built.

As for the 1948 refugees problem, when the War of Independence broke out, the leader of the Palestinian Arabs was the Mufti of Jerusalem, Haj Amin al-Husseini, one of the most fanatical supporters of Hitler. He had organized the anti-Jewish terror in Eretz Israel and had flown to Germany, where he conferred with Hitler, broadcast from Radio Berlin appeals to the Arabs to overthrow the British, organized and recruited espionage teams, mobilized Moslems in East Europe to the Nazi ranks and supported the Nazis' extermination of the Jews. At a rally in Berlin, in November 1943, he declared: "The Germans know how to get rid of the Jews."

He visited Auschwitz, Majdanek and other death camps to study closely the grisly techniques of incineration; he received a promise from the Nazis that a representative of Eichmann would arrive in Jerusalem to serve as his — the Mufti's — personal adviser, after the Mufti's return there upon the Axis' victory. The Mufti exhorted the Arabs of Palestine to take brief refuge in the neighboring Arab States not to hinder the advance of the invading Arab armies; he promised them an early return, after the Jews had been thrown into the sea.

Broadcasts from Cairo and Amman, from Damascus and Beirut, announced that "any Arabs who did not withdraw from Palestine would be hanged as collaborators with the Jews." So, the Arab states set in motion the events out of which the Arab refugee problem developed. Their aim was to thwart the establishment of the Jewish State, but they did not succeed. Israel's statehood was reborn.

The Arab states in effect cajoled or coerced 550,000-560,000 Palestinians into exodus, and at the same time they oppressed and terrorized 650,000 Jews into fleeing Arab lands where they had lived for centuries in loyal citizenship. In utter destitution, stripped of all that they possessed, most of these Jewish refugees were welcomed and integrated by Israel. It was an exchange of population. Jewish refugees from Arab lands transferred to a country with a Jewish majority; Arab refugees from Israel went to Arab countries: an internationally accepted transfer.

Since the end of World War II, exchanges of populations have taken place in various parts of the world. 4,000,000 of Moslems moved from India to Pakistan; the same number of Hindus made the reverse trip from Pakistan to India. 3,000,000 Sudeten Germans were expelled from Czechoslovakia: 2,000,000 settled in West Germany and Austria, 1,000,000 in East Germany. Between 1949-1961, there were in West Germany 2,739,000 refugees from East Germany. 6,750,000 Germans left the territories annexed by Poland. Over a million French or pro-French Arabs escaped from North Africa before and after Algeria's independence. When Vietnam was divided, 800,000 North Vietnamese went over to South Vietnam. Over 1,000,000 refugees from North Korea settled in South Korea. Over 1,000,000 refugees from Communist China arrived in Hong Kong. Masses of refugees from Nigeria, Biafra, Ethiopia, Eritrea, Cyprus, Cambodia were settled elsewhere.

Over 60,000,000 persons have become refugees since World War II, and most of them were settled and rehabilitated in the countries where they sought refuge.

The civilized world considers the absorption and settlement of refugees as a top priority moral obligation, and this has found its expression in a series of international laws and regulations. The Arab states, however, with all their wealth and space, have not absorbed the Arab refugees, who are their kin in blood and faith. They dismissed Israel's offer to open peace talks — as envisaged in the armistice agreements — and to discuss the refugee problem, on humanitarian grounds, as first item on the agenda. They abjured Israel's proposal to convene an international conference on the issue, to be attended by representatives of their own, of Israel, of the United Nations agencies that have been handling the problem and of nations contributing to refugee funds, with a view to working out a five-year plan of solution, even before peace talks.

While Israel gave the Jewish refugees a new home, the Arab states perpetuated the Arab refugee problem. They deliberately kept the Palestinian refugees in camps and used them as tools in their war against Israel. They kept the refugees in quarantined ghettoes, forbidden to resettle, denied integration into the economies of the host-countries, and used as political pawns.

In arithemtic text-books, they taught the children in the camps exercises like: "In a concentration camp there were 1,000 Jews; the Arab police in the camp killed 850 of them; how many remained alive?" They insisted that the refugees return to Israel, and Gamal Abdel Nasser, the President of Egypt, did not hesitate to reveal his motive: "If the refugees return to Israel, Israel will cease to exist."

For Israel to let the Arab refugees return would, therefore, be suicidal. The Arab terrorists could then choose whether to shell Israel from across the borders or destroy it from within. National suicide, however, is neither an international, nor a moral, obligation.

As for the Lebanese issue, Israel was paying in southern Lebanon a heavy price in casualties, almost every day for 18 years. That war, which was supposed to end within days, has become a deadly quagmire. IDF soldiers in southern

Lebanon, like their officers, excelled in high motivation. They were among the bravest the IDF had ever known. But our political leadership, from left and right, and the senior command of IDF, were unable to crystallize an effective fighting doctrine against the *Hizbullah* terrorists whose level of daring was constantly rising. The head of Northern Command, General Gabi Ashkenazi said: "One must say the truth: we have difficulties to locate the *Hizbullah*."

General Amos Malka, head of military intelligence, said that the terrorist acts of the *Hizbullah* were all the time improving, and there was no answer to it. *Hizbullah*'s successes became more numerous. In 10 days — in November 1998, seven IDF soldiers were killed. During the last week of February 1999, six soldiers and the Israel radio correspondent Ilan Roi lost their lives. Among the losses that week were the commander of the paratroopers' reconnaissance patrol, Major Eytan Belchassan, and the commander of the liaison unit to Lebanon, Colonel Erez Gerstein. Whether the Lebanon War was a political mistake or a military failure, its opponents argued that nowhere in the world has a regular army succeeded in defeating guerrilla fighters.

Minister for Internal Security Avigdor Kahalani made the frightening comparison between IDF soldiers and the clay ducks which serve as an easy target on a shooting range. While IDF soldiers were located in fixed positions and were focuses for raids and attacks, the *Hizbullah* terrorists were on the move between friendly villages, carried out ambushes, shot from open areas and escaped into the village houses.

The *Hizbullah* terrorists were safe from IDF's long arm because, according to the understandings following "Operation Grapes of Wrath," IDF was limited in the perimeters of its movements and actions and was not allowed to return fire towards populated areas, while *Hizbullah* was permitted to attack our soldiers freely. When the *Hizbullah* activated the explosives against the convoy of Colonel Gerstein and his troop, it was not considered a violation of the "Operation Grapes of Wrath" understandings which protected only civilians from combat. Moshe Arens, as Minister of Defense, raised the question of abandoning those understandings which, according to him, tied IDF's hands while granting immunity to the *Hizbullah*.

Minister Avigdor Kahalani supported a far-reaching military initiative and the harming Lebanon's economic infrastructure. Following *Hizbullah* attacks, he said: "I don't understand why we don't extinguish the lights in Beirut. I don't understand why there are no funerals in Lebanon." Following the terrible rise in attacks in southern Lebanon, public demands increased to find a solution to the problem by renewed negotiations with Syria. Syria had received from Russia more sophisticated and precise long range missiles, and, according to press reports, was to receive from them also a nuclear reactor.

Following the Israeli-Syrian negotiations in December 1995, at Wye Plantation, Assad claimed that Yitzhak Rabin was ready to evacuate the Golan Heights, to the June 4, 1967, border in exchange of full peace. Prime Minister Netanyahu reported to a government meeting, on return from a visit to the United States, that Yitzhak Rabin had never given a written statement to withdraw, under certain conditions, from the Golan Heights to the June 4 lines. Netanyahu announced publicly Israel's readiness to withdraw from Lebanon if the Lebanese Army would deploy in the south, would take over the territory, would maintain law and order, would prevent the organized terror there and from that territory against Israel, and would ensure the interests of the South Lebanon Army (SLA). Assad invited Lebanon's President and Prime Minister to Syria and ordered them to reject Netanyahu's proposals.

Before visiting Paris, in July 1998, Assad declared that, if the problems with Israel were resolved, there could be normal relations. On another occasion, he said that peace is even more important for Syria than it is for Israel, but also added a threat, that a freeze in the peace process would cause a war. Syria's Foreign Minister Farouk Shara followed up and said: "If a proposal were now made in a serious manner for a real comprehensive peace, stressing especially Israel's withdrawal from the entire Golan to the June 4 border, we would not hesitate."

There was nothing new in the Syrian position. Following the Yom Kippur War, Assad said to American Secretary of State Henry Kissinger: "I want the Israelis to withdraw from the territories. If they want to withdraw, we will make peace. If they want to hold occupied territory, let them keep it. We will continue with our struggle, maybe not five years but 50 years. As long as the occupation will continue, we will fight."

The U.S. continued to act for the renewal of the negotiations between Israel and Syria, and at the funeral in Amman of King Hussein — whose heir is his oldest son, Prince Abdullah — Clinton spoke about it with Assad. After the leader of the Democratic Front for the Liberation of Palestine, Naef Hawatmah, shook hands with Israel's President Ezer Weizman, he went up to the Syrian president and told him that Weizman wanted to shake hands with him, too. Assad replied: "Not now, not here."

While Yitzhak Rabin's principle in the talks with Syria was "the depth of the withdrawal will be like the depth of the peace," Netanyahu's formula was "the depth of the withdrawal will be like the depth of the security." According to both formulas, Israel considers the Golan Heights a vital strategic asset for its security. The Knesset, in the meantime, approved (53 for, 30 against) a law which requires a majority of 61 Knesset members and a majority in a nationwide referendum for the handing over of land in Jerusalem and on the Golan Heights.

The difficulties and fateful decisions awaiting Israel after the elections made one yearn fervently for an outstanding leader like David Ben-Gurion. It is not because in his time our situation wasn't difficult, nor because he didn't make mistakes. It is because David Ben-Gurion was a superb leader who broke new ground and gave people a sense of direction. He inspired confidence in his actions and, with his sincerity, gained trust in his ability and power to decide. All this is so sorely lacking now.

In Ben-Gurion's time, during the first years of the state, in the years of the tent camps, austerity regime and the many personal hardships, in the days of an American arms embargo and when the contributions of the Jews to Israel were measured in pennies, we enjoyed political independence which enabled Ben-Gurion to say: "It is not important what the Gentiles say, it is important what the Jews do," and he stood firm that the Arab-Israeli conflict must be resolved by direct negotiations. All Israeli governments have traditionally insisted on direct negotiations, assuming that an Arab leader's readiness for direct contact with Israeli negotiators was an essential first step in arriving at a peace agreement.

With Netanyahu, direct negotiations continued to take place between Israeli and Palestinian representatives at the lower political echelons. In the military domain, there existed a certain level of confidence between Israeli and Palestinian officers to solve local problems. But at the highest echelon, there was only American mediation. At Wye Plantation, with Netanyahu's approval, the United States moved from being an "honest broker" to playing the role of "facilitator" and eventually to arbitrating between Israel and the Palestinian Authority.

The American arbiter has become a supervisor. In order to speak with the Palestinians on political issues, Israel needs Dennis Ross; to reach an agreement with them in the security field, Israel needs the good offices of the C.I.A., and for the government to take decisions, the American president is required to intervene.

Bill Clinton is considered by Israel a most friendly American president. What a pity that there was no chemistry between him and Netanyahu who, immediately after his election as Prime Minister, made an ill-conceived declaration that he would not adjust Israel's interests to fit the relations with the U.S.A.

True, Clinton differentiated between his attitude towards Netanyahu and his attitude towards Israel, but here and there, his relations with Netanyahu had implications which brought about the granting of benefits by the Americans to the Palestinians and the establishment of close and even intimate relations between the Clinton administration, Arafat and the Palestinian Authority. Inherent in this is a certain danger.

PART SEVEN

SOUL-SEARCHING

RE-ASSESSMENTS

In 1992, on the eve of the parliamentary elections, Yitzhak Rabin said in the Knesset that "the most important thing was to grant, through a permanent peace settlement, maximum security and defensible borders to the 4,800,000 Jews living in the State of Israel" — Israel's Jewish population in that year. Rabin continued: "If the choice is between the 'whole of Eretz Israel' — which, we believe, the Jewish people have the right but its result is a binational state with two and a half million Palestinians — and a state in smaller territory, which will be a Jewish State, we have to prefer a Jewish State in which at least 80% of its citizens will be Jews."

During a visit to the U.S. after his election as prime minister, he cautioned: "While the entire Moslem world is making an enormous effort to develop nuclear arms and other weapons for mass destruction, Israel might find itself in seven to ten years in a much greater danger than ever." Six years after that warning, nuclear arms were approaching the Middle East. The first to arrive in Islamabad after Pakistan's nuclear test was Iran's Foreign Minister, and Palestinian spokesmen declared that the day of the Pakistani explosion was a holiday for the Palestinian people. The Pakistani explosion was presented as a counterbalance to the Israeli atomic reservoir.

For years, the world has been certain that Israel has developed a nuclear capability as its preeminent means of deterrence to safeguard itself from threats to its existence. Initialy, Israel categorically denied the rumors about its atomic reactor in Dimona. Eventually, the existence of that campus for nuclear research could no longer be disavowed. Shimon Peres, who acquired the atomic reactor from France, in 1957, explained why Dimona was chosen as the site for that installation: it was a vacant, relatively spacious area, as well as empty, so that, in case of a radioactive leakage, the catastrophe could be contained.

Much information has been published abroad about Israel's nuclear power. Details were published by Mordechai Vanunu, who had worked as a technician at the Dimona reactor. The London weekly "Sunday Times" disclosed that Vanunu was kidnapped in October 1986 on the high seas by an agent of the *Mossad*, Sindy, after she succeeded in persuading him to come from London to Rome, for a supposed romantic encounter. He was brought to trial, was convicted and sentenced to 18 years imprisonment. According to the "Sunday Times," Vanunu worked in Dimona in the production of plutonium for nuclear bombs and he smuggled out abroad about 60 photographs taken by him secretly at the reactor. On the basis of those photographs, the "Sunday Times" concluded that Israel possessed between 100 and 200 nuclear bombs, ten times more than atomic experts in the world had believed. That made Israel the sixth largest nuclear power in the world.

According to publications abroad, the crude uranium for the production of the bombs reached Israel from South Africa, Niger, Gabon, the Central African Republic, Argentina, and also from a plant in the United States.

When I served in Argentina, I visited in 1965 the uranium mines at Malargue, near the town of San Raphael, in the province of Mendoza.

When Israel was asked about its nuclear arms, its spokesmen replied — in the framework of its policy of "ambiguity," or deterrence through vagueness — that "Israel won't be the first to introduce nuclear weapons in the region." Since 1969, an understanding has existed with the Americans according to which Israel won't reveal its nuclear capability and the United States will consider Israel an exception to its global disarmament policy and will not pressure it to join the Nuclear Non-Proliferation Treaty (NPT). After the waves of nuclear tests in India and Pakistan, President Clinton reaffirmed in a letter to Netanyahu, following the Wye Plantation agreement, the American commitment as long as Israel will continue its policy of "ambiguity." Netanyahu considered this letter as one of his most important achievements.

During a visit to Jordan after the Pakistani nuclear test, Shimon Peres said: "We have not developed the nuclear option to conduct a Hiroshima, but to reach Oslo. We thought that the reason for Israel's being attacked five times without any provocation on her part, was the belief of some of our neighbors that they could overcome us. So we wanted to make sure that this temptation should not exist any more. I think that without it we would not have the Oslo agreement."

The danger exists that the Pakistani nuclear test will also benefit Iran, in addition to Iraq and Libya, after Russia supplied Iran with nuclear knowledge and signed with her an agreement for the acceleration of the construction of her nuclear reactor. It's only a question of time until Iran becomes a nuclear power.

Despite the United States' contacts with Iran, following the election of Muhamad Hatemi as its president, and the American activity to reach a normalization with Iran, Israel continues to consider Iran as a real threat to her existence. The threat became especially tangible after Iran executed successfully, with the help of the Russians and of North Korea, a test of the "Shihab 3" missile with a range of 1,300 kilometers. The Iranians say that this missile can reach any site in Israel. The "moderate" President of Iran, Muhamad Hatemi, presented that missile as "an answer to the Zionist force." When the "Shihab 3" missile was shown during a military parade in the streets of Teheran, a banner was hoisted on the truck carrying it which said: "It is necessary to erase Israel from the map."

The Russians are helping the Iranians to develop the next generation of that missile, the "Shihab 4" model, with a range of 2,000 kilometers. The Iranians are also making efforts to develop — with Russian help — chemical and biological weapons and even a nuclear warhead for their missile.

The head of Israel's military Intelligence, General Amos Malka, said in the Knesset Foreign Affairs and Security Committee that, in combination with the Iraqi missiles, the Iranian long range ballistic missiles constitute a significant threat to Israel. All this only confirms Yitzhak Rabin's appraisal of the Iranian danger, and Israel's main possible countermeasures are assiduous vigilance and stepped up efforts to thwart terror and military deterrence.

Former deputy chief-of-staff, General Matan Vilnai, said Israel's military doctrine, established in Ben-Gurion's days, has become obsolete, and, if not updated, Israel will not be able to provide answers to the strategic problems of the hour or obtain a decisive victory in a confrontation with the Arab world.

In 1999, the arms balance between Israel and its main neighbors seemed to be as follows:

Country	soldiers	tanks	artillery	missile launchers	war planes	helicopters
Israel	631,000	3,895	1,348	12	624	289
Egypt	699,000	2,785	3,510	36	498	224
Iran	868,000	1,520	2,640	39	145	243
Iraq	1,082,500	2,000	1,950	34	180	366
Jordan	154,000	872	788	–	101	68
Libya	76,000	746	2,220	128	166	127
Palestinian Authority	34,000	–	–	–	–	2
Saudi Arabia	185,000	865	404	12	346	160
Syria	512,500	3,700	2,575	62	365	295

Parallel to the re-assessment of our military superiority, a political review has taken place of our approach to the reality of the Palestinian problem. In the past, the very mention of a possible establishment of a Palestinian state was considered a taboo and whoever tried to ignore it would do so at his peril. This was the conception of Israel's governments at both ends of the political spectrum. "A Palestinian people does not exist," — thundered Golda Meir from a party rostrum — "I am a Palestinian." "We will talk with the PLO only through the barrel of a gun" — declared Moshe Dayan. Ezer Weizman (then Minister of Science and until recently the President of Israel), was investigated by the police on his contacts with the PLO. Abie Natan was jailed for violating the taboo of contacts with the PLO.

Menachem Begin maintained an adamant position against any contacts with the PLO. In August 1980, my wife and I arrived in Israel, from our post in Bucharest, for the wedding of our son Meir with Shelli, the daughter of David and Tamar Kochav. During our stay in Jerusalem, I met with Prime Minister Begin who sent with me a message to Ceausescu. Begin asked me to tell the Romanian president that Israel would never negotiate with the PLO and quoted from the *Fatah* decisions adopted in those days in Damascus.

Those resolutions stated that "the goal was to liberate all of Palestine and to liquidate the political Zionist entity economically, militarily, culturally and ideologically." On my return to Bucharest, I met with the President and gave him Begin's message. Ceausescu suggested ignoring the *Fatah* decisions because he had personally spoken with Arafat, who had assured him that he favors a peaceful solution of the conflict.

When I met with Ceausescu before my return to Israel at the completion of my five-year mission in Romania, the President asked me to transmit to Begin, Shamir and Peres his recommendations that Israel recognize PLO, negotiate with it and agree to an independent Palestinian state. On my return to Israel, I reported to the three of them, but none was ready to accept Ceausescu's recommendations.

When Israel agreed, in 1991, to participate in the Madrid Conference, it was only after it reached an understanding with the U.S.A. that the PLO would not be part of the process either directly or indirectly. Even after Israel recognized the PLO, in 1993, it continued to oppose the establishment of a Palestinian state. Still during the discussions in the Knesset — in September 1993 on the Declaration of Principles and in May 1994 on the "Gaza-Jericho First" agreement — Shimon Peres ruled out a Palestinian state and said: "With the establishment of the autonomy we prevented the establishment of a Palestinian state." But recently, Peres reversed himself: "A Palestinian state — yes or no? The answer must be in a clear voice — a state. Why? Because we cannot take upon ourselves the responsibility for the fate of three million Palestinians."

The PLO is today a legitimate partner to negotiations in the eyes of both Labor and Likud: both now regard the reality of the Palestinian problem, including the eventual establishment of their state, in a way that in the past was considered almost a national betrayal. The Palestinian state is no more a taboo.

At the U.N. General Assembly in 1997, the Arab bloc presented a proposal to grant the PLO the status of a state. Not only Israel was opposed to it. The Americans, too, considered this Arab initiative as a violation of the accords between Israel and the PLO. The Americans formed a rare American-European-Russian front and thwarted the initiative: 57 states voted for the proposal, 65 against, 32 abstained. Having failed to push through this proposal, the PLO tried to pass a resolution at the U.N. which would raise its status from observer to that of representative of "almost a state." It didn't succeed in this either. But 124 countries — against four (Israel, the United States, Micronesia and

Marshall Islands) and ten abstentions (Bulgaria, Honduras, Zambia, Liberia, Malawi, Poland, Paraguay, Congo, Rwanda and Romania) — voted in favor of the addition of exclusive privileges for the PLO observer. Those additional privileges are defined "technical," but the Palestinians, on their part, already see themselves as being on the way to join the family of independent Arab states.

Thus will be realized the U.N. resolution of November 29, 1947, on the creation of two states in Palestine — a Jewish one and an Arab one. But for the Arab rejection then of the U.N. partition plan — which was, no doubt, their biggest mistake — a Palestinian state would have been in existence long ago, and wars and much bloodshed would have been avoided.

Arafat announced he would proclaim the Palestinian state on May 4, 1999. But there is no doubt that a unilateral proclamation of a Palestinian state would be without a legal foundation.

The White House spokesman declared that the United States does not support a unilateral Palestinian proclamation of their state. Bill Clinton himself

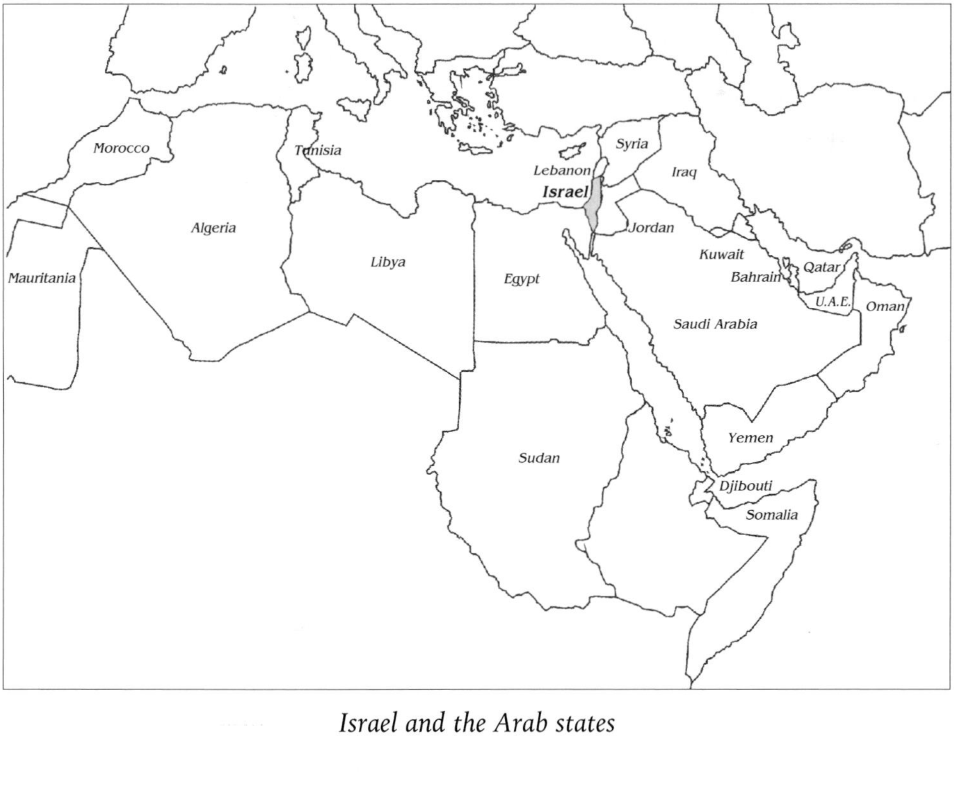

Israel and the Arab states

American Vice-President, Al Gore, at Israel's 50th anniversary celebration, with Prime Minister Benjamin Netanyahu, President Ezer Weizman and his wife Reuma

declared at his meeting with Arafat, following his meeting with Netanyahu in January 1998, that the Palestinians have the right to live as a free people.

Vice-President Al Gore refrained from referring to the subject when he arrived in Israel for its 50th anniversary celebration. He limited himself to saying that the United States would do everything to ensure Israel's security.

At the Wye Plantation Summit, Arafat refused firmly to commit himself not to proclaim the state on May 4, and following the Summit, he said he had reached an understanding with President Clinton that, if there would be no progress in the negotiations on the permanent settlement, the United States would not oppose the proclamation of a Palestinian state.

In the meantime, at the end of November 1998, a conference of the countries contributing to the Palestinian Authority was convened in Washington. Arafat was received there with much warmth by Bill Clinton and Madeleine Albright, and declared that "the time has come for the Palestinian state and this will happen very soon, very soon."

PALESTINIAN STATE

Arafat had his reasons for declaring a state on May 4, 1999. He did not believe that the interim track would lead to a state. He thought that the Israeli Government was not ready to reach an arrangement to the Palestinians' liking — a state with Jerusalem as its capital. One must also not ignore Arafat's personal situation: his advanced age (70) and poor health, perhaps made him feel that he had little time to reach significant achievements of historical value. On the eve of President Clinton's visit to Gaza, Arafat said: "I don't know whether I will be alive in a year or two."

Certainly, Arafat also had serious misgivings about unilaterally proclaiming the state on May 4, 1999. His main consideration was the fear lest such a step — which was contrary to the agreements established in Oslo and Wye Plantation — cause a bloody clash and an absolute collapse of the peace process, for which he would be blamed by the Americans and the Europeans. This would also cause a delay in American aid and even affect Arafat's achievement of having instilled into the consciousness of the world the inevitability of a Palestinian state.

The fear also existed that the proclamation would provide Israel with an opportunity to nullify the Oslo agreement and to take unilateral countermeasures, some of which would be irreversible.

At the U.N. General Assembly Netanyahu warned that Israel would consider a unilateral proclamation of a Palestinian state as an essential violation of the Oslo Agreement, and in response Israel might abolish it. Arafat knows that Israel has almost all the bargaining cards in her hands: she keeps the territories, the Palestinian prisoners are in her jails, the supervision over the border passages is in her hands, she supplies the territories with electricity and water, and almost their entire economy depends on Israel. At the same government meeting which approved the Wye Plantation Agreement, it was also decided that, if the Palestinians would proclaim their state on May 4, 1999, Israel would be free of all the obligations contained in the Oslo Agreement and in the Interim Agreement. In face of a Palestinian unilateral step, Israel would apply Israeli law and jurisdiction on all the territories under her control. Israel could annex all the settlements, their immediate surroundings and the roads leading to them.

In addition, Israel could impose an all-out closure on the territories of the Palestinian Authority: to absolutely forbid the entrance of Palestinian workers into the area of the green line, prevent the entrance of tourists to the Palestinian Authority's areas, close the passages to Jordan and Egypt, stop the transfer of money to the Palestinian Authority, delay the transfer of their goods by closing the harbor and the airport and cause a dangerous decline in the Palestinian Authority's functioning. Israel could also increase her military presence in area B and annex land in areas B and C, in which she is interested for security reasons, and this would be seen in the eyes of many as justified because it would be done as a countermeasure to a Palestinian unjustified unilateral step.

Arafat knew that his dependence on Israel would not diminish with the proclamation of the state and that the poor economic situation of millions of Palestinians would not improve, maybe even the contrary. Arafat was also aware of the pressures by the populace he would face when the hunger of the inhabitants is stronger than their national pride. Arafat had, therefore, many good reasons to think twice before crowning with the title of "State" his small autonomous enclaves. He had much to lose. On the other hand, in view of the upcoming elections in Israel, he could wait patiently until after their conclusion, in the hope that Barak would win and he would receive from his hands the yearned-for state.

The United States and the countries of the European Union asked Arafat to postpone the proclamation of the state. Arafat did not reject their request; he only asked for something in exchange — a guarantee, or at least a promise — that they will recognize the Palestinian state when it is proclaimed in the future.

Arafat was mainly interested in a formal public recognition by President Clinton of the Palestinian rights to a state. On the other hand, the American

Congress exerted pressure on the president to declare publicly and unequivocally that the American administration was opposed to the unilateral proclamation of a Palestinian state. The American Senate approved by an immense majority (98 voting for, 1 against) a decision warning Yasser Arafat against the proclamation of the state since it would be a basic violation of the Oslo agreement. This decision was also approved by the House of Representatives by a majority of 381 votes, 25 against.

With America's tacit consent, the European Union expressed support for the option of an establishment of a Palestinian state at a future date, in light of the talks between Israel and the Palestinians on the final peace. It was also clear to Arafat that only if he would postpone the proclamation, the enormous Palestinian investments for the reception of the large number of pilgrims for the celebrations of Jesus' 2000th birthday would not be completely lost. The Pope had already confirmed his coming in March 2000.

For the millennium celebrations to succeed and to bring the Palestinians

President Bill Clinton, his wife and daughter — accompanied by Mr. and Mrs. Netanyahu — on Mount Massada

political prestige and substantial financial income, quiet was necessary in the territories.

On December 12, Clinton arrived in Israel, accompanied by his wife Hillary and daughter Chelsea. The same day, the judicial committee of the American House of Representatives decided on the impeachment of the President because of the Monica Lewinsky affair, but, ultimately, the President was not deposed.

During his visit to Israel, the President repeated his firm friendship for Israel and his deep commitment to its security.

On December 14, President Clinton attended the special Palestinian assembly in Gaza, as agreed at Wye Plantation, which reaffirmed the letter sent on January 22, 1998, by Yasser Arafat to President Clinton and to Prime Minister Peres concerning the nullification of the Palestinian Covenant's paragraphs, that are inconsistent with the letters exchanged between the PLO and the Government of Israel on 9-10 September 1993. Arafat's letter was sent following a resolution by the Palestinian National Council (PNC) in Gaza, during the days 22-25 of April, 1996.

The PNC abolished then, by a great majority, all the Palestinian Covenant's paragraphs which are contrary to the agreement of mutual recognition between Israel and the PLO. According to the press, 504 members of the PNC voted for the abolition while 54 voted against. Following Arafat's letter to Peres, the Israeli Labor Party decided, on the eve of the Knesset elections in May 1996, to omit from its political platform the opposition to the establishment of a Palestinian state. Now, in Gaza, the participants at the assembly reconfirmed the abolition of the paragraphs by raising their hands and applauding.

President Clinton defined the abolition as "full, final and forever." In Israel, too, the majority considers the matter as closed.

In his speech before the assembly, Clinton repeated Israel's right to live in security and his recognition of the legitimate rights of the Palestinians, as determined in the Camp David agreements. He declared that the Palestinians now had the opportunity to decide their future on their land, and Arafat called Clinton a President whom the Palestinian people love and respect, he being the first American president to visit the territory under Palestinian rule.

Arafat, who for years was called a terrorist and was a persona non grata in the United States (the ally of Saddam Hussein who only a few years earlier was prevented from stepping outside the territory of the U.N. enclave in New York), was now the host of an American president in a state ceremony. The landing of President Clinton at the Gaza international airport, his reviewing, together with Arafat, the military guard of honor, and the exchange of official addresses — all that gave the Palestinians the most important international recognition and constituted a historical moment for the 500 million Moslems watching it on their home screens.

The President's lighting of the Christmas tree in Bethlehem, had to be considered by Christians all over the world as an indirect recognition by the American president of a Palestinian state, and Arafat presented it in this light. Clinton's visit was, therefore, an important strategic Palestinian achievement.

A day after Clinton's participation at the Gaza gathering, a tripartite summit meeting was held at the Erez checkpoint: Clinton, Netanyahu, Arafat. The meeting ended without a press conference and with a dispute between Israel and the United States on the withdrawal issue. Netanyahu repeated his opposition to the establishment of a Palestinian state.

Whatever the time, circumstances and borders, if and when the Palestinian state is established, politicians will argue and historians research who and what led to its establishment. Even if it was the dynamics of the historical process, there were those who during this process did contribute to its realization.

King Hussein of Jordan rejected in Paris, in September 1965, Golda Meir's proposal to sign an Israeli-Jordanian Peace Treaty with the then borders of Israel, when the entire West Bank was in Hussein's hands.

Had Hussein not rejected Meir's proposal, wars would have been prevented, the death of thousands of human beings avoided, and the developments in the Middle East would have been different. Five years later, Hussein again missed an opportunity of peace.

Hussein considered Israel as his insurance policy, for the preservation of the sovereignty of his Hashemite Kingdom and for his remaining on his throne. A few times, the Israeli *Mossad* brought to his attention plans to depose or kill him, and when the Syrians tried once to intercept his plane, Israel's air force sent up planes which drove away the Syrian aircraft. In September 1970, the Palestinian organizations tried to produce a revolution against the Hashemite Kingdom and even proclaimed the establishment of their government at Irbid, headed by Yasser Arafat. IDF reinforcement on the Syrian border deterred the Syrian tanks from invading Jordan to join the rebels in Irbid. Hussein butchered Palestinians and expelled them. When he met Yigal Allon in November of that year, he thanked him for Israel's help, but rejected Allon's plan for peace with Israel which would have left Hussein with 70% of the West Bank, and would have prevented the establishment of a Palestinian state.

When Hussein passed away, Israeli citizens were effusive in their expressions of love and admiration for him. Israel's deep yearning for peace made her forget and forgive Hussein's past hostile acts.

Not only Hussein, but Israel's leaders, too — each in his own time and his own way — contributed to the developments that we are witnessing today — a Palestinian state in formation.

Levi Eshkol evaded meeting King Hussein, following the Six-Day War, when Hussein asked to meet with him personally or to send Moshe Dayan to him. Eshkol refused both requests. By this refusal, Eshkol missed an oppportunity to reach a political arrangement with Hussein which Dayan defined "honorable and mutual," based on significant border amendments, the emigration of the Arab refugees to remote lands and a solution of the issue of the Holy Islamic places in Jerusalem as a united city.

Menachem Begin recognized at Camp David, in September 1978, the legitimate rights of the Palestinian people. He signed an arrangement for Judea, Samaria and the Gaza Strip which determined a full Palestinian autonomy with a strong police for five years. Begin distinguished at Camp David between territories held by Israel by force of virtue — Judea and Samaria — which were vital to her interests, and territories held by her by virtue of force — Sinai — on which it was possible to bargain. By this, Begin created a precedent of evacuating settlements and surrendering territory to the very last milimeter.

Yitzhak Shamir rejected in 1987 the draft of the "London Agreement," which was prepared by Shimon Peres and King Hussein and which was intended to bring about a peace agreement with Jordan and the Palestinians. Afterwards, the *intifada* broke out and King Hussein gave up his claim to the West Bank and granted the Palestinians his blessing for independence. In 1991, Shamir arrived at the Madrid peace conference and paved the way for the Oslo agreement.

Yitzhak Rabin and Shimon Peres recognized the PLO — in Oslo, in

September 1993 — and converted Yasser Arafat into a partner to a dialogue. They signed the Declaration of Principles, the "Gaza-Jericho First" agreement and the Israeli-Palestinian Interim Agreement. They thus officially adopted a territorial compromise and determined afresh the partition of Eretz Israel and the separation between the Israeli and Palestinian populations.

It was Netanyahu's commitment to implement the Oslo Agreement that brought him to power in 1996. Both before and after the elections, Netanyahu declared — even from the Knesset rostrum — that his government was committed to the agreements signed by the previous government. He was fully aware that he would have to implement the territorial compromise which the left had dreamt about but was not able to execute.

Sharon claims that the mother of all sins is the autonomy accord signed by Menachem Begin at Camp David, and he stated that it would be better to have a Palestinian state in part of Judea and Samaria rather than a Palestinian autonomy in the whole of Judea and Samaria, as long as the state is reached by an agreement, not a unilateral act, and there is no army there — just a demilitarized zone with restrictions on the size of the police force and the number of heavy weapons.

Benjamin Netanyahu — who, on his election as Likud chairman, in January 1994, stated that if the Likud were to come to power, it would not honor the agreement with the PLO — was the first rightist leader to shake hands with Yasser Arafat.

Netanyahu, who in the past described the Oslo Agreement as a "document of capitulation" and as a "national disaster," stuck to the reciprocity principle and became a devout adherent to the implementation of all the paragraphs in the agreement with the PLO. As one who demanded from others allegiance to accords, he couldn't free himself from his obligations to fulfill all their paragraphs, and Netanyahu began to implement the territorial compromise by signing the "Hebron Protocol."

In a letter to King Hussein, Netanyahu expressed his readiness for the establishment of a Palestinian entity with independence in the fields of demography, geography, politics and economy. In addition, Netanyahu spoke publicly of the development of the Palestinian Authority into a state like Andorra, a small state, a member at the United Nations, although — by his

Prime Minister Benjamin Netanyahu shaking hands with Yasser Arafat

demand for its demilitarization from heavy weapons — Netanyahu continued to advocate something "less than a state."

The distinction between a "state" and "something less than a state" is one of semantics by somebody who is a prisoner of his own conception. However, Netanyahu's demand for demilitarization is designed to ensure Israel's security. Israel will be secure if Jerusalem will be its undivided capital forever; there will be no return to the June 4, 1967, borders; the Jordan Valley will be Israel's strategic border; Israel will not give up control of airspace, water sources and the area overlooking the centers of population and strategic targets; there will be warning stations and Israel will not allow a Palestinian army equipped with heavy weapons or non-conventional arms to form west of the Jordan; and there will be no return of the Palestinian refugees.

It is vital to ensure that Yasser Arafat, and his successors, will have to fulfill his statement at the Stockholm Conference on December 5, 1998, that the Palestinian state will not conclude military alliances with foreign countries and will not invite Arab armies. It is essential that the Palestinian state's air and sea ports not serve for the import of arms and various means of sabotage, and that the free passages between the Gaza Strip and the West Bank — via roads passing through Israeli areas — not endanger Israel's security. Maximum security collaboration between Israel and the Palestinian state is crucial, as is a halt to the anti-Semitic and anti-Israeli propaganda in the educational institutions and in the news media of a Palestinian state.

In a television interview, Netanyahu explained that what frightens him in a Palestinian state is not the flag, the hymn and the passports nor bilateral agreements with the United States and the European countries. What really scares him is the idea that an armed Palestinian sovereign state will sign an agreement with Saddam Hussein. Moshe Arens, then Minister of Defense, also voiced Israel's fear that a Palestinian state might sign alliances with other Arab countries. This fear is absolutely justified and understood by anybody who remembers how the PLO leadership stood on the roofs during the Gulf War and applauded the falling of Iraqi Scuds on Israel. Moshe Arens was Minister of Defense at that time also.

In those days, the people of Israel were relieved that all Israeli governments withstood all pressures for the establishment of an independent Palestinian state. For rejecting the idea of a Palestinian state, the Israelis were accused of being stubborn and inflexible. If insistence on survival is being stubborn and inflexible, we plead guilty to those sins. It was our good fortune to be so. It saved us from a horrible disaster that would have befallen us, if the Palestinian state had been in existence when Saddam decided to launch deadly missiles against Israel.

Instead of launching the Scuds from a distance of 700 kilometers — while being bombarded by the mighty American air force — Saddam could have attacked Israel from across the border, endangering its very existence.

On May 4, 1999, Arafat had intended to proclaim an independent Palestinian state. But the Central Council of the PLO decided to postpone the proclamation temporarily, after Arafat received a letter from President Clinton nicknamed in the news media "a kind of Palestinian Balfour Declaration." In his letter to Arafat, Clinton repeated what he had said in Gaza, that he supports the aspirations of the Palestinian people to decide its future on its land, and referred to the principle of "land for peace" among the aims of the peace process. Clinton called both sides to refrain from taking unilateral actions to change the status of the West Bank and Gaza Strip, while mentioning Jerusalem and the refugees among the subjects to be negotiated.

On May 17, elections took place in Israel. Out of 4,285,428 eligible voters, 74.51% took part in the elections. Ehud Barak won by receiving 1,791,020 votes (56.08%), against Netanyahu's 1,402,474 votes (43.92%).

It was an astounding victory for Barak. Netanyahu congratulated Barak and resigned from the Likud leadership and from membership in the Knesset. Ariel Sharon was elected temporary chairman of the Likud Party. Barak made his victory speech at the Rabin Square in Tel-Aviv, and the following day went to the Western Wall in Jerusalem where he made a wish. Barak promised to follow up on Rabin's heritage and act for the achievement of peace. He repeated his election promise to withdraw the IDF from Lebanon within a year.

Ehud Barak declared: "I intend to be prime minister of all. Whatever differences of opinion exist among us — we are brothers. We are brothers — and brothers walk together."

President Bill Clinton was among the first to congratulate Barak on his

Ehud Barak making a wish at the Western Wall

victory and promised the firm support of the United States and his devotion to accelerated efforts towards achieving a permanent, lasting peace settlement.

Yasser Arafat, too, telephoned Barak and in their conversation both committed themselves to continuing the process of implementation of the agreements already achieved.

According to people close to Arafat, he was not pleased with Barak's statement, in his victory speech: on the status of an undivided Jerusalem as Israel's eternal capital, on the non-return to the 1967 borders, on the non-admission of a foreign army west of the Jordan river, and on most settlers remaining in blocs of settlements in the territories under Israel's rule.

Ehud Barak's test was to be whether in the negotiations on the permanent settlement he will fulfill what he promised before the elections, namely "if the result of a permanent arrangement will be a Palestinian state, it is necessary to ensure that the Palestinian state's security and political restrictions which are agreed upon, should reflect the vital interests of Israel." This means that the Palestinian state will be most limited in its military capability and will not endanger the existence of the State of Israel.

THE NEW CHRISTIAN-JEWISH RELATIONSHIP

On September 4, 1999, three and a half months after Barak's election as Prime Minister of Israel, the Israeli-Palestinian Memorandum on the implementation of the timetable of the signed agreements and the resumption of the permanent status negotiations was signed at Sharm el-Sheikh.

The government of the State of Israel and the Palestine Liberation Organization committed themselves to full and mutual implementation of the Interim Agreement and all other agreements concluded between them since September 1993 as well as all outstanding commitments emanating from the prior agreements.

The Israeli side undertook in this memorandum to carry out further redeployments and to release Palestinian and other prisoners who committed their offenses prior to September 13, 1993, and were arrested prior to May 4, 1994. Agreements were also being reached on the safe passages and on Hebron issues: the opening of the Shuhada Road for the movement of Palestinian vehicles, the opening of the wholesale market Habashe, and the convening of a committee to review the situation in the Tomb of the Patriarchs. The two sides also agreed on the principles to facilitate construction works on the Gaza Sea Port.

The two sides agreed to act to ensure the immediate, efficient and effective handling of any incident involving a threat of act of terrorism, violence or incitement, and to resume the permanent status negotiations in an accelerated manner, with an effort to conclude a framework agreement on all permanent

Signing of the Sharm el-Sheikh Memorandum.
From left to right: Gilad Sher, Israeli negotiator; King Abdullah of Jordan; Ehud Barak, Prime Minister of Israel; Hosni Mubarak, President of Egypt; Madeleine Albright, American Secretary of State; Yasser Arafat, Chairman of the Palestinian Authority; Dr. Saeb Erakat, Palestinian negotiator.

status issues by February 13, 2000, and a comprehensive Israeli-Palestinian peace agreement by September 13, 2000.

On December 15, 1999, Israeli-Syrian talks began at the White House in Washington. The Israeli delegation was headed by Prime Minister Ehud Barak and the Syrian delegation by Foreign Minister Farouk Shara. After two days of discussions, in a cold and tense atmosphere, without a Barak-Shara handshake, it was agreed to continue the negotiations in the United States on January 3, 2000. They reopened in Shepherdstown, West Virginia, where the Americans submitted to the two sides a draft of an Israeli-Syrian Peace Treaty from which the main points of contention between Israel and Syria were evident:

1. **Borders.** Syria's position: Israel must withdraw to the June 4, 1967, border. Israel's position: the June 4 line is not a border, but rather the

cease-fire line on the eve of the Six-Day War, and the final border should take into account security and other vital interests of the parties.

2. **Security.** Syria demanded parallel and equal security arrangements and rejected the establishment of an Israeli ground station. Israel demanded more expansive demilitarized zones on the Syrian side and for Israel to maintain an early-warning ground station on Mount Hermon to give her reasonable advance warning of any aggressive re-deployment of the Syrian army.
3. **Normalization.** Syria was ready to establish ordinary peaceful relations between two neighboring states, but refused to sign agreements between the two governments regarding normalization. Israel demanded the opening of borders and exchange of embassies immediately after the start of withdrawal.
4. **Water.** Syrian position: land and borders should be discussed before water resources, which can be discussed only in the context of a Syrian-Israeli-Lebanese-Jordanian framework. Israeli position: the Golan water resources constitute one-third of Israel's resources; a pledge not to obstruct the flow of water is equivalent to the issues of security and normalization. Israel must have full control of the Kinneret-Jordan river basin so that water sources remain under its sovereignty.

The second round of Israeli-Syrian talks ended after a week exactly like the first one — without any agreement, without any conclusions, without any compromise or concession, and in a sour and frosty atmosphere. The third round of talks was to take place at Shepherdstown on January 19, 2000. But on the eve of the departure of the delegations for the United States, the Syrians published changes they demanded in the American draft-treaty and announced the suspension of the talks.

As a condition for renewing the peace talks, Syria demanded that Israel commit itself to a withdrawal from the Golan Heights to the June 4, 1967 borders, which would mean Syrian control of the Jordan River, part of the shoreline of the Kinneret (Sea of Galilee) and Hammat Gader. Syria also stipulated that there would be no Israeli presence in early warning stations, and

Shara declared that if a peace treaty is signed, no sign will remain of the Jewish settlements on the Golan. Shara asserted that a peace agreement with Israel would be nothing like the accords Israel signed with Egypt and Jordan and called the eventual agreement "part of the plan of phases for liberating all of Palestine." Syria also made it clear that the issue of the Palestinian refugees must be included in the negotiations and that it wants the disarmament of the Middle East of all weapons of mass destruction — nuclear, chemical and biological. Syria refused to commit itself to preventing acts of violence against Israel from territories under its control and to refraining from cooperation with any third party in a hostile alliance of a military character. It also rejected Barak's call for a meeting with Hafez Assad.

Contrary to the behavior of Egyptian President Anwar Sadat and King Hussein of Jordan, Syrian President Hafez Assad humiliated Barak twice: he did not "condescend" to meet the Israeli Prime Minister and did not authorize Farouk Shara to shake Barak's hand. While Barak is Israel's most senior decision-maker, Assad sent his Foreign Minister who had a lower political rank and couldn't make any decision without approval from Assad.

The Israeli-Syrian negotiations at Shepherdstown
From left to right: Prime Minister Ehud Barak, Secretary of State Madeleine Albright, President Bill Clinton and Foreign Minister Farouk Shara

From the pictures released by the Americans, it became clear that Shara never sat next to Barak — an American always sat between them.

Someone not acquainted with the real situation in the Middle East might think that Syria was victorious and Israel defeated and forced to surrender.

But the facts are that the Syrians were the losers in the 1967 Six-Day War, proved a failure in the 1973 Yom Kippur War, were defeated in the 1982 Lebanon War and lost both the Golan Heights and Mount Hermon. According to the 1999 annual Middle East Military Balance, issued by Tel-Aviv University's Jaffe Center of Strategic Studies, the strategic balance between Israel and Syria has never been so tilted in Israel's favor and Damascus has no real military option. In addition, the Syrian economy is deeply in trouble, the collapse of the Soviet Union left the Syrian military high and dry, and economic progress in Israel and advances in Israeli military and civilian technology have provided the Israeli defense forces with an overwhelming advantage over the Syrian military.

The paradox in the situation was that the anticipated U.S. military aid to Syria, after an agreement with Syria has been signed, will redress the military balance between Syria and Israel in Syria's favor — and what is no threat at the present time could turn into a threat in the years to come, which neither demilitarization of the Golan Heights nor early-warning devices can prevent.

Hence the impressive show of power by the pro-Golan lobby on the day the Shepherdstown talks ended. Between 150,000 and 180,000 demonstrators, many of them youngsters wearing knitted skullcaps, filled Rabin Square in Tel-Aviv, defying cold and rainy weather, to protest against any peace treaty with Syria that would require Israel to give up the Golan Heights. Relinquishing the Golan Heights and forcing 18,000 Israelis to leave their homes was considered by many a blow to the very foundation on which Israel is built — a self-inflicted wound that will not heal easily in the years to come.

In a preliminary plenum reading, the Knesset approved — with 60 members voting for, 53 against and one abstention — a Likud amendment to the Basic Law on the Golan Heights Referendum. According to the amendment, a majority of 50% of all eligible voters is required in the referendum for the approval of a withdrawal from the Golan Heights.

Hafez Assad, on his part, decided to pressure Israel into making concessions by exacting from it a price in blood. Weapons shipments from Iran to *Hizbullah*, passing through Damascus, were increased, with Syria's authorization and blessing, in the midst of Israel's negotiations with the Syrians.

On January 25, 2000, for the first time in over four months, a soldier was killed in South Lebanon — Rafael Zangwill was the victim of a missile attack on an IDF outpost. Five days later, Israel suffered a major blow in Lebanon when Colonel Akl Hachem — the number-two man in the South Lebanon Army (SLA), designated to succeed its commander, General Antoine Lahad — was killed by the *Hizbullah*.

The following day, three Israeli soldiers — Major Tidhar Templehoff, Staff Sergeant Lior Niv and Staff Sergeant Tzachi Malka — were killed in a *Hizbullah* missile attack. The same day, in an unusually harsh editorial, the official Syrian newspaper "Tishrin" compared Israel to the Nazis, claiming that Zionism "created the Holocaust myth to blackmail and terrorize the world's intellectuals and politicians and is now dealing in the same way with Arabs in the occupied Syrian Golan Heights, Palestine and South Lebanon."

IDF officers demanded to retaliate, saying: "Israel must act forcefully and transfer the dilemma from Jerusalem to Damascus." But the Israeli cabinet approved only an assassination attempt on Ibrahim Ikal — *Hizbullah*'s top military commander in South Lebanon — which unfortunately failed. Hassan Nasrallah, the *Hizbullah* leader, warned that his organization's *katyushas* were ready for reaction: an Israeli soldier, Staff Sergeant Yedidya Gefen, was killed and seven wounded, four of them seriously. Tension was increasing and Israel was losing the impressive qualitative edge it had gained in Lebanon since June 1999, when it lifted the Grapes of Wrath restrictions on IDF operations in Lebanon and its air force bombed Lebanese infrastructure targets, thus achieving a sharp drop in *Hizbullah* activities and a considerable decrease in IDF casualties.

Barak decided to resume Israel's adherence to the Grapes of Wrath understandings but failed to have the Syrians agree that, while there is talking, there can be no shooting. Barak's misreading of Assad's tactics brought about a resumption of full-scale *Hizbullah* operations, and, when the situation became intolerable, Barak ordered Israeli warplanes to launch a wave of strikes, in the early hours of Februay 8, against suspected *Hizbullah* strongholds in Lebanon. Three power plants — near Beirut, near Baalbek and near Tripoli — as well as parts of Beirut, were plunged into darkness.

Hizbullah fired an antitank missile at the Dla'at outpost from a house in the suburbs of Nabatiyeh and killed Staff Sergeant Amir Meir. Sergeant Tzahi Itach, killed at the Israeli army base at Beaufort, was the seventh casualty of the IDF in Lebanon within two weeks, but Barak again refrained from ordering a harsh response out of fear that this would make more difficult the resumption of the Israeli-Syrian talks.

After having failed on the Syrian track despite having yielded, in principle, to Assad's demand to return to the June 4, 1967 line, Barak claimed there was nothing new in his position: according to him, four of his predecessors had already agreed, in negotiations with Syria, to the June 4 line.

He said that Yitzhak Shamir, who began the talks with Syria at the Madrid Conference in 1991, had accepted U.N. Security Council Resolution 242, and the Syrians construed this to mean Israeli readiness for a withdrawal from the Golan. Yitzhak Rabin gave the Americans a commitment, which they passed on to the Syrians, that if they fulfilled Israel's demands, it would return to the line of June 4, 1967. Shimon Peres, said Barak, conducted talks with the Syrians while confirming Rabin's commitment, and Netanyahu held negotiations, with June 4 as the basis, seeking control two miles east of the line at one point along the border, and along the rest of the line at a significantly lesser distance eastward.

Shamir and Netanyahu categorically denied what Barak said about them. Peres did not confirm Barak's statement and said that Israel cannot agree to a return of the Syrians to the Kinneret. Leah Rabin declared that her late husband always insisted that the Kinneret must remain in Israel's hands.

On January 20, 2000, Arafat and Clinton met in Washington and following that meeting, the Palestinians presented to the Americans a proposal on a final status agreement. The proposal included the establishment of a Palestinian state in the West Bank and the Gaza Strip, in accord with the pre-1967 borders, claiming that 90% of the West Bank should end up in their hands. According to the Palestinian proposal, Jerusalem was to remain united, but sovereignty and municipal administration would be divided in a fashion consonant with the demographics of each neighborhood. In lobbying for international support for his idea of sharing undivided Jerusalem and creating a Vatican-style sovereignty in the Old City, Arafat met on February 15, 2000, with Pope John Paul II and a basic agreement was signed between them.

The preamble of the agreement declares that an "equitable solution" for Jerusalem based on international resolutions is "fundamental for a just and lasting peace." It also says that "unilateral decisions and actions altering the specific character and status of Jerusalem are morally and legally unacceptable." By that agreement, Arafat was officially recognized by the Vatican — interested in a special international status for Jerusalem — as a partner in determining Jerusalem's future.

With the day of Pope John Paul II's visit to Israel approaching, he asked on March 12 — in a Day of Pardon Mass at St. Peter's Basilica at the Vatican — for God's forgiveness for the sins committed by Roman Catholics over the centuries, including those against Jews. This was met with criticism and disappointment from Jewish and Israeli quarters, for its failure to make specific mention of the Holocaust or the sins of the Church as an organized body. Instead it referred only to the guilt of "Christians" and avoided any reference to the historical connection between Christian anti-Semitism and the Holocaust. While the Holocaust was conceived and perpetrated by Hitler, the Jews see the Church's indifference to it as an open sore in Vatican-Jewish relations.

The Pope touched down in Israel, on March 21, for a six-day visit. On his arrival, he called for an end to prejudice between Christians and Jews, dialogue among Jews, Moslems and Christians and peace in the Middle East. The day after visiting Bethlehem (revered as the birthplace of Jesus), and a nearby refugee camp at Deheishe, the Pope celebrated a private Mass in the Last Supper room at the Dormition Abbey on Mount Zion in Jerusalem. Then he proceeded to Heichal Shlomo, the seat of the Chief Rabbinate in Jerusalem, where he met briefly with Israel's Ashkenazi Chief Rabbi Israel Meir Lau and Sephardi Chief Rabbi Elyahu Bakshi-Doron. Aftrwards, he met with President Ezer Weizman at the president's residence, and then went to Yad Vashem Holocaust Memorial on Mount Herzl for a ceremony attended also by Prime Minister Ehud Barak.

During the ceremony, held in the Hall of Remembrance (a stark structure where the names of the death camps are engraved on the floor), the Pope rekindled the eternal flame — its smoke wafting out of an opening in the ceiling eerily recalled the smoke of the crematoria — and placed a wreath on a slab under which are buried the ashes of Jews from six of the extermination camps.

In his speech, the Pope said: "I have come to Yad Vashem to pay homage to the millions of Jewish people who, stripped of everything, especially of their human dignity, were murdered in the Holocaust. More than half a century has passed, but the memories remain. As Bishop of Rome and successor of the Apostle Peter, I assure the Jewish people that the Catholic Church is deeply saddened by the hatred, acts of persecution and displays of anti-Semitism directed against the Jews by Christians at any time in any place."

These words of the Pope were an unequivocal response to the Holocaust deniers who a short while afterwards were struck an additional blow when in London British historian David Irving lost his libel suit against American historian Deborah Lipstadt for accusing him of denying the Holocaust and distorting history. The ruling of the British High Court is a milestone in the struggle against the denial of the Holocaust.

The Pope said at Yad Vashem that "there are no words strong enough to deplore the terrible tragedy of the *Shoah*" and declared that the lesson of the Holocaust is "to ensure that never again will evil prevail, as it did for the

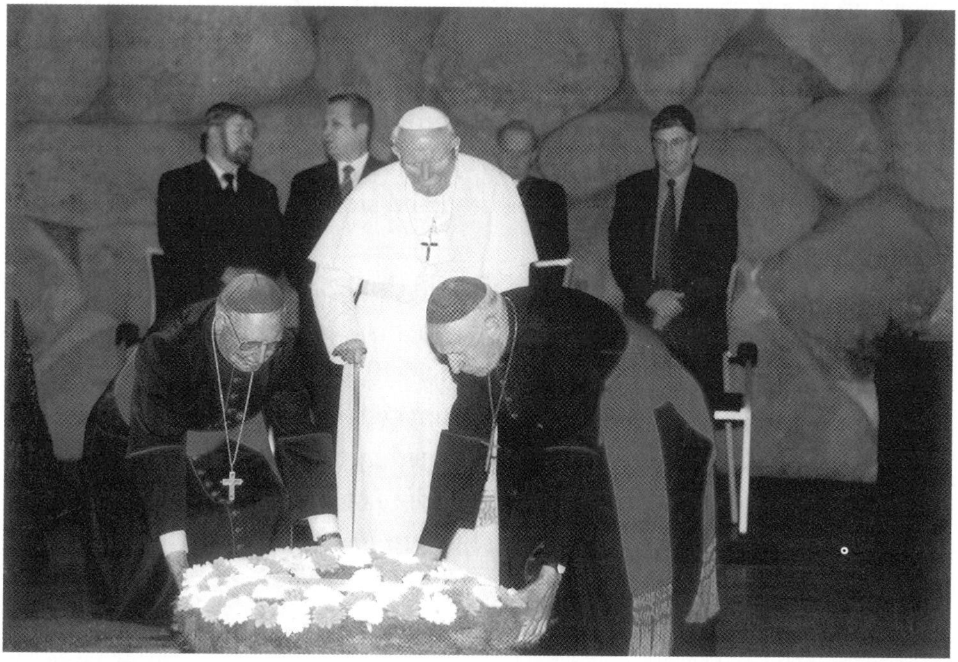

Pope John Paul II placing a wreath in the Hall of Remembrance at Yad Vashem Standing behind him, from left to right: Shevah Weiss — Chairman of Yad Vashem Council, Prime Minister Ehud Barak and Avner Shalev — director-general of Yad Vashem

millions of innocent victims of Nazism." He added: "Our prayer is that our sorrow for the tragedy which the Jewish people suffered in the twentieth century will lead to a new relationship between Christians and Jews." This new relationship began with Pope John XXIII. Pope John Paul II deepened and redefined the relationship between Judaism and Christianity.

The Pope, however, stopped short of the apology the Jews had hoped for, for the silence of the Catholic Church and of Pope Pius XII during the Holocaust.

The next day, the Pope spoke on the Mount of Beatitudes, near Moshav Korazim, to a crowd of 100,000, who had flocked in from across the globe: Africa, Europe, the Far East and the Americas. The Pope drew the faithful to Mass on the shores of the Sea of Galilee where tradition says Jesus worked miracles and preached to his first followers gathered there.

On Saturday, the Pope traveled to Nazareth, revered by Christians as the place where Jesus was born and grew into manhood. Several thousand faithful attended a celebratory papal Mass in the Basilica of the Annunciation — the site Catholics revere as the place where Angel Gabriel appeared to Mary with the news that she would give birth to Jesus.

On his last day, Sunday morning, the Pope visited the cavernous Church of the Holy Sepulcher, believed by many Christians to be the site of Christ's entombment and resurrection, and the Temple Mount. Before departing, he went to the Western Wall, bowed his head and stood silently. He then placed a prayer in the Wall.

The prayer he inserted had been prepared in advance and it appeared to sum up in a few lines his appreciation for Judaism, his feelings about the persecution of Jews, and his aspiration for a new dialogue with the Jewish people. The prayer said: "God of our fathers, you chose Abraham and his descendants to bring Your Name to the Nations. We are deeply saddened by the behavior of those who in the course of history have caused these children of yours to suffer, and ask Your forgiveness. We wish to commit ourselves to genuine brotherhood with the people of the Covenant."

At the bottom of the prayer was his signature.

The Pope ended his historic six-day pilgrimage by being flown home on an El Al plane named Jerusalem.

WITHDRAWAL FROM LEBANON

The next visitor to place a wreath in the Hall of Remembrance at Yad Vashem was China's President, Jiang Zemin. He arrived in April to Israel for a historic six-day state visit. On his arrival, the Americans expressed displeasure over Israel's sale of Israeli-made Phalcon spy-planes to China. Similar to the American-made AWACS, the Phalcon system gives early warning of an approaching attack aircraft. The U.S. feared such a sale would upset the delicate balance of power between China and Taiwan, America's protégé. The Americans also canceled a joint exercise of the U.S. and Israeli air forces, which they had been conducting for a few years.

Members of the House Appropriations Committee sounded some of the stiffest warnings yet to Israel. They said that if the Phalcon sale goes ahead, it will jeopardize not only $250 million (the amount of the deal) in military assistance, but all future U.S. aid. In a bipartisan unanimous vote, the committee approved an amendment to the 2001 Foreign Appropriations Bill that strongly urged Israel to cancel the deal. Barak was compelled to inform China that under the current circumstances Israel would not be able to carry out the Phalcon project, but would continue to look for ways to implement it, in consultation with the U.S., should the circumstances change.

In its relations with Israel, it is in China's interest to obtain the technological cutting edge, otherwise only available from the United States which severely limits Chinese access to its military technologies. For Israel it is important not only for economic reasons, but also because they give Israel a certain leverage when discussing Beijing's policies vis-à-vis Iran and Syria.

Iran has a military deployment in Lebanon and has sent long range rockets

From left to right: Ezer Weizman, Jiang Zemin and Ehud Barak

there which are being stored by Iranian personnel and this constitutes a serious development. The rockets, which have a range of about 70 kilometers, were brought there with the explicit purpose of threatening Israel for which it is a military issue with strategic importance, whether peace ensues and certainly in case of a confrontation. By its successful test of Arrow-2 anti-ballistic missile (which intercepted and shot down a simulated Scud ballistic missile) Israel was increasing its deterrent power on enemy plans to strike against her surface-to-surface missiles.

Iran has directed the *Hizbullah* to prepare an infrastructure to carry out acts of terrorism inside Israel. It has also opened in the city of Shiraz, behind closed doors, the show trial of 13 Jews on charges of spying for Israel. Three of them were acquitted, 10 others got jail terms between four and 13 years.

Israel's High Court of Justice, on its part, ordered the liberation of 13 pro-Iranian Lebanese detainees held in Israel as "bargaining chips" to secure the navigator Ron Arad's release. The Court's decision raised much criticism in

Israel and Ron Arad's mother accused the judicial system of "betraying Ron." His family filed an appeal at the Court asking that these detainees remain in prison as "bargaining chips" for the missing Israeli soldiers, but the appeal was rejected. Israel continued to hold Sheikh Abdel Karim Obeid and Mustapha Dirani — "Amal" security chief, when Arad disappeared.

With the number of IDF casualties increasing, Barak passed a resolution in the Cabinet to end Israel's long military presence in Lebanon until July 7. Unfortunately, in Lebanon in particular and in the Arab world in general, *Hizbullah* succeeded in presenting this decision by Israel as a surrender to pressure under fire. As the IDF was accelerating its preparations for the withdrawal, *Hizbullah* was looking for any pretext to escalate the fighting in order to stain the IDF with blood and depict its withdrawal as a victory.

Military logic — especially with the escalation in fighting — demanded as rapid a redeployment as possible, without waiting until July. But Barak's diplomatic logic required more time to see if the Syrians would return to talks and in the hope that the pullback could be made part of an agreement. Barak was waiting for the miracle of resumption of the negotiations with the Syrians and heaped praise on the tyrannical Syrian leader offering him far-reaching concessions, but Assad remained as stubborn as in the past. When he met Clinton in Geneva, he told him that Syria's position was that it has the right to get back every inch of land which the Syrian soldiers held on June 4, 1967. Syria's position thus remained: total Israeli withdrawal from the Golan Heights to June 4, 1967, lines; Syrian sovereignty on the shore of the Kinneret, and the right to part of the sea.

In supporting unilateral withdrawal, the Israeli Cabinet promised not to abandon Israel's long-time allies in the security zone — the members of the South Lebanon Army, their families and those who worked in Israel or with the civil aid authorities. The estimate was that about 20,000 people had allied their fate with Israel and among them was wrought an atmosphere of anxiety with the *Hizbullah* deliberately targeting them to undermine their morale and bring about the militia's collapse before the completion of the withdrawal.

The SLA Commander, General Antoine Lahad, called on Lebanon's President, Emile Lahoud, to grant amnesty to all members of the SLA and their families — except himself. But Lebanon's Prime Minister, Salim Hoss, rejected

Lahad's demand urging him to surrender to the authorities. Colonel Nabi Abu-Rafi — Druze second-in-command in the SLA — declared: "We haven't accomplished anything. What a waste of lives, what a waste of 25 years."

Since the beginning of the Lebanon War, in June 1982, until the day of that Cabinet decision, 1,547 soldiers were killed in Lebanon. 320 of those victims died since Israel withdrew from Lebanon, in June 1985, to the security zone. 73 fighters were killed in the disaster of the collision of the two helicopters above Shear Yishuv, on their way to IDF positions in South Lebanon, and 12 were Naval Commando's fighters killed on September 4, 1997, north of Tyre in a clash with terrorists.

Colonel Bashar Assad (Hafez Assad's son) was quoted saying that a unilateral withdrawal is not a solution. If not the *Hizbullah,* he said, "the Palestinians will fight on." Syria — in addition to adding new long-range North Korean-made Scud missiles to its arsenal — was doing everything to push Palestinians into activities against Israel, including their training for cross-border attacks following the withdrawal. Ahmed Jibril's Damascus-stationed "Popular Front for the Liberation of Palestine" (PFLP) was gathering outdated Soviet-made tanks. The IDF was concerned that those tanks were to be passed on to *Hizbullah,* and Israel's air force attacked the tank depot base inside the Syrian-controlled Beka'a Valley in Lebanon, three kilometers from the Syrian border, and at least 10 Soviet-made T-55 tanks were destroyed in the attack. Israel's Deputy Defense Minister, Ephraim Sneh, issued a reminder to Syria that, in case a war erupted between Israel and Syria, the IDF is "closer to Damascus — which is within the IDF's artillery range — than the Syrian army is to Jerusalem, even closer than the Syrian army is to Tiberias."

Israel proposed to the U.N. that the UNIFIL (the U.N. force in Lebanon since the 1970s) control the key areas Israel will leave behind when it withdraws, in compliance with U.N. Security Council Resolution 425. The United Nations accepted Israel's request, and the Security Council welcomed the withdrawal, increased the UNIFIL force from 4,513 to 7,935 and called on Lebanon's army to ensure that all national territory falls under the effective authority of the Lebanese government. The Lebanese and Syrian governments were warned that the U.N. would consider Beirut responsible for the safety of the South Lebanon Army members following Israel's withdrawal.

The U.N. support to Israel's withdrawal occurred symbolically at a time when a half-century anomaly was being rectified in U.N.-Israel relations. Israel was the only U.N. member state that was not a member of one of the regional groupings, which meant it had no chance of being elected to serve on main U.N. organs. This was due to the objection of certain states to Israel's joining its natural regional group of Asia. So now, the European grouping decided to include Israel in it. Thus ended the clear violation of the principle of sovereign equality of member states embodied in the Charter of the United Nations.

Hizbullah, however, vowed to continue its struggle. A rain of *Hizbullah* Katyusha rockets killed Sergeant Major Shaked Ozeri and wounded 26 Israeli civilians, most of them residents of Kiryat Shmona. In retaliation, Israel bombed Lebanese power stations, and strikes were carried out on the Beirut-Damascus road and on a weapons and ammunitions warehouse.

On May 22, 2000, a central pillar of Israel's strategic defense policy in South Lebanon collapsed with the desertion of hundreds of members of the SLA *Shi'ite* battalion from the security zone, forcing the IDF to conduct a hasty retreat. This began in chaos and humiliation, but ended orderly, with neither casualties nor hitches. Thus ended Israel's 18-year-long military presence in Lebanon, changing the defense concept for the north by redeployment on the international border and protecting the border from within Israeli territory.

In the aftermath of the Israeli withdrawal, U.N. officials set the "line of withdrawal" between Israel and Lebanon, establishing a new security regime in the region, and U.N. peacekeepers were deployed in that border region. Meanwhile, a Lebanese military court began to sentence pro-Israeli Lebanese militiamen who surrendered to Lebanese authorities to stand trial while thousands abandoned their homes and ran for life — in fear, fatigue, hunger, confusion and anger. More than anything, they felt betrayed. About 7,000 refugees arrived in Israel.

Initially, most of them were taken from the Rosh Hanikra and Good Fence crossing points to Amnun Beach near Capernaum. As the numbers grew, alternative accomodation was found in hotels, hostels and apartments in Tiberias, Safad, Afullah, Acre, Haifa, Haderah, Netanyah, Ashkelon and in various kibbutzim (collective settlements). A massive campaign of aid poured in from all parts of the country: baby food, disposable diapers, mineral water, clothes and other items. Israel has a moral obligation towards those who were her allies. Prime Minister Barak pledged that every assistance would be given to help those who had sought refuge in Israel — whether to stay here, to try to find homes in other countries, or return to their homes when the situation calms. The Interior Ministry announced that all families would be provided with one-year residency permits and the right to work, health insurance and other social benefits.

When *Hizbullah* (in the immediate proximity of Israel's towns and villages within sniper range and flushed with its "victory" over the IDF) threatened to continue and attack Israeli targets, Prime Minister Barak warned he would hold Syria and Lebanon responsible for any attacks across the northern border. He said: "I don't advise anyone to test our reaction once we're deployed at the international border." Foreign Minister David Levy warned in the Knesset: "If Kiryat Shmona burns, Lebanese soil will burn."

Those warnings indicated that, if Israel's forces or civilians were to be hit after the withdrawal, all forces in Lebanon, including the Syrian army, would be targets for retaliation. Israel tried to convince the Lebanese and the Syrians that IDF military strikes would then be more painful than anything Lebanon had known in the past. Barak's view was that respecting full Lebanese sovereignty over the evacuated area would justify a "full-strength" Israeli response, if it continues to be subject to attacks.

By ordering the withdrawal of the IDF from the security zone in southern Lebanon, Barak made good on his election campaign promise and many Israelis hoped it ended what Barak had termed "the Lebanese tragedy." Following the deployment of the Lebanese army and UNIFIL troops along the border, thereby filling the vacuum left behind after the IDF withdrawal, Barak had hoped that quiet would reign along the border in the north.

Four-and-a-half months after the withdrawal came the test. On October 7, *Hizbullah* guerrillas attacked Israeli army posts in the north and kidnapped three soldiers — Staff Sgt. Omer Suaed, Staff Sgt. Avraham Binyamin and Sgt. Adi Avitan. A week later, *Hizbullah* announced the abduction of a fourth Israeli — "a colonel, a member of the *Mossad*." Israeli spokesmen stated that Elhanan Tannenbaum was a private businessman, a colonel in the reserves, with no link whatsoever to Israel's security establishment.

Those who had opposed the IDF withdrawal accused Barak of having made a bad bet. Barak was faced with the challenge of fulfilling the warning he made on the eve of the withdrawal — that in case of any hostile action by the *Hizbullah*, the Israeli retaliation would be swift and drastic. To do so meant reopening the Lebanon front, without any chance the soldiers could be rescued. So Barak opted for the exchange of hostages and began to negotiate a deal.

FATEFUL PERMANENT PEACE DECISIONS

Some Palestinian Authority officials confirmed Israel would hand over 90% of the West Bank, including the Jordan Valley, to the Palestinians. Barak himself declared that keeping 80% of the settlers under Israeli sovereignty would constitute a "historic achievement." The obvious implication of this declaration was that 20% of the settlers (about 50,000) would find themselves outside Israel sovereignty. They would thus be faced with the choice of being transferred from their homes or living under Palestinian rule. Thousands of settlers protested at Barak's reported plans to dismantle settlements and force others to live under Palestinian Authority's control.

At the same time, State Comptroller, former Supreme Court justice, Eliezer Goldberg, published his damning report on party financing of the 1999 elections. Attorney General Elyakim Rubinstein announced that he was instructing the police to launch a criminal investigation, principally directed at the illegal activities of the fictitious pro-Barak non-profit associations into which were funneled illegally various funds.

This came after a criminal investigation into the activities of the former Prime Minister Netanyahu — on a handyman's bill for 440,000 NIS for services he rendered to the Prime Minister and gifts belonging to the State which the Netanyahus took for themselves. This coincided with a police criminal investigation of President Ezer Weizman for accepting thousands of dollars in cash gifts from French businessman millionaire Edouard Saroussi. Attorney General Elyakim Rubinstein and State Prosecutor Edna Arbel, presented a report criticizing Weizman for acting contrary to the law and ethical norms and agreed with the police findings that Weizman could have been indicted if the statute of limitations on his offenses had not expired. They decided to close the file after toning down the report because of Weizman's failing health and his public announcement that he would retire within the year 2000.

The Attorney General also decided to close Netanyahu's file due to the absence of sufficient evidence for criminal indictment, but in his public report, Rubinstein said there was a measure of "ugliness" in the way Netanyahu acted.

Following Weizman's retirement in July, the Likud candidate Knesset member Moshe Katsav was elected the eighth President of Israel. Katsav was born in Iran in 1945, immigrated to Israel at the age of five and grew up in a tent camp for immigrants. He began his political activity as a student at the Hebrew University in Jerusalem. He is a resident of Kiryat Malachi, a development town in the south where he became the youngest-ever mayor at 24 and is now the youngest-ever President at 55. He was elected to the Knesset in 1977 and served as Labor, Transportation and Tourism Minister.

From left to right: Prime Minister Ehud Barak and his wife Nava, President Moshe Katsav and his wife Gila, Knesset Speaker Avraham Burg and his wife Yael

Then there was the police investigation into the accusation against Transport Minister, Yitzhak Mordechai (leader of the "Center" Party). The Attorney General decided to charge him on sexual harassment. Aryeh Deri, former Minister of the Interior, SHAS' (Sephardi religious party) strongman, became the first ex-minister in Israel's history to go to jail, sentenced to three years for bribery, fraud and breach of trust. So, a scandal was pursuing a scandal. Half a century after the establishment of Israel it seems as if this has become a way of life.

In the meantime, the hours ticked by in Barak's tight timetable to obtain, between mid-February and September 13, 2000, a framework agreement and a permanent status accord with the Palestinians, and the PLO's Central Council decided to declare Palestinian statehood on September 13, on the basis of the Sharm el-Sheikh Memorandum. Barak made the mistake of fixing in that Memorandum September 13 as the target date for a permanent status accord. His pledge that within 15 months he will achieve peace with Syria was just as unrealistic. Following Hafez Assad's death, his son Bashar stated that Syria would not yield to Israel even one inch of Syrian territory. At the same Central Council, the Palestinians restated their red lines: Israel must withdraw to the 1967 borders, including East Jerusalem; the Palestinian refugee problem must be solved in accordance with U.N. Resolution 194 calling for the right of return and compensation for those who don't; the Palestinians must be in control of their borders with Egypt and Jordan; and all the Jewish settlements must be dismantled.

Following those PLO decisions, President Clinton invited Barak and Arafat to Camp David on July 11. Barak pledged publicly his red lines: there will be no return to the 1967 lines; Jerusalem will remain united and under Israeli sovereignty; no foreign army will be west of the Jordan River; the majority of the settlers will be in settlement blocs under Israeli sovereignty; and Israel has no moral responsibility for the Palestinian refugees.

SHAS, Yisrael b'Aliyah (the Russian immigrants' party) and the National Religious Party suspected that Barak filled his briefcase with concessions damaging Israeli security interests and national assets. So, on the eve of his departure for Camp David, their ministers resigned from the Government and in the Knesset, the Likud won a no-confidence vote by 54 to 52. But the

Government wasn't toppled because the Likud didn't muster the needed 61 votes. However, never before has a national leader embarked on such a crucial mission amid such domestic weakness. Barak was going to a Camp David summit with the purpose of shaping the permanent borders of Israel and end the long conflict with a Government in collapse and without parliamentary support.

Even his Foreign Minister David Levy refused to accompany him to the summit. Barak himself compared the Palestinians to crocodiles (the more you give them to eat the more they want). The Palestinians did not comply with their obligations given to Israel in Oslo I, Oslo II, Hebron, Wye Plantation and Sharm el-Sheikh agreements.

Barak departed for the summit in the wake of pushing forward the "Yeshivah" students draft bill through the Knesset, legalizing in effect draft-dodging. He argued that when, as opposition leader, he submitted a bill to conscript all "Yeshivah" students and promised the "one nation — one draft," he was unaware of the complexity of the issues involved. Political observers wondered whether Barak was aware of the complexity of the fateful decisions to be taken in a permanent peace treaty with the Palestinians.

Over 150,000 demonstrators converged on Tel-Aviv's Rabin Square to protest against Barak making broad concessions at Camp David to the Palestinians. The Council of Jewish settlements decided that "all settlements in Judea, Samaria and Gaza will stay where they are under any circumstances and under any conditions, and will never leave their homes." In the Knesset, the opposition inflicted, in preliminary readings, several stinging defeats on the government on peace-related issues. By a vote of 51 to 40, the Knesset passed a bill that would require the government to immediately annex security and settlement areas in Judea, Samaria and the Gaza Strip in the event that the Palestinians unilaterally declare an independent state. It would also result in the cancellation of any economic agreements with the Palestinian Autority. By 64 to 40, the Knesset passed a bill that will force the government to repeal the Oslo Accords if the Palestinians unilaterally declare a state.

By 49 to 37 a bill was passed to bring any permanent peace accord to a referendum. By 50 to 38, a bill was passed requiring approval of 55% of participants in a referendum for concessions in Judea, Samaria, Gaza and the

Opening Camp David Summit.
From left to right: Ehud Barak, Bill Clinton, Yasser Arafat

Jordan valley. By the same majority (of 50 to 38), a bill was passed requiring a final-status framework agreement or a peace deal with the Palestinians involving Judea, Samaria and Gaza to be approved by 61 Knesset members and then by a special majority of registered voters in a referendum.

The summit collapsed because Arafat did not want to declare the end of the conflict and presented unlimited claims. Barak had no other choice but to write to President Clinton stating that "he has reached the conclusion that the Palestinian side is not conducting negotiations in good faith and is not prepared to discuss in a serious fashion."

Barak also claimed that all concessions he was prepared to make would be invalid if no agreement was reached. But Israel's vital interests have already been severely prejudiced by those concessions which have set down a marker. Foreign Minister David Levy resigned from the Government saying that Barak's commitments at Camp David were "in contradiction to the very soul of the people." He was referring specifically to Barak's readiness to divide Jerusalem. "This would take us back to a situation in which Jews would have to go through a pathway to get to the Western Wall," he said.

Levy rejected Barak's assertion that his concessions are invalid without a full accord. "When the discussions are renewed" — Levy said — "they will start from the point where they left off." Or those concessions will serve as an obstacle to further progress in the peace process. That was what happened with Rabin's "playing" a theoretical game, at Wye Plantation in 1995, about an eventual withdrawal, under certain conditions, from the Golan Heights to the June 4 lines. The Americans hinted to Assad that Rabin's game might be real and since then, the Syrians have insisted that the negotiations be renewed only from that point.

Barak did not show political wisdom at Shepherdstown or Camp David. He revealed all the concessions he was prepared to make and in both cases was left in the lurch without an agreement. At Camp David, Barak raised to the top of the agenda the core issues of the Israeli-Palestinian conflict — Jerusalem, the Jordan Valley, refugees and the Palestinian state. Barak is the first Israeli Prime Minister to break the taboo on Jerusalem and has dared to negotiate Jerusalem and its heart and soul — the Old City and the Temple Mount.

Exactly like Netanyahu, when the chips were down, Barak tried to form a national unity government, to avoid early elections, informing the Likud that all that had been agreed at Camp David was invalid. He changed almost on a daily basis his pronouncements on an imaginary "secular revolution," jumping from one topic to another on his "national agenda" with its receding deadlines making everyone dizzy by his zigzags.

President Clinton told Israeli Television, following the Summit's failure, that it would be a "big mistake" if Yasser Arafat were to declare statehood unilaterally. If that happened, he would review America's entire relationship with the Palestinians. Faced with this American position, the PLO's Central Council decided to postpone the unilateral declaration of statehood on September 13.

It took Benjamin Netanyahu's Government over two years to start to disintegrate. It took Ehud Barak a little more than a year to lose 11 ministers out of 23. His bureau collapsed as a result of infighting, friction and a messy method of government.

AT A CROSSROADS

Barak tried to reach an agreement during the United Nations' Millennium Summit in New-York, when Clinton met separately with him and Arafat, but Arafat remained adamant on Jerusalem, refugees and borders. He continued to deliver inflaming speeches strewn with illusions, repeating what he had already said in the past: "All of Jerusalem will be the capital of the Palestinian state and our flags will be flying everywhere in the city. Anyone who does not like it — let him drink the water of the Dead Sea."

When he said it on his return from Camp David, incited Palestinians burned Israeli flags and set fire to photographs of Barak with swastikas plastered over them. When he repeated it on his return from the Millennium Summit, the worst Palestinian-Israeli fighting erupted in 14 years — since the rioting in September 1996 over the opening of the Western Wall tunnel, when for the first time Palestinian policemen fired at Israeli soldiers.

According to Prime Minister Barak, it was Arafat who orchestrated the rioting which began on September 28, 2000, following his interview with a Saudi daily newspaper in which he said that "while the Palestinian Authority wants peace, it won't hesitate to engage in war on Israel." After an Israeli medic was killed near Netzarim junction and an Israeli border police officer shot dead by a Palestinian Authority policeman, while on joint patrol in Kalkilya, the Moslem Friday prayers on the Temple Mount ended with heavy stone throwing on the Jews praying at the Western Wall.

Arafat used Likud leader Ariel Sharon's visit to the Temple Mount as an excuse to launch plans he had drawn up to intensify the conflict. It wasn't Sharon's first visit there and it was his right to do so. The Arab Knesset members put themselves at the forefront of the protest against Sharon's visit, setting the tone of the rioting and playing a key role in its escalation.

Arafat continued to fan the flames despite clear promises made to Barak and the Americans to stop them. Various world leaders told Barak that they recognized Arafat's fingerprints on the start of the riots and they assumed that he cynically dispatched children to the frontline using them as shields in gun battles because it is easy to secure the sympathy of the world with a photograph of a dead child. Near Joseph's Tomb in Nablus, border policeman Sergeant Major Madhet Yosef succumbed to injuries and died. Palestinian Authority's officers had refused to allow Israeli medics to evacuate him.

After Palestinian Authority security forces vowed to safeguard the holy site, the IDF withdrew from Joseph's Tomb. As soon as the Israeli troops were removed, thousands of Palestinians stormed the site, looted it and set it on fire. Later, they murdered Rabbi Hillel Lieberman, a settler from Elon More and a teacher at Joseph's Tomb Yeshivah, a father of seven. Rabbi Lieberman was a second cousin to the Democratic candidate for the U.S. presidency, senator Joseph Lieberman.

The bloody incidents spread from the West Bank and the Gaza Strip to towns and villages of Israeli Arabs, numbering in the year 2000 over a million. Of this figure, 81% are Moslem, 10% Christian and 9% Druze. An upward surge of extreme nationalism was clearly noted among Israel's Arabs. Their demands have taken on a more assertive and ultra-nationalistic trend and periodically also violent. Arafat succeeded in dragging the Israeli Arabs into the so-called "Al-Aksa *intifada*." They termed it *intifada* to make the events seem like a popular uprising with demonstrations and strikes, but it was real war and not the kind of legitimate protest acceptable in a democracy.

Thousands of Israeli Arabs rioted in the heart of the country: main roads and junctions were blocked, Jews were pelted with stones as their cars were torched, and there was vandalism. Israeli Arabs cut off some areas from the rest of the country and inflamed the situation while Palestinians fired at soldiers and policemen leaving dozens of injured. Israel could not — no state could — tolerate it, and reacted forcefully. The IDF sent in tanks, armored personnel carriers and helicopters and eased the regulations for opening fire, in order to restore law and order.

Only after 50 Palestinians and 13 Israeli Arabs had lost their lives, a cease-fire was agreed on October 3, and U.S Secretary of State Madeleine Albright invited Barak and Arafat to meet with her the next day in Paris in an attempt to end the fighting and return to the table of negotiations. They both accepted the invitation, but no agreement was signed. On his return to Jerusalem, Barak sent a sharply worded letter to a hundred world leaders, in which he stated that the Palestinian Authority and Arafat are responsible for the continuation of the violence having encouraged incitement and hatred in the Palestinian media. He called upon the world leaders to immediately work toward convincing Arafat to put an end to the violence. Barak was compelled to recognize publicly that Arafat was no longer a peace process partner, and on the eve of Yom Kippur 2000, he gave Arafat a 48-hour ultimatum to put an end to violence.

The effect of this ultimatum was about as effective as the threats he made at the time to *Hizbullah* and the Lebanese and Syrian governments. Violence continued and murderous incitement against Jews was aired on Palestinian media and at mosques.

The IDF wrecked the Palestinian "twin towers" buildings which had facilitated Palestinian gunfire attacks against the IDF outpost at the Netzarim junction and also demolished a factory and a Palestinian Authority police post near that junction. Israel also shut down the Gaza International Airport to all flights apart from those transporting Yasser Arafat.

There was one day of relative calm, and then gun battle broke out again and the Palestinian Authority released almost all *Hamas* and *Islamic Jihad* prisoners.

In Ramallah, two IDF reservists who blundered into the town — Yosef Avrahami and Vadim Nourezitz — were brutally lynched and mutilated by a Palestinian mob at the local police station as the police stood by or joined in. An Italian TV crew showed the Palestinians tossing the body of one soldier out of the second-story window to the ground, where another mob continued to beat him. The other soldier was still alive when the mob tied him to a car and dragged him through the main street of Ramallah. British photographer Mark Seager, who witnessed the lynching, reported in the Sunday Telegraph: "It was the most horrible thing that I have seen. It was murder of the most barbaric kind." The Palestinian Authority has fully shown itself as having inhuman values and not belonging to the community of enlightened and civilized nations.

Israeli commandos hunted down and captured a number of Palestinians suspected in connection with the barbaric lynching of the two Israeli reserve soldiers in Ramallah, including the man who was seen around the world on television as he triumphantly held up his hands covered with blood after the murders. Israel's Deputy Defense Minister Ephraim Sneh declared that "justice will get to those who did the brutal lynch, just like it came to perpetrators of the massacre of the Israeli athletes at the 1972 Olympics in Munich."

Barak called on Likud leader Ariel Sharon to join a "national emergency government." He showed Sharon a plan for a "unilateral separation" between Israel and the Palestinians — a gradual withdrawal from parts of the West Bank, in which Israel would station itself along the places it needs to defend, leaving the final-status dispute unresolved. Barak suggested that the plan serve as the basis for the unity government. Sharon asked to see the maps, but requested Barak to renounce the concessions he made at Camp David. Barak proposed to take a "time out" from the peace process to re-evaluate the political situation.

When the Oslo Accords were brought by Yitzhak Rabin, in 1993, for approval by the Knesset, 61 members voted for them — only half the population of Israel supported the Oslo peace process. It was Benjamin Netanyahu, the Likud Prime Minister, who contributed to the crystallization of a great majority of the Israelis supporting it.

When Netanyahu was elected Prime Minister in 1996, he offered no alternative to the policies of Yitzhak Rabin who had an almost hawkish image. Rabin had served as hardliner Defense Minister in Shamir's National Unity Government during the *intifada* and fiercely opposed the return to the 1967 borders. It was only because he held those positions that Rabin was able to lead Labor to victory in the 1992 elections.

Netanyahu continued Rabin's road: he withdrew from almost all of Hebron, the city of our Patriarchs and the first capital of the Jewish people. King David was crowned there, and it is the second-most important city in Jewish history, after Jerusalem. Netanyahu adopted at Wye Plantation the principle of "land for peace." He gave up areas in Judea and Samaria, the cradle of the Jewish people. Netanyahu renounced one of the foundations of the Likud Party — the whole of Eretz Israel as a supreme value.

In the 1999 elections, therefore, the popular belief was that Madrid process and Oslo Accords erased the Likud-Labor political differences. Barak stated that even with a microscope it was difficult to see the ideological differences. This was also why in those elections many politicians roamed from one party to another. There was no political ideology in 1999, an anti-Netanyahu ideology took its place. Unfortunately, he did not radiate credibility. Many of his actions were grasped as a gimmick, while Barak, Israel's most decorated soldier, radiated trust.

However, Barak abandoned all red lines he had pledged and — without getting anything in return — deviated from Rabin's legacy regarding Israel's vital national interests: he agreed to divide Jerusalem, relinquish the Golan Heights and the Jordan Valley, evacuate Jewish settlers, and discuss the return of Palestinian refugees to Israel. Barak's amazing victory at the polls evaporated and the people began losing faith in him.

Even Shimon Peres, Rabin's closest partner and architect of the Oslo process, thought Barak had conceded too much at Camp David: it was wrong to debate the division of the Old City and give the Palestinians sovereignty over Judaism's holiest shrine, the Temple Mount.Yitzhak Rabin's widow, Leah, said Barak was an absolute disappointment and that her late husband "would be turning in his grave if he could see what concessions Barak had offered."

On October 16, 2000, a Barak-Arafat summit meeting took place at Sharm el-Sheikh, with the participation of U.S. President Bill Clinton, President of Egypt Hosni Mubarak, King Abdullah of Jordan, U.N. secretary-general Kofi Annan and European Union representative Javier Solana. At the summit, Arafat and Barak pledged to issue public statements unequivocally calling for an end of violence and to take immediate concrete measures to end the current confrontation.

Since the Oslo peace process began, Arafat has made repeated commitments to resolve all issues relating to the permanent status by peaceful negotiations. He made a promise in writing to Rabin that he would refrain from resorting to violence each time the negotiations become stalemated. However, his "violence card" has always been on the table, with the purpose of achieving political gains.

He continued to make insatiable political demands at the negotiating table and his security mechanisms in the territories were engaged in preparing extensive acts of violence which led to the Ramallah atrocities and confirmed what Major-General Moshe Ya'alon, Commander of IDF's Central Command, had said: "Although the Palestinians are striving for statehood, they behave like hooligans."

Not even 48 hours had passed after Arafat's pledge to end violence and shots were fired into the Gilo neighborhood in Jerusalem from the neighboring Palestinian village of Beit Jala. There were nightly attacks against the Jewish quarter of Hebron and in Bethlehem. Two of Arafat's personal guards were killed in an explosion, and Israeli sources suspected that it was a bomb being prepared for a terror attack that exploded prematurely. The same day, Rabbi Binyamin Herling, a resident of Kedumim and father of eight, was killed and four Israelis were wounded when Palestinians opened fire on a group of Israeli men, women and children, on a tour trip at Mount Eval near Nablus. Arafat decided to get to the Arab League summit in Cairo with the territories still ablaze. And, indeed, during the weekend of the summit, violence escalated and at least 12 Palestinians were killed and over 500 injured.

At the summit itself, vociferous attacks against Israel were made by all participants, and it called on Arab countries to consider cutting their ties with Israel. Morocco, Tunisia and Oman froze the relations. Qatar closed Israel's interests office. Egypt recalled its ambassador and Jordan delayed the appointment of a new ambassador. Mauritania's ambassador continued to function. Arafat was most extreme in his speech, and when Barak announced the "time out" to re-assess the peace process, he declared: "Let Barak go to hell."

After the summit, the violence continued and, amid fierce fighting, Shimon Peres met with Yasser Arafat. An agreement was reached that the next day Arafat and Barak would issue a joint call "to refrain from violence, incitement and the use of force in order to restore peace and calm." This agreement brought about a freezing of the retaliatory steps determined overnight by Israel's military Cabinet. But the next day, Arafat did not make the agreed call. Instead, a powerful car bomb, claimed by the *Islamic Jihad*, went off in the center of Jerusalem killing two Israelis and wounding ten. Barak placed responsibility for the bombing on the shoulders of the Palestinian Authority saying that the attack was the result of the release of *Hamas* and *Islamic Jihad* prisoners.

The number in Israel of those who think that true peace with the Arabs is wishful thinking, an illusion, an assumption lacking any ground in reality, has been growing. They believe that for the Arabs the peace process is only a stage in their aspiration to liquidate the State of Israel. In one of his interviews, Arafat referred to the "phased plan": in the first phase, to achieve a Palestinian state in part of Palestine, and in the second phase to act from that state for the elimination of Israel. We are witnessing Israeli Arabs articulate a passionate identification with their brothers and sisters beyond the Green Line with the cry "Death to the Jews!" and encourage the creation of an independent State of Palestine with the cry "With blood and fire we will redeem Palestine!"

Israeli Arabs are saying they would like to transform Israel from a Jewish state with a Zionist ideology into a "State of all its citizens." There is fear that they might in the future demand political and educational-cultural autonomy, with the aim of having a State of Palestine beyond the pre-1967 borders and a bi-national state within these borders. The basic Arab position in regard to Israel is an integral part of Islam's attitude towards the Jews and of its perception of peace with the enemy.

Islamic law rules out the possibility of the existence of an independent Jewish State and does not grant peace to its rivals as equals. Therefore, there can be no agreement of true peace with enemy states and also armistice agreements are not solid but only tactical. Peace with non-Moslem enemies is temporary and not binding, and Moslems are free to violate and nullify those agreements if they believe they have accumulated enough force to prevail over the enemy.

Arafat himself compared in 1998 the Oslo Accords to the Pact of Hudaibiya which the Prophet Mohammed made, in the year 628, with a rival tribe in Mecca agreeing to a 10-year period of peace. Two years later Mohammed took over the city by force of arms, violating the agreement. That violation has been recognized in Islam as legitimate tactics and wisdom and Arafat has been acting accordingly. During his war against the Hashemite Kingdom of Jordan in the early 1970s, he reached 22 cease-fire agreements, each of which he subsequently broke. He dealt in the same manner with his Lebanese rivals a decade later. Where Arafat is concerned, agreements were never made to be honored and he, therefore, violated all the key clauses of the Oslo Accords.

Barak responded to the cruel lynching of the two Israeli soldiers in Ramallah by bombing some empty buildings, whose occupants — who were directly responsible for the murders — were warned beforehand. Arafat concluded that violence pays. Barak's sweeping concessions on Jerusalem, constant restraint to the *intifada,* successive abortive ultimatums, repeated declarations that Arafat was no longer a partner to peace talks (although the next day he secretly sent emissaries to him to negotiate even with the territories ablaze) — were interpreted by Arafat as weakness and degraded Israel's deterrent power.

On November 13 Israel sustained its highest daily casualty toll since the September 28 rioting had erupted: two soldiers and two civilians. Israeli security forces arrested fifteen "Fatah" gunmen (among them policemen), suspected of involvement in those killings. On November 17, Arafat declared that he had ordered an end to shooting attacks on Israeli positions from areas under Palestinian security control. The next day, a Palestinian security officer killed two Israeli soldiers in the Gaza Strip. Two days later, near Kfar Darom, the Palestinians attacked a schoolbus. Miriam Amitai Bone, mother of four, and Gavriel Biton, father of six, were killed in the roadside bomb attack. Among the nine injured were five children, three from the Cohen family: Orit — 12, Tehila — eight, and Yisrael — seven. All three lost limbs.

Israeli helicopters and navy gunboats attacked nine Palestinian Authority targets, but a Palestinian sniper killed a youth as he was hitching a ride, and in Haderah a car bomb killed two people and wounded 61. About 100,000 people participated at a rally in Jerusalem's Zion Square, under the slogan "Let the IDF win," protesting against Barak's policy of restraint.

On December 8, 2000, the Palestinians marked the 13th anniversary of the first *intifada* in 1987 and it was among the bloodiest days since the new *intifada* had erupted: three Israelis were killed. Among those killed was Rina Didovski, 50, a teacher, mother of six. Two weeks later, Palestinians killed 30-year-old Elihau Cohen on the road between Jerusalem and Modi'in. A Palestinian suicide bomber wounded three Israelis in an attack at a roadside cafe in the northern Jordan Valley, a bomb exploded on a bus in Tel Aviv wounding 14 and 34 Israelis were wounded in a car-bomb attack in Netanyah. In the southern Gaza Strip, Captain Gadi Marsha and Border Police Sergeant-Major Yonatan Vermullen, a Christian volunteer from The Netherlands, were killed. Near the settlement of Ofra in the West Bank, Palestinians murdered Binyamin Kahane and his wife Talia and five of their six children were injured. Binyamin was the son of the late

Rabbi Meir Kahane, founder of the Jewish Defense League in 1968 to combat anti-Semitism in the U.S. and assassinated in New-York in 1990.

The assessment of the IDF was that violence in the territories was likely to continue, even if there was a drop in the number of incidents after 347 Palestinians had lost their lives and over 10,000 were wounded. The Lebanon front, too, could heat up again. Chief-of-staff General Shaul Mofaz told the Knesset Foreign Affairs and Security Committee that the likelihood of a full-scale regional war was now higher than at any time in the past and that such a war could potentially result from an intensified conflict with the Palestinians or a crisis on the Lebanese border caused by the *Hizbullah*. In the meantime, three important bills were discussed in the Knesset.

In the third and final reading, 84 to 19 votes approved the bill requiring a majority of 61 Knesset members to change Jerusalem's municipal borders or transfer any authorities in the city to a non-Israeli entity. The bill defines Jerusalem as Israel's undivided capital with boundaries according to the municipality's 1967 expansion. In the largest gathering in the history of Jerusalem some 300,000 people thronged the streets around the walls of the Old City of Jerusalem in a massive rally for the unity of Jerusalem. With the words "Jerusalem, I pledge" projected onto the wall near Yafo Gate and torches blazing along the ramparts, the crowd sang in unison, "If I forget thee, O Jerusalem, let my right hand wither."

In the third and final reading, 90 to nine votes supported the bill establishing that Palestinians who became refugees in 1948 and in 1967 will not be allowed to return to the State of Israel without the approval of a majority of 61 Knesset members. The bill was submitted by the Likud and was supported by all parties except the Arab ones.

In the first reading, 79 to 29 votes supported the dissolution of the Knesset. Two more readings were necessary to decide on a date for the early elections. Barak announced his resignation and, if the prime minister resigns, a special election for the prime minister only must take place within 60 days. February 6, 2001, was fixed as date for that election with two candidates for Prime Minister — Ehud Barak and Ariel Sharon — and it is worthwhile quoting what Sharon — as Foreign Minister in Netanyahu's government — wrote on October 30, 1998, following the Wye Plantation Summit Agreement, to the secretary-general of

Sharon at Wye Plantation.
From left to right: Natan Sharansky, Yitzhak Mordechai, Benjamin Netanyahu, Bill Clinton, Al Gore, Ariel Sharon, Madeleine Albright.

the United Nations on the Israeli-Palestinian settlement: "The transfer of the territories in Judea and Samaria will bring to the control of the Palestinian Authority on 40% of the land of Judea and Samaria (areas A and B) and to the activation of its legal authority over 98% of the Palestinian inhabitants."

Because of the manner Barak had chosen to pursue the goal of peace and for reacting with too much restraint to the new *intifada,* all polls showed that Sharon would defeat Barak. Even Ezer Weizman declared he would vote for Sharon.

Yitzhak Rabin had once said that a final settlement of the conflict was impossible because of the Jerusalem issue. Barak did not heed the warnings that he was committing the sin of hubris in rejecting the idea of a graded permanent settlement and imposing the over-ambitious goal of an "end of the conflict" on the gradual process that is at the very heart of the Oslo Accords.

The Oslo process was to be one of gradual accomodation entailing an entire series of obtainable interim goals, in the hope that the gap separating Israeli and Palestinian positions on the really knotty questions could be narrowed at a later stage — namely, after a relationship of mutual trust is already in place. Barak, however, clung to wishful thinking and illusions that within 15 months he would solve all the problems.

He also ignored Yitzhak Rabin's legacy that the Israeli public could not withstand the pressure of simultaneously giving up territories in the Golan Heights and in the West Bank. Former American Secretary of State, Dr. Henry Kissinger, wrote in the Los Angeles Times that Barak's iron-willed determination to achieve an instant solution simply accelerated the explosion of violence in the territories. Thinking things out properly is preferable to hasty action, counseled Kissinger.

Barak, the very same leader who filled our hearts with such high hopes in the 1999 elections has proven to be a novice of political inefficiency and, with him as Prime Minister, the Israel ship was sailing in stormy seas without a captain. By resigning, he conceded the total failure of his policies and ability to rule.

For one who voted for Barak, it was painful to read that Barak would be well advised to take a time out because he needs a break and the country needs a leader who has the opportunity as well as the interest to do a little soul-searching and draw the right conclusions from Barak's colossal failure in running the country's affairs. In such a soul-searching at a crucial crossroads, the people of Israel will have to settle decisively in the forthcoming elections the debate existing between its doves and hawks on the political road to follow — appeasement or deterrence.

Since the Six-Day War, the doves have been saying: assuage the Palestinian grievances; give them land, a militia, their own state and we will have peace. The hawks have been saying: the grievances are not satisfiable; the Palestinians don't just want a state in Gaza and the West Bank, they also covet Israeli territories within the Green Line; they claim not just Jericho but Jerusalem also; if you make concessions and show weakness, you invite war.

Since Oslo, the dove theory has been in command. In 1993 Israel brought the defeated and exhausted Arafat out of exile in Tunisia and gave him recognition, international legitimacy, self-government, weapons, foreign aid and an end of occupation for 98% of the Palestinian population. At Camp David, Barak offered the Palestinians concessions so sweeping that even the U.S. negotiators were astonished. Arafat refused and the most pro-Palestinian, dovish Israeli government in history became the target of the most virulent, most frenzied anti-Israel violence, with wild crowds in Arab countries calling — as it was on the eve of the Six-Day War — for the final battle to destroy Israel.

The hawks claim that Arafat has proven with blood and fire how right their theory was and how wrong, outlandish and naive, the conception of the doves was to give the Palestinians power, rifles, ammunition and large portions of the Land of Israel. In their view, Arafat made a strategic choice of pushing for a war of attrition, in the hope of generating international involvement in the negotiations that would bring enough pressure on Israel to enable him to dictate terms. Israel's hasty and disorganized withdrawal from Lebanon has become the model. If the Israelis could be driven out of Lebanon, reasons Arafat, he can drive them out of Palestine.

With the election approaching, the Knesset approved in a preliminary reading a bill, by 49 to 48, that would block Barak from signing or initialing any diplomatic agreements as long as he doesn't have the support of 61 Knesset members. Barak, however, decided to try and reach some kind of agreement with Arafat before the end of Clinton's term of office and to turn the vote in the election into a peace referendum. Attorney General Eliyakim Rubinstein — in a letter to Barak — questioned his moral authority to engage in fateful peace negotiations just prior to the election. All the more, wrote Rubinstein, when speaking of a minority government with a prime minister who has resigned.

On January 14, the very day Barak resumed the talks with Arafat, the Palestinians murdered 30-year-old Roni Tsalah from the Kfar Yam settlement in the Gush Katif area. Ofir Nahum, 16, from Ashkelon was murdered by Palestinians near Ramallah after being lured to a meeting by a girl he met on the Internet. While talks continued, Palestinians abducted Israeli restaurateurs Motti Dayan and Etgar Zeitouny as they were dining in Tul Karem, took them out to a field and murdered them. Akiva Pashkos, father of five, was murdered while driving his car in the Atarot Industrial Zone north of Jerusalem. Arieh Hershkovitz from Ofra, father of four and grandfather of four, was shot dead in the same area. On February 1, two Israelis were murdered: 23-year-old Lior Atia

U.S. President-elect George W. Bush, during his visit to Israel in November 1998 as Governor of Taxas, with the then Prime Minister Benjamin Netanyahu

from Afula and Dr. Shmuel Gilis, a senior hematologist at Hadassah Hospital, father of five. A day before the elections, St. Sgt. Rujia Salame was killed by a Palestinian sniper near Rafah in the Gaza Strip. Salame, a Christian Arab from the village of Tur'an in the Galilee, served in the Bedouin reconnaissance battalion. The death toll of the Israelis rose to 54. Barak's last moment attempt to reach some kind of agreement before the elections has failed.

No agreement with the Palestinians was reached and in the election, out of 4,504,769 eligible voters, 62.28% took part. Ariel Sharon won a crushing victory by receiving 1,698,077 votes (62.39%), against Barak's 1,023,944 votes (37.61%), and became Israel's new Prime Minister.

In the meantime, Republican President-elect George W. Bush and Vice-President Dick Cheney entered the White House.

As a Holocaust survivor, I was an eyewitness of the help given by American officers and men to the Jewish refugess to surmount obstacles and circumvent obstructions in their determination to reach the shores of the Land of Israel. As a diplomat of the independent Jewish State, I was privileged to observe closely the amity of the American people and the constant aid of its governments to Israel since its creation.

The United States is committed to the survival and security of Israel and to strenghten Israel's defensive possibilities, ensuring its qualitative military edge. On announcing the appointment of Colin Powell as new Secretary of State, President-elect George W. Bush declared that a lasting peace in the Middle East must be based on a secure Israel. The American commitments and the American-Israeli strategic agreement to enhance Israel's deterrent capabilities, are for the Jewish State a source of fortitude and hopefulness. A strong Israel is the key to achieving peace and the key to sustaining peace. Israel must, therefore, stand firm on any issue on which we cannot, dare not, yield.

We may be destined to gain the longed-for permanent peace with security by proving our capacity to bear its absence, our brother Jews in the Diaspora standing steadfast with us, close and vigilant, guarding our joint future. This was clearly expressed also at the annual General Assembly of thousands of activists and representatives from Jewish federations across North America held in Chicago in the middle of November 2000, in difficult days for the people of Israel. Both Prime Minister Ehud Barak and opposition leader Ariel Sharon addressed the convention which turned into an impressive show of support for and identification with Israel. The love being heaped upon Israel at that event was a heartwarming sight and it demonstrated that Jewish unity is indeed alive and well — something every Jew can only rely on and hold precious.

The Chicago General Assembly took place after a solidarity visit to Israel of 1,500 North and Latin American Jewish leaders. When the participants met with Israel's President Moshe Katsav, he said to them: "We are more united than at any other time of our past. Our feeling is that you are behind us — we are one family. And because of that we can overcome the problems and challenges before us."